Group Processes in the Classroom

Group Processes in the Classroom

Second Edition

Richard A. Schmuck
Patricia A. Schmuck

UNIVERSITY OF OREGON/EUGENE, OREGON

WM. C. BROWN COMPANY PUBLISHERS
Dubuque, Iowa

Copyright 1971, 1975 by Wm. C. Brown Company Publishers

Library of Congress Catalog Card Number: 74-78454

ISBN 0–697–06089–6

Second Printing, 1976

Printed in the United States of America

TO *Bob Fox* AND AGAIN TO *Ron Lippitt*

Contents

List of Figures

Preface

While we were revising the first edition of this book, our son arrived home after the first day of his kindergarten class to report that the teacher really was *not* a teacher after all. He made his observation this way, "She said that we were all the teachers and she would help us teach one another." The words of our son's kindergarten teacher succcinctly summed up one of our own perspectives on teaching and learning. Students learn from the myriad of interpersonal stimulations and challenges that occur within the classroom. Teaching is not only carried out by the adult who is designated formally as teacher. A great deal of teaching and learning takes place within the interplay of the peer group.

From our point of view, classroom learning constitutes a transactional process, involving the exchange of a school curriculum between teachers and students and among the students. Thus, teaching and learning transactions are particular kinds of *interpersonal relationships*. How students experience the curriculum is influenced, not only by their relationships with the teacher, but also through their contacts with peers. The teacher typically has been singled out as the most influential classroom participant since he or she is formally charged with presenting the curriclum and with improving interpersonal relationships. In contrast, we focus here on the classroom as a group which includes the teacher as a member, not as a group with the teacher as a separate participant.

The prevailing historical model of putting greatest emphasis on the teacher has led to certain blind spots among educators. It has promoted a way of viewing the classroom as if it were composed of two-person units—the teacher and individual student in interaction. The history of this model contains two phases that have been described by Glick.* The first phase led to research on the relationships of teachers' personality characteristics to the achievement or attitudes of students. This research, on the whole, came to no useful conclusions. The second phase took a major step forward by researching teachers' behavior rather than their personality characteristics. It is our aim in this book to contribute to the development described by Glick by focusing upon a third phase, that of bringing together recent research on teacher behavior and the theories and research of social psychology and group dynamics.

Glick has proposed the term *mediational model* for what we have in mind. The mediational model views the effects of a teacher's behavior as being mediated by classroom group processes and not as occurring in two-person units. For instance, when a teacher gives the class a direction, responses to it are influenced, not only by the teacher's relationship with the students as individuals, but also by the feelings, attitudes, and relationships that are shared within the peer group. Every classroom manifests group influence of one sort or another, and whatever the teacher does, the group gets involved in mediating that behavior for its members.

We hope that this book will bring greater awareness of these mediating group processes to teachers. A teacher who is aware of the group processes in the classroom should be better able to pursue behavioral objectives. The teacher should not view peer group processes as only nuisances or detriments to student learning. A teacher who is aware of the informal interactions among peers might transform what seems to be endless chatter into useful opportunities for learning. Awareness of the student who is influential in the peer group, for example, can lead to constructive use of that influence in learning. Recognizing student strengths and using them within the group processes challenges the assumption that only the teacher can help students learn.

We are *not* preparing this book to equip teachers with preventative measures to foster classroom order and control. In fact, teachers who use group processes effectively may not see the traditional picture of an orderly, well-controlled classroom; rather, they may see an active interpersonal environment in which a variety of interactions is occurring. Group processes, whether they are visible or covert, are operating within all classrooms. Hopefully, some knowledge about them can help the teacher to mobilize them effectively to foster student learning.

Evidently, these points of view are rapidly picking up adherents. We have been very pleased and encouraged by the wide use of the first

*See O. Glick, "The Educational Process in the Classroom." *The School Review*, September, 1968, pp. 339-351.

edition of this book. We are grateful especially for the many gracious letters and phone calls we have received from readers. Clearly, interest in finding ways of helping all classroom participants to act at the same time as teachers and learners has become widespread.

However, building a bridge between the understanding of group processes and their effective use can be exasperating and frustrating. Knowledge does not necessarily, or even easily lead to changes in behavior. Behavioral change is a very complex phenomenon involving cognitive change, emotional involvement, behavioral tryouts, and feedback. Our experience in the classroom and working with teachers has indicated that information alone, such as that which is communicated in this book, is not sufficient to improve classroom group processes. Often, teachers become enthusiastic about a new idea, but their plan fails terribly the first few times it is tried. Frustration must be expected if teachers are going to try to think and behave in different ways.

Although this book may encourage new ways of thinking about the classroom, it will not automatically lead to new behaviors. Too often, we find that educational textbooks imply that if a teacher plans carefully, takes the needs of students into consideration, is sure about his or her goals, and implements the plan carefully, then the new teaching strategies will turn out as planned. In reality, plans often are incomplete, problems that will arise are difficult to anticipate, and it is almost impossible to consider the psychological states of students when one's own needs are so paramount. Teaching is a difficult activity, especially when one has authentic hopes, goals, and expectations for both students and oneself.

Notwithstanding our cautious point of view concerning the power of cognitive knowledge for behavioral change, we do hope that this book will bring insights and that it will stimulate the reader intellectually. We hope, too, that it will be especially valuable to teachers in preservice training programs who are in the process of developing a repertoire of ideas and behaviors that they eventually will use in the classroom. They might use the book in their curriculum, instruction, or educational psychology courses. We also hope that experienced teachers will find here ideas that will be useful in broadening their view of the classroom and that they will make use of the book in in-service training sessions. For the teacher to be knowledgeable and aware of what is happening within the classroom is at least one starting point for constructive change.

While this second edition includes most of the material that was in the first edition, major changes and additions have also been made. Two chapters—Chapter 9, Sequential Stages of Development, and Chapter 10, The School Organization (formerly Chapters 8 and 9)—have been substantially revised and considerably expanded. Chapter 3, Expectations, is a new chapter written for this edition which we believe adds to understanding about classroom group processes. The entire book has been brought up to date and more attention has been placed on action ideas for change. We estimate that this second edition is about forty percent changed from the first edition. We hope these many modifications are improvements.

We acknowledge the assistance of Greg Starling and Rosemary Briggs in the preparation of this manuscript.

R. A. S.

P. A. S.

CHAPTER 1

Basic Concepts

This book is about how the processes of group interaction combine to help or hinder cognitive and affective learning in the classroom. We believe that what really happens in classrooms involves interpersonal complexities and subjective depths of meaning that challenge any teacher's imagination. Because classrooms are replete with so many facets of social life, no single theory of teaching or of learning to account for all of the dynamics involved can be proposed. Instead, we will present numerous concepts about interaction in the classroom along with the available research on those concepts expressed in practical terms. This chapter lays the groundwork for the rest of the book by offering a social psychological perspective on classroom group processes.

The Importance of Group Processes

There are several reasons why group processes in the classroom have become a primary concern of most educators. The increasing complexity of social conditions and the large concentrations of people have brought to the forefront the need for and the importance of learning to work effectively in groups. Modern life, particularly in the cities, places a premium on the ability to relate well with others, and future adults will be compelled to deal with interpersonal tensions and conflicts—not merely

1

to avoid them but to handle them constructively and creatively—if some of the social problems of America are to be solved.

As a result of societal changes during the past several decades, schools have an increased responsibility for helping students learn behavioral skills that will equip them to fill responsible and useful roles in society and contribute maximally to the productivity of groups. As viewed here, this means that concurrent with the teaching of an academic curriculum, schools should be concerned with the development of skills in interpersonal relationships, with the adequacy of the student's relationship to classmates and teachers as well as to self.

Another dimension of group life is the important part it plays in the developing self-concept of individuals. Positive self-esteem is influenced by the manner in which important people in a person's environment respond to that person. This appears to be true for very young infants, children and adolescents, as well as for adults of all ages. Everyone makes use of the reactions of other people in formulating their opinions of themselves. People rely on others for the gratification and rewards which make them feel worthwhile and esteemed, or for the punishment and disapprovals which lead them to feel inadequate and worthless. It is primarily other people—in person or in the images one holds of them— who are able to make an individual feel secure and happy or lost and unhappy. Students' concepts of themselves are built up primarily through the accumulated bits of feedback that they receive from those with whom they come in contact in school.

At the same time, persons are not passive receptacles being pushed into behaving by social influences. Thomas et al. (1963) have shown that babies differ in their behaviors at birth. Some are very active in their squirming and kicking; others lie more or less passively in their bassinets; some have strong tendencies to approach physical stimuli; others withdraw from these stimuli or avoid them and some seem to manifest generalized moods of happiness, while others appear to be unhappy. Even attention spans differ significantly for babies just after birth. Some babies also show unique ways of either reaching out or holding back in relation to others. Such active social striving or censoring influences the ways in which others respond to the infant. Clearly, behaviors of teachers or of peers in school to individual students will have varying effects on those students, depending on their behavioral individuality.

Although each person experiences unique social influences and responds to them in unique ways, there are some developmental stages which all persons go through as they mature. Erikson (1950) conceived a sequence of stages which enumerates the developmental difficulties faced by everyone. How the problems posed at each of these stages are resolved by the individual depends in part on what has happened to that individual in his or her past. People are continuously growing psychologically and such development emerges out of a past which itself influences the growth process. Even though all persons face similar developmental problems, each one seems to solve them in very special, individualistic ways. The dynamics of the group processes of the family, the peer group, and the school provide powerful environments in which each developmental problem will be solved.

Five-year-old children have already developed varying degrees of trust or distrust in others. They have a sense of independence or dependence in relation to others and their personal feelings of competence are based on their past achievements and failures. They come to school with concerns for being accepted, being influential, and being competent. These three motivational areas play a major role in how they cope with group processes. In turn the social climates of the school and classroom influence how they will behaviorally execute their needs for affiliation, power, and achievement. Unless children's early experiences have been unduly harsh, they also come to school with strong drives to understand their environment. Most children are eager, curious, and exploratory, and they take pleasure in discovering and solving problems. Thus the school receives active, highly motivated children and over a number of years is instrumental in helping to point these propensities toward salutary or debilitating goals.

Classroom Life

The classroom is not a depersonalized setting; it abounds with emotion between teachers and students and between students and their peers. It is primarily members of the peer group who respond most to a student's affective needs. A close friend can help a student to overcome anxiety and loneliness in a large and complex school. The combination of teachers' responses to students' personal needs and the peer group's interaction with them constitute the core of group processes in the classroom.

Peers are especially influential in shaping the group processes of a classroom. They provide emotional support as students attempt to break free from dependency on their family and other adult figures. Peers directly influence one another's information and attitudes toward success, power, prestige, respect, and ways of affiliating with others. As they give and take from one another, they learn ways of relating to persons of all ages with some degree of empathy and reciprocity. Peers also help shape some of a student's own attitudes, values, aspirations, and social behaviors. For instance, sons of manual workers are more likely to adhere to middle-class aspirations if they attend classrooms with predominantly middle-class peers, and conversely, professional men's sons aspirations for a college education become lower if they attend school with mostly working-class peers (Wilson 1959). Other research has indicated that students are more likely to aspire to higher education and actually to attend college if their best friend also plans to go to college (Alexander and Campbell 1964).

Although the peer group is very important, the classroom is made up of much more. It is a meeting ground for the peer group taken collectively, the teacher, the individual students, and the academic curriculum. Teaching and learning are complementary acts that involve a host of interpersonal processes. When this process takes place in the classroom it is complicated and affected by the relations among students, and between the students and the teacher. In some classrooms the learning process is enhanced by peer relations that actively support a productive learning atmosphere; in others, it is inhibited by peer relations. The teacher's instructional style and the curriculum, the students' feelings about themselves and their academic abilities, and the nature of the interpersonal relations in the classroom are major influences on this teaching-learning process.

Each member of this classroom social configuration brings to it a special, unique set of characteristics, and since the classroom is only one part of the lives of its members, it is vulnerable to the influences of social forces surrounding it. The classroom group is directly and indirectly influenced by the total organization of the school building, the characteristics of the district in which the building lies, and the dynamics of the community in which the district is located. The different sociological environments of social class, race, and rural-urban differences create variances in the classroom's constitution. To implement identical classroom programs in large city schools and small rural schools would probably be unwise, if not impossible, because of these important differences.

Even though these sociological factors can play a significant role in what happens in any classroom, this book will *not* focus on them. Rather, we are interested in describing and explaining the classroom group processes themselves, whatever the varying inputs from the sociological surroundings might be. We know that students and teachers bring to the classroom many personal characteristics which set the stage for the group processes that are played out. But what goes on in the classroom is more than a simple summing up of the individuals' characteristics; the group processes themselves, in many ways, take on a life of their own.

Perhaps the most useful point of view the teacher can adopt is that all members of the classroom are at the same time quite different and quite similar. Natually, the individuals are different. They have had different experiences, they have acquired different skills and abilities, and their attitudes and personalities have developed differently. At the same time, all persons, whether they are students or teachers, have certain interpersonal needs and desires that must be gratified. Each of the classroom members wants to feel included, influential, and loved. Each wants respect and a feeling that he or she is important and relevant. For us, the classroom and its group processes are exciting and challenging to study precisely because of this complexity and intense humanity. The human group, and especially the classroom group, is a splendid myriad of different individual styles and emotional experiences. It is virtually impossible to spend any time in classrooms or with other groups of people, for that matter, and not to recognize a host of personal desires which in some basic sense are common to all of us.

The Class as a Group

Even with increased interest in group processes, there still exists a lack of clarity regarding them, and many different points of view on the role they play in the classroom. From our point of view classrooms are *not necessarily* groups. Each classroom should be conceived of as being placed on a dimension with the quality of groupness; and to the extent that a collection of classroom members lies near the group end of that dimension, it can be better understood by applying group dynamics theory and research.

To illustrate the groupness of a classroom let us describe two quite different classes which are involved in learning foreign language. One class uses an individualized programmed procedure; students are allowed to proceed at their own rate and in their own unique way. All students are seated in their own separate booth which does not allow for much face-to-face contact. Assignments are presented to each student by a teacher or teacher's aide, and all students use an audiotape for their lesson and are finished with each tape as they answer correctly questions presented to them. The second class varies significantly and contrastingly from that format. There, small groups of students gather to discuss a topic in the foreign language that they are learning. Exchanges of information, paraphrasing, and some repetitive practice in the foreign language are attempted in the discussions. At given intervals the teacher asks students to divide into groups of three or four to help one another with new words and pronunciation. After such interchanges, students return to the larger groups to discuss what they have learned with the teacher leading the group. In this second class, interpersonal contacts are paramount and group processes are pervasive.

Both of these classrooms are commonly found in American public schools. Perhaps the most typical classroom would combine both procedures. The same collection of persons in a single classroom could be doing programmed instruction part of the time and group discussion other times. These two types of classes are not antithetical to each other. Whether the "groupy" type of classroom format is in a separate class or the same class as the more individuated one is irrelevant to our discussion. While it is proceeding it represents more groupness than the programmed instruction class, and therefore what goes on in it can be better understood by applying knowledge from group dynamics.

Let us now look at some of the properties of groups that we have in mind when we speak of classroom groupness.

Interaction and Interdependence of Persons

A group is a collection of interacting persons with some degree of reciprocal influence over one another (Gibb 1964, and Bany and Johnson 1964). This property of groupness excludes aggregates in mere physical proximity, such as persons at a football game or in a lecture hall, or collections of persons with something in common such as redheads or all of the citizens of the United States. The second group-oriented class described above had more interaction and interdependence of students than the first programmed instruction class. This is not to argue that the programmed instruction class did not have some interaction between the students. As will be seen later in this chapter, the mere presence of others can have a significant impact on intellectual performance. Moreover, we know that even the physically separated cubicles allow for noises, giggles, whispers, and note-passing. We should also keep in mind that students' carry around within themselves images of others in the class and concepts about themselves. And it is primarily images of these other persons which influence a student's feelings about the classroom and the curriculum. Nevertheless, the second class was more interdependent and had more interpersonal interaction.

Two theoretical approaches to characterizing the interdependence of persons in groups seem to be useful for describing interaction in classrooms. The sociologist, Parsons (1951), suggested that there are five basic interaction modes for describing groups: the dimensions of *affective-nonaffective* which focuses on the emotions involved in the interaction; *self-collective* which describes whether the interaction is intended to satisfy personal motives or for achieving group goals; *universalism-particularism* which describes how consistently and uniformly persons in similar roles are defined by one another in the interaction; *achievement-ascription* which has reference to how persons gain status—whether by performance or by some inherent characteristics; and finally *specificity-diffuseness* which has reference to the degree to which the interaction in a content domain is focused.

Classrooms can be described as ranging along these five dimensions. In some classes expressions of feelings are welcomed and supported, but in many others the students are encouraged to keep feelings of happiness and displeasure to themselves. Some classes are self-oriented, as is the individuated, programmed learning class described above; others engage in many group activities in which students are asked to achieve group tasks. In some classes the teacher treats all students alike, sometimes supporting an expectation for uniform performances and behaviors; other teachers take heed of the relevance and importance of individual differences by expecting varied performances and behaviors. In most American classrooms, one's high standing with the teacher is achieved by dint of personal effort. In some, however, the status one enters by way of one's sex, social class, and skin color can influence the status eventually arrived at in the classroom group. Finally, for many teachers, class discussions must be intently focused on the proper content of the curriculum; for others, a broader array of topics, including very personal ones, are legitimate and seized upon as learning experiences.

A second and different theoretical system for describing modes of interaction in groups was developed by Schutz (1958). His psychological theory assumed that group activities are predictable from knowledge of the person's interpersonal needs and the principles governing their interaction. He computed compatibility scores for pairs of persons in terms of their needs for *inclusion, control,* and *affection.* Scores on these three motives are derived in two ways: the person's expression of these needs, and how much of each kind of need he or she desires from others. Compatibility of classroom groups can be gauged by estimating whether or not each of these needs is expressed in sufficient amount to satisfy student wants. Classes can have involvement problems if inclusion responses are lacking, power problems if students are either competitive or apathetic about expressing influence, and emotional support problems if too little warmth and love is expressed.

One recent empirical study on third grade classrooms pointed directly to the importance of peer group interaction and interdependence (Calonico and Calonico 1972). These authors showed that the more frequently third graders interacted with one another, the stronger were their feelings of friendship for one another. The research also corroborated the common hypothesis that friendly people receive supportive feedback and unfriendly people receive negative responses. Indications were that the friendly third graders received support from their peers, while those third graders who expressed a great deal of unfriendly aggression received rejecting responses from their peers. Also pointed up was the fact that the higher the sociometric status of a third grader, the more likely that student was to conform to the norms of the peer group.

These findings underscore the concepts and importance of student interaction and interdependence in the classroom. The teacher who discourages peer interaction is neglecting one of the main resources of classroom learning. Calonico and Calonico emphasize that the major implication of their study is that teachers should encourage rather than discourage interaction between students. We concur, believing that a teacher who constructively uses the inevitable chatter and idea-sharing among students can accomplish more educational tasks than the teacher who sets rules that discourage interaction. The latter teacher spends too much time and energy working to get students to refrain from talking with one another.

Interaction Around Common Goals

Groups are constituted of several potentially antagonistic pulls. They have tasks to accomplish and work to produce, but they also must maintain cohesiveness and an optimal level of morale. There also exists in all groups persistent pulls between group goals and individuals' motives. Group goals describe a preferred or desired state which guides the behaviors of group members. The learning of subject matter is an example of a group goal in the classroom. Various dimensions for describing group goals have been advanced but the dichotomies of task-social emotional and group-individual have been most popular. When these dichotomies are used to construct a matrix, four categories emerge: task-group, task-individual, social emotional-group, and social emotional-individual. Industrial work groups in which completion of tasks requires concerted effort and in which the persons who work are viewed as interchangeable are examples of groups with task-group goals. Classroom groups have learning tasks to accomplish but typically the focus is on individual students' learning and therefore, most of the time, classes are in the task-individual goal category. T-groups or group dynamics seminars which concentrate on emotional processes in groups are in the social emotional-group category, while group therapy would be illustrative of the social emotional—individual category.

Groups can become more effective as they are able to fulfill more than one of these goal categories. A project in which an industrial work group analyzes its social emotional processes can enable the group to produce higher economic gains (Kuriloff and Atkins 1966). In classrooms, an individual's interest in learning the academic curriculum can be strengthened by helping the class to set group tasks to perform (Schmuck 1971). At the same time, classroom group processes can be improved by satisfying the social emotional needs of individuals (Schmuck 1966). Students who are liked by at least a few other classmates typically feel more secure and are better able to expend energy on the task-group and task-individual goals.

In theory the classroom with the greatest degree of groupness in its goals would have small groups of students working on subject-matter projects (task-group); individuals working alone but in parallel on subject-matter (task-individual); discussions in which group expectations and feelings were made public (social emotional-group); and informal relationships of warmth and security that are satisfying to the individual students (social emotional-individual). See Figure 1.1.

Interaction Through a Structure

Groups also can be categorized according to their structure. Structured interaction is regular, repetitive, and to some extent expected and predicted by the participants. Getzels and Thelen (1960) have proposed two basic structures for the classroom: *nomothetic* roles which are formalized and institutionalized and *idiographic* aspects of structure which bear on personal dimensions. For those authors, the nomothetic structure is characterized by persons in roles carrying out the functions of a social system. Examples would be teachers and students carrying out their responsibilities and duties apart from any consideration of their personal characteristics as individuals. From this perspective, it is possible to make an abstract analysis of what goes on in a classroom and to predict the gross behaviors of members without ever really knowing the individual persons. The idiographic dimension also must be included in such an analysis before a complete view of the living classroom can be understood. In actuality, no two roles are carried out identically; a personal component is always present.

Walberg (1968; 1969) and Walberg and Anderson (1968) have executed a series of empirical studies using the conceptual framework of Getzels and Thelen. Their research showed some of the blends that occur in classrooms between the idiographic and nomothetic dimensions. For instance, background interests and peer group norms (nomothetic) of students are important in determining the style of culture in the classroom, while the personality characteristics (idiographic) of teachers make a difference in how daily routines proceed. Anderson (1970) also showed how the normative climate of the classroom in turn affects the academic learning patterns of individual students.

	Task	Social-Emotional
Individual	Programmed Instruction Independent Assignments Reading Alone	Supportiveness Acceptance Helpfulness
Group	Group Projects Content Discussions Setting Learning Goals with the Class	Discussions about Classroom Procedure Making Group Agreements About Classroom Rules

FIGURE 1.1   /   *Examples of Classroom Goals.*

The salient analytic feature of using nomothetic and idiographic aspects of structure lies in the proportion of each in the classroom. If the class maximizes the nomothetic, it will emphasize the academic tasks and the disciplinary rules of the school. Classrooms with a high nomothetic emphasis do not allow for the unique and varied expressions of individuals. Emphasis on the idiographic assumes that each student will seek what is relevant and meaningful to him. It will emphasize individuality and variation. From the group process point of view, both dimensions are inevitably a part of the classroom. The classroom group is part of a formal institution with certain prescribed goals, while at the same time it is made up of different personalities. Effective group processes are those that work through a balanced blend of the nomothetic and the idiographic in the classroom.

Group Dynamics Theory

Our theory of classroom group processes is based on ideas and research findings from four different historical traditions in social psychology. These traditions are summarized below with some attention given to relating them to the classroom group.

Perspective 1: Informal and Formal Aspects of Groups

The first perspective that sheds light on classroom group processes originated in classical sociological theory (Cooley 1956). It emphasizes the reciprocal influences between the intimate, informal aspects of a group on the one hand and the formal role requirements, performances, and goals of the encompassing organization on the other. Classroom groups, like other groups, have both formal and informal aspects. The formal aspects have to do with the ways in which various members work toward carrying out the official or specified goals. In the classroom, for instance, one formal feature is the way in which any child performs the nomothetic role of academic student, as it is defined by the teacher, school system, and adult community at large.

The informal aspects of a group involve the idiographic ways in which each member relates to other members as persons. In the classroom an informal feature would be the way affection, or students' friendship for one another, is distributed. These informal relationships often have an important bearing on the way formal processes are carried out. Many of them, such as the amount of friendship members have for one another or their willingness to help and support one another, may be thought of as positive and enhancing classroom group processes.

Early sociological research on industrial organizations pointed to the importance of informal relationships in small work groups for accomplishing goals of production (Roethlisberger and Dickson 1939). Employees in industry were not viewed primarily as "economic men," but rather as "ego men." What the employees hoped for, above all else as "ego men," was credit for work done well, interesting and stimulating tasks, appreciation, approval, and congenial relations with their fellow workers. Industrial administrators were encouraged to look at the informal, person-to-person relations on the job because the emotional lives of the employees were seen as being importantly related to the production goals of the organization.

Ideas similar to those pointed out in studies of industrial management have been developed in other branches of sociology to describe the interconnectedness between formal and informal group processes. Moreover, these two pulls in group life are reflected in a philosophical debate concerning people's rational and emotional natures. In sociology, rationality is emphasized in those processes through which a group solves the problems of adaptation to its environment. By rationally generating a nomothetic organizational structure and role definitions, a group is able to use the knowledge and skills available to make an optimal adjustment to its external world. Supportive emotionality, on the other hand, does not help in the solving of external problems but is conceived, instead, as the medium through which a group maintains its internal viability with a minimum of strain and tension. The terms *secondary* and *primary* relations reflect this difference and, in the literature of group dynamics, there are many other terms which stand for it, such as *formal* and *informal, external* and *internal, socio* and *psyche, task* and *maintenance, task* and *social emotional,* and *instrumental* and *expressive.*

One important study that dealt with informal processes in groups was one made of the German army (Shils and Janowitz 1948). The researchers showed that the breakdown of the German army was not due to any flaws in its formal organization, but instead, arose out of the dissolution of friendships among small units of soldiers. The informal, supportive relationships of closeness among the soldiers were quite necessary for a full realization of the formal goals of "winning the war."

Much the same thing was found by Goodacre (1953) in his study of differences between good rifle squads and poorly performing ones in the American army. He found that the turnover rate was not significantly different in the two types of squads, but that the men in the "good" squads reported their group as having a significantly greater number of men "buddying around" together on the post after duty hours, having fewer disagreements among the men in the squad, and as having an attractive group from the points of view of other soldiers on the post.

Moreno (1934) vigorously advocated that the management of organizations take into consideration the feelings and informal interpersonal relations of the members. He argued that affective relations between persons are inevitable in any formal organization, and that if the formal organization failed to take such informal relations into consideration, discord, strife, and conflict would appear at the formal level of functioning. Classroom group processes support Moreno's argument. If informal group processes, in the form of peer relations and norms, are not supportive, considerable tension can occur, and the learning of the formal curriculum can be deterred. We have shown that classroom groups with supportive friendship patterns enhance academic learning, while more hostile classroom environments reduce learning (Schmuck 1966). The research has indicated that student academic performances were conditioned by emotional contents associated with their self-concepts as peers and students, and these self-concepts were influenced, in part, by the students' friendship and influence relations with their classmates. Informal group processes in the classroom do make a difference in the accomplishment of the formal goals of the school.

Perspective 2: Emotional Aspects of Small Groups

The second perspective, complementary to the first, grew out of the tradition of psychoanalytic theory and emphasizes the deeply emotional tone of face-to-face relations in small groups. The writings of Bion (1948) and Thelen (1954) best express this perspective by their stress on the unavoidable affective nature of all interpersonal relationships. They maintain that the first interpersonal relationships a person experiences in the family are saturated with feelings and that it is from the family setting that a person learns basic ways of relating with other people. People who must be in prolonged daily contact with others will tend to relate in ways similar to the emotional styles they learned in their families. Emotionality and affective interpersonal ties are viewed as inevitable within a group of people who meet regularly.

A case in point is the classroom in which high levels of feeling exist daily. As students interact, and students and teachers relate, they communicate, however indirectly, their feelings about one another. Such gestures of affect influence how students view themselves, their abilities, their likeability, and their general worth. These feelings or evaluations of self make up students' self esteem and have impact on the degree to which they use their intelligence and how they form their current educational aspirations. In addition to having difficulties in academic performance, youngsters with poor self-images tend to dislike and be disliked by other students and so to perpetuate uncomfortable interpersonal relations. Students involved in these unproductive relationships often are unable to work on their academic subjects with concentrated effort and vigor. Their perceptions sometimes become so distorted that they are unable to study effectively. The greater the threat students feel in the presence of their peers, the more pronounced the restricting and distorting effect is on their thoughts and perceptions of their academic work. Classroom disturbances tend to proliferate when students have poor self-images and, at times, teachers unwittingly exacerbate such tensions by scolding or punishing, thereby perpetuating negative self-images and unacceptable classroom behavior.

Perspective 3: Group Effects on the Self-Concept

Some social psychologists have argued convincingly that people's self-concepts develop through relations they have with other people. According to Mead (1934), Cooley (1956), and Sullivan (1948), human beings develop in a sequential and systematic manner, not because of the gradual unfolding of instinctual tendencies, but because they experience a regular sequence of interpersonal interactions in their lives. The family, the peer group, close friends, brief and prolonged formal and informal contacts, marriage, parenthood, and an ever-changing array of people offer grist from which the self is formed and reformed. In the development of a self-concept, communication with others makes possible taking the role of the other by providing a set of common meanings and a form of behavior in which people can become objects to themselves. The learning process that occurs involves first one person imagining how he or she looks to a second person, followed by the first person's estimating how the second reacts, resulting in the first's internalizing a new view of self based on his or her view of the second person's reactions.

Mannheim (1957) tested this theory about the development of the self-concept with an analysis of extensive questionnaire data collected from college students. She concluded that students' self-images tended to be similar to the self-image reflected to them by members of their dominant reference group, which in most cases was their living unit. Her analysis also revealed that changes in one's reference groups were associated with changes in one's self-concept, both positive and negative.

Students' self-concepts are influenced strongly by the reflections they derive from the reactions of their teacher and their classmates. Unfortunately, students who receive unfriendly reactions from these others develop a poor view of themselves, and such a negative self-concept can have several debilitating effects. First, the way students feel about themselves is an important determinant of their behavior toward others. Thus, students who hold negative feelings about themselves tend to hold negative feelings toward others, and their aggressive reactions toward others merely support the others reacting negatively in turn. Secondly, students with low levels of self-esteem in the classroom are apt to slip into daydreams or misbehave when they are in school, and to attempt to drop out of school as soon as possible. Students whose self-esteem in school is low, or for whom self-esteem is unrelated to school achievement, are on the way to becoming dropouts unless corrective interventions are made by creative teachers.

Perspective 4: Group Effects on Intellectual Performance

The mere presence of other persons who are working on a similar task has been shown to have significant effects on the intellectual and motor performances of an individual. This tradition of psychological research, referred to as the psychology of social facilitation, is best represented by F. Allport (1924) and Dashiell (1935) who gave attention to the effects of groups of people upon the individual person. Their method of investigation compared the achievements of individuals who were performing with other persons being physically present with those of individuals working on the same tasks alone.

Most of this research showed that the mere presence of other coacting persons had a detrimental effect on intellectual functioning and a facilitating effect on simple motoric performances. One important dimension in this research was the psychological complexity of the task to be performed. The presence of other persons had more negative impact on the individual as the task became more complex. Although the point on such a dimension at which time the presence of persons becomes detrimental is still unclear, the research is convincing in pointing out that the intellectual activity of individuals can be influenced negatively by the presence of others doing similar tasks.

A related theory developed by Snygg and Combs (1949) argued that when individuals feel anxious or fearful in the presence of another, they have difficulty in accurately perceiving the world. The greater the threat individuals feel from another, the more pronounced the restricting and distorting effect is on their thoughts and perceptions of their surroundings. Their perceptions may become so distorted that they are unable to behave efficiently. An experiment performed by Combs and Taylor (1952) illustrated this phenomenon. Belligerent examiners introduced mild degrees of personal threat while students were performing a task requiring intellectual functioning. The researchers predicted that this personal threat would result in an increase of time required to complete the task, as well as an increase in errors in performance. The fifty participants in this experiment were given the task of translating sentences into a simple code. With only one exception, the students required longer time periods to complete the coding procedure when they were working under threatening conditions than they would have needed otherwise, and they also made a greater number of errors of translation than in a comparable, nonthreatening situation.

It is not difficult to predict what might happen to students who again and again are presented with interpersonal situations that are threatening to them. One of the possible effects of having others working close by, especially others with whom students feel insecure, is a reduced level of performance on complex, cognitive learning activities. The extent to which such students use their intelligence is likely to be considerably reduced in so threatening a classroom situation.

Group Dynamics Theory and the Classroom

The preceding four historical perspectives from group dynamics help us acquire a rudimentary understanding of the role of group processes in the classroom. The students in a classroom can be regarded as a collection of individuals who relate to one another formally and informally simultaneously. They perform in the physical presence of one another in order to develop themselves intellectually and emotionally. Their informal relationships of friendship, influence, prestige, and respect can have decided effects on the manner in which the more formal requirements of the student role are accomplished by the individual youngsters. At the same time, informal relationships in the peer group are often fraught with emotion and involvement and some sort of an interpersonal hidden world is inevitable for every student. As these informal peer relations increase in power and salience, the individual student's definition and evaluation of self become more and more vulnerable to peer group influence. Each student's self-concept is on the line within the classroom setting where the quality of informal relationships can be either threatening and debilitating, or supportive and enhancing to the development of self-esteem. The more threatening or supportive the interpersonal relationships in the classroom become, the more likely the individual student's academic learning and classroom behavior will be affected. In short, emotionally-laden interpersonal relationships that occur informally can affect the student's self-concept which, in turn, can influence his or her intellectual performance.

References

Alexander, C., and Campbell, E. "Peer Influences on Adolescent Aspirations and Attainments." *American Sociological Review* 29, no. 4 (1964):568-75.

Allport, F. *Social Psychology*. Boston: Houghton Mifflin Co., 1924.

Anderson, G. "Effects of Classroom Social Climate on Individual Learning." *American Educational Research Journal* 7, no. 2 (1970):135-52.

Bany, M., and Johnson, L. *Classroom Group Behavior*. New York: Macmillan Co., 1964.

Bion, W. R. "Experiences in Groups, I." *Human Relations* 1 (1948):314-20.

Calonico, J., and Calonico, B. "Classroom Interaction: A Sociological Approach." *Journal of Educational Research* 66, no. 4 (1972):165-69.

Cohen, A. K. *Delinquent Boys*. New York: Free Press, 1955.

Combs, A. W., and Taylor, C. "The Effect of the Perception of Mild Degrees of Threat on Performance." *Journal of Abnormal and Social Psychology* 47 (1952):420-24.

Cooley, C. H. *Human Nature and the Social Order*. New York: Free Press, 1956.

Dashiell, F. F. "Experimental Studies of the Influence of Social Situations on the Behavior of Individual Human Adults." In *A Handbook of Social Psychology*, edited by C. Murchison. Worcester, Mass.: Clark University Press, 1935. Pp. 1097-1158.

Erikson, E. H. *Childhood and Society*. New York: W. W. Norton & Co., 1950.

Getzels, J., and Thelen, H. "The Classroom Group as a Unique Social System." In *The Dynamics of Instructional Groups*, 59th Yearbook, part 2, edited by N. Henry. Chicago: National Society for the Study of Education, 1960.

Gibb, J. "Climate for Trust Formation." In *T-Group Theory and Laboratory Method*, edited by L. Bradford, J. Gibb and K. Benne. New York: John Wiley and Sons, 1964. Pp. 279-309.

Goodacre, D. M. "Group Characteristics of Good and Poor Performing Combat Units." *Sociometry* 16 (1953):168-78.

Kuriloff, A., and Atkins, S. "T-Group for a Work Team." *Journal of Applied Behavioral Science* 2 (1966):63-94.

Mannheim, B. F. "An Investigation of the Interrelations of Reference Groups, Membership Groups and the Self-Image: A Test of the Cooley-Mead Theory of the Self." *Dissertation Abstracts* 17 (1957):1616-17.

Mead, G. H. *Mind, Self, and Society*. Chicago: University of Chicago Press, 1934.

Moreno, J. L. *Who Shall Survive?* Washington, D. C.: Nervous and Mental Diseases Publishing Co., 1934.

Parsons, T. *The Social System*. New York: Free Press, 1951.

Roethlisberger, F. J., and Dickson, W. J. *Management and the Worker*. Cambridge, Mass.: Harvard University Press, 1939.

Schmuck, R. A. "Some Aspects of Classroom Social Climate." *Psychology in the Schools* 3 (1966):59-65.

———. "Influence of the Peer Group." In *Psychology and Educational Practice*, edited by G. Lesser. Glenview, Ill.: Scott, Foresman & Co., 1971. Pp. 502-29.

Schutz, W. *FIRO: A Three-Dimensional Theory of Interpersonal Behavior*. New York: Holt, Rinehart & Winston, 1958.

Shils, E. A., and Janowitz, M. "Cohesion and Disintegration in the Wehrmacht in World War II." *Public Opinion Quarterly* 12, no. 1 (1948):280-315.

Snygg, D., and Combs, A. W. *Individual Behavior: A New Frame of Reference for Psychology*. New York: Harper & Row, 1959.

Sullivan, H. S. "The Meaning of Anxiety in Psychiatry and in Life." *Psychiatry* 3 (1948):1-17.

Thelen, H. A. *Dynamics of Groups at Work*. Chicago: University of Chicago Press, 1954.

Thomas, A.; Chess, S.; Birch, H.; Hertzig, M.; and Korn, S. *Behavior Individuality in Early Childhood*. New York: New York University Press, 1963.

Walberg, H. J. "Personality Correlates of Factored Teaching Attitudes." *Psychology in the Schools* 5 (1968):67-74.

———. "Predicting Class Learning: An Approach to the Class as a Social System." *American Educational Research Journal* 6, no 4 (1969):529-42.

Walberg, H. J., and Anderson, G. S. "The Achievement-Creativity Dimension and Classroom Climate." *Journal of Creative Behavior* 2, no. 4 (1968):281-92.

Wilson, A. "Residential Segregation of Social Classes and Aspirations of High School Boys." *American Sociological Review* 24 (1959):836-45.

CHAPTER 2

Group Processes: An Overview

Group life in schools cannot be compared directly with group experiences in any other institution in our society. Although studies from industry, government, and the military have been helpful in generating insights and perspectives, there is no substitute for research done directly in public schools for understanding classroom group processes.

History

Much of the current thinking and research about classroom group processes have grown out of two separate but interrelated historical movements. One of these stems from the influences of John Dewey who emphasized the social aspects of learning and the role of schooling for training students in problem-solving and democratic, rational living. The other historical movement stems from the empirical research of Kurt Lewin and the subsequent development of scholars and practitioners of group dynamics. The Lewinean movement stressed the collection of scientific data which undergirded the philosophical work of Dewey and introduced the action techniques for improving group processes.

Dewey's primary contribution to a study of group processes in the classroom developed from his focus on the *process* of learning rather than its *content*. He argued that if children were to learn to live democratically, they would have to experience the living process of democracy itself in the classroom. Life in the classroom, according to Dewey, should be the democratic process in microcosm. It should be democratic not only in the ways that students are involved in making choices and engaged in carrying out projects collaboratively, but also in their being taught directly to empathize with others, to respect the rights of others, and to work together rationally. His contributions are unquestionably profound, especially from the point of view of classroom group processes, but many would argue, and with accuracy, that Dewey's ideas have remained largely on philosophers' shelves rather than having reached into the realities of everyday classrooms.

One of the keys for unlocking Dewey's major contributions lies in the development of group dynamics as a subdiscipline of social psychology. Group dynamics, while it also has value as a philosophical orientation, has contributed more than Dewey's work to the knowledge of group operation by scientifically gathering evidence on the functions and processes of small face-to-face groups. Until recently most of this research had been carried out to a greater extent in industry and government than in classrooms or school organizations. But during the past twenty-five years, there has been a gradual accumulation of scientific research on classroom groups. An article by Trow et al. (1950) compared with one by Getzels (1969) clearly reveals the large number of studies on classroom groups carried out during the decades of the fifties and sixties. The differences between these two articles are striking. The 1950 article consisted mostly, if not solely, of theoretical propositions. The 1969 article, on the other hand, presented substantial empirical evidence derived from research done directly on classroom groups and school organizations.

Research on group processes in general burgeoned during the last twenty years. In 1955, Hare and others annotated a bibliography of 584 items on small groups. By 1959, Raven had collected 1445 references related to group processes; in 1962, Hare published a *Handbook* consisting of 1385 items; and by 1966, McGrath and Altman had presented a bibliography of 2699 items. During the same period, classical books on small groups were being brought up to date. Cartwright and Zander's 1953 edition was revised in 1960 and again in 1969. The book by Hare and others (1955) was considerably altered with 20 additional articles in 1965. Other analyses were published indicating both the magnitude and interest in group processes (Golembiewski 1962; Luft 1963 and 1970; Napier and Gershenfeld 1973; Olmstead 1959; and Shepherd 1964). Only a few of these, however, focused on the classroom or the school (Miles 1959; Thelen 1954 and 1960).

A more significant trend relative to public education was the direct application of group research on improving personal learning and organizational processes. A notable invention was the technique for educating adults referred to as the training group (T-group) utilized by the National Training Laboratories: Institute for Applied Behavioral Science. Important books relevant to the T-group are Bradford et al. (1964), Schein and Bennis (1965), Dyer (1972) and Lieberman, Yalom, and Miles (1973). A number of contributions on organizational group processes that included many applied studies were also related to the development of T-group technology (Argyris 1972; Katz and Kahn 1966; Likert 1961; March and Simon 1958). Although researching classrooms and school settings directly continues to be underplayed in relation to group research on other settings, there has been increased emphasis on the application of group processes to educational settings. The 59th Yearbook of the National Society for the Study of Education (Henry 1960) provided social psychological theory about classroom groups and proposed ways of using research findings to improve instruction. Three separate textbooks published within the last several years apply social psychology to the study of education (Backman and Secord 1968; Guskin and Guskin 1970; and Johnson 1970). Other books and articles have focused on empirical data about group processes in the classroom and the school (Bany and Johnson 1964; Glidewell et al. 1966; and Lippitt et al. 1964), while other publications have used data to make recommendations for improving teaching and classroom group processes (Schmuck, Chesler, and Lippitt 1966; Fox, Luszki, and Schmuck 1966; Chesler and Fox 1966; Amidon and Hunter 1966; Schmuck and Schmuck 1971; and Schmuck and Schmuck 1974).

The continually increasing number of studies on public education have been due in part to increased federal funds and foundation grants. From 1950 to 1960, federal funds for educational research and development increased tenfold. Funds for educational researchers continued to increase even at a more rapid rate during the early 1960s. This increased funding was due primarily to the need for answers to such imminent situations as the evident and growing problems of schools in heavily populated urban centers; widespread bureaucratization and duplication of services; inequalities in educational opportunities; and a growing awareness of the need for flexible managers of complex technology.

Since the late sixties, however, there has been a notable leveling-off of federal funding for school improvement even though these societal problems still remain. This leveling-off in part has been a reflection of the low priority that education holds alongside other national and international goals as well as the critical analyses of many people that educational institutions have not improved because of this massive spending. We believe that substantial school improvement has not occurred because the interpersonal relationships within schools have been largely ignored by educational researchers and change agents. Even though a great deal of study has been carried out on new teaching methods, curricula, educational hardware, and architectural designs for school buildings, improvements in the quality of human interaction in our schools has gone largely unheeded.

Current Social Movements

During the 1970s several social movements have emerged which point out many of the damaging aspects of our public schools. The representatives of these social movements criticize neither curriculum materials nor innovative teaching methods; instead they aim their concerns at the dehumanizing and demeaning relationships—for faculty as well as students—that exist in schools. The writings of Kozol (1967), Kohl (1969), Dennison (1969), Herndon (1971), and Postman and Weingartner (1971) represent the "educational romantics." They have brought the devastating effects of some public schools out into the open with clear and shocking prose. The title of Kozol's book, *Death at an Early Age*, succintly typifies the destructive picture that many "educational romantics" paint of our schools. A similar theme is also presented by more dispassionate observers; the three year Carnegie-sponsored study by Silberman (1970), a detailed, documented view of the schools, portrays very well the same themes of the decay and stagnation of public schools.

In addition to the social movement of the "educational romantics," there are the advocates of the British Infant Schools. They offer a ray of hope to those who believe humanistic change is possible. After many years of very traditional academic education the British have revolutionized some of their schooling for very young children. The Infant Schools in England emphasize the diversity of interests and skills of young people; teachers are viewed as facilitators or managers of the school environment working with students on an equalitarian basis. Teachers are not regarded as one-way transmitters of information or wisdom (Brown and Precious 1968); instead all participants—adults and children—are expected to act both as teachers and learners.

Corollary to contemporary criticisms of the demeaning atmospheres of American public schools and of the emergence of the British Infant Schools has been the creation of numerous alternative schools in our country. Although some of these organizations—often called free schools —are alive and flourishing today (Kozol 1972; and Render, Moon and

Treffinger 1973), many of them have not done much better to improve relationships than their public school counterparts. Others have failed in the wake of organizational inefficiencies or economic disaster. We should note, however, that some public school districts have successfully implemented alternative schools within the public schools while others have searched for new ways to solve the problems of human interchange through the introduction of new forms of school management (Chesler 1973). The lasting influence of this brand new alternative school movement on public schooling can not yet be assessed.

It is evident nowadays, especially from participants in these social movements, that there are strong demands for better human relationships in schools. Many of these social demands and their attendant hopes for our nation's schools have reached a wider audience than just educators; in fact parents in community after community are demanding more from their local schools. As one parent put it, "I didn't realize schools could be different until I read Silberman!" One prerequisite necessary to the fulfilling of such hopes for humanistic change is a more complete understanding of the dynamics of groups within educational settings.

Classroom Climate

Even the most casual observer of schools can perceive the differences in feeling tones of different classrooms. Some are quiet, formal, and tense while others are pleasant, active, and exciting. We use the term *climate* to refer to the feeling tones of a group. Most research on classroom groups corroborates the view that a positive social climate in the peer group enhances students' self-esteem and their academic performances. Classrooms that have a climate of competitiveness, hostility, and alienation cause anxiety and discomfort and do not facilitate the intellectual development of many students. Classrooms in which students and teacher support one another facilitate the development of self-esteem and provide the opportunity for students to use their intellectual capacities to their utmost. The interpersonal power that students feel in relation to their classmates, or the levels of skill and competence students see in themselves also encourage positive feelings about school and increased involvement in classroom tasks. The relevance of positive classroom climates for optimal school adjustment of students is now commonplace for most educational practitioners.

Even though there is general agreement about the significance of social climate, few direct and detailed empirical analyses have been made of the characteristics of positive or negative classroom climates. The concept, classroom social climate, has generally been of a summary nature.

It has been abstract and vague and seldom clearly defined. For the purposes of this text, *a positive classroom climate is one in which the students expect one another to do their intellectual best and to support one another; where the students share high amounts of potential influence—both with one another and with the teacher; in which high levels of attraction exist for the group as a whole and between classmates; where norms are supportive for getting academic work done, as well as for maximizing individual differences; wherein communication is open and featured by dialogue; and where the processes of working and developing together as a group are considered relevant in themselves for study.* In such a classroom we would expect to find strong student and teacher motivation for accomplishing mutual goals, feelings of positive self-esteem, relaxed feelings of security, high involvement in academic learning, agreeable feelings of being influential with the teacher and other students, and a high degree of attraction to one's classmates, class, and school.

While each separate property of climate is important by itself, the climate of a classroom is more than the sum of its properties. The term "climate" describes *how* each of the properties is integrated and working in relation to one another. For us, the concept of climate summarizes the group processes that are worked out by a teacher in interaction with students and between the students in the classroom. Climate is *what* the classroom activity is in carrying out educational goals; it is *how* the curriculum and learning materials are actually used through the human exchange; and it *is* the styles of relating among the members of the classroom group.

This book deals primarily with research on the climate of the classroom —the group dynamics of classrooms. Most of the concepts presented have been derived from empirical research on interpersonal relations, group dynamics, and organizational psychology. Unfortunately, much of this research has not been carried out in public school settings. Some of the material that will be presented represents strong hunches, extrapolated from other settings but not yet directly empirically tested in classrooms. At the same time, liberal use will be made of research on classroom settings by Richard Schmuck, and of material from the research of other social psychologists of education. Attempt has been made throughout to keep the reader clear on the distinction between empirically tested findings and our authors' strong hunches based on theory.

The core content of this book (Chapters 3 through 9) lays out what empirical research indicates are the essential properties of classroom climate. Chapter 3 tells how interpersonal expectations—especially expectations for achievement—become patterned and influential in the classroom. Chapter 4 shows how leadership or interpersonal influence is exerted; it is concerned with power as a feature of classroom climate. Chapter 5 describes how friendship patterns affect the classroom; it is concerned with attraction and hostility as features of classroom climate. Chapter 6 focuses on explaining how group norms work for or against educational goals, and is concerned with the effects of interpersonal expectations and pressures on the climate. Chapter 7 describes how communication patterns occur in the classroom and how the different patterns relate to positive and negative climates. Chapter 8 deals with a cohesive classroom group, how it is created and maintained; cohesiveness is a central feature of classroom climate. Chapter 9 shows how class members might be expected to react at different stages of the classroom group's development. Chapter 10, the final chapter, deals with the relationships that exist between the organizational processes of the school and the classroom group. How the classroom climate can be affected by the interpersonal relationships and norms of the professional staff has been fully delineated. Each chapter also includes plans for action so that teachers can implement specific instructional activities based on group dynamics principles.

The remainder of this chapter is devoted to summarizing some research on each of the properties of classroom climate, in this way presenting an overview of Chapters 3 through 10.

Expectations

Interpersonal expectations and the social psychological dynamics of the self-fulfilling prophecy have stimulated the imagination of many educational researchers and practitioners during the past few years. Most social behavior involves both the motivations and intentions of an individual as well as that person's expectations about how others in the immediate environment will behave. An expectation is a prediction of how another person will behave. All people develop expectations for themselves as well as for other people with whom they interact over a period of time.

As an example, Carl, a fifth grader, may see another student, Paul, struggling with a problem that he, Carl, has already solved. Carl is pleased with his success and wishes to be helpful. His act of offering help to Paul attests to his own firm feelings of self-regard. Carl may make a rather neutral comment to Paul such as, "I see you're having trouble with this problem, maybe I can help you." Paul's response depends in great part on the expectations he has for Carl. If Paul sees Carl as a "wise-guy" or a "show-off" who enjoys building himself up at the expense of others, he will most likely refuse the offer of help. However, if Paul views Carl as supportive and friendly, he probably will accept the offer for help.

Most of the systematic research on expectations in the classroom has been focused on a teacher's expectations for students. Some dramatic instances of the self-fulfilling prophecy have been documented by researchers. For example, Palardy (1969) showed that first grade teachers who expect girls to read better than boys have classes where girls read better than boys at the end of the first grade. In contrast, classes of teachers who do *not* expect sex differences do not have any substantial differences between girls and boys at the end of the year. In another study on the self-fulfilling prophecy, Doyle, Hancock, and Kifer (1971) showed that students who are rated by their teachers as possessing high I.Q.'s perform better than students who are rated as low, even when the I.Q.'s of the students in both groups actually are *not* different. At the same time, other studies have found no difference in students' performance based on teachers' expectations (Claiborn 1969) and consequently a debate rages on as to whether teacher expectations make a real difference for student performance.

Taken as a whole, the research evidence indicates to us that the self-fulfilling prophecy can operate in many classrooms. Good and Brophy (1973) have offered a theoretical sequence to explain the effect of interpersonal expectations in the classroom: (1) teachers naturally expect different achievements from different students; (2) teachers behave differently toward individual students as a function of their different expectations—when they place an expected troublemaker near their desk, for example, or call on a student who, they expect, will have the answer when a visitor comes to the classroom; (3) over a period of time the teachers' differential treatments of students communicate to the students what behaviors their teachers expect them to perform, and (4) the students' behaviors come to conform more and more to the expectations that their teachers continually communicate.

In enumerating these four processes involving interpersonal expectations we have focused on interaction between teachers and students. Patterns of interpersonal expectations are, of course, also visible in the family, in the peer group, and in other school situations outside the classroom. Young people begin to develop their self-concept through the reflected appraisals of their parents and brothers and sisters. Later in psychological development, the classroom—in terms of interactions with the teacher and with peers—can have equally strong impact on students' self-image. Classrooms that foster healthy self-development are featured by interpersonal expectations that emphasize an individual's strengths rather than weaknesses. In such healthy classrooms, expectations for different members' behavior are varied, changing, and mostly positive. There is a deliberate effort to support all students in displaying their unique strengths and competencies.

Leadership

The most fruitful way to think about leadership in the classroom is as a set of influence functions; as an interpersonal process rather than as an attribute of a person. Leadership is leading; it is a verb rather than a noun. In this sense, leadership is viewed as behaviors which help the group move toward its objectives. Leadership consists of actions by group members; actions that aid in setting group goals, moving the group toward its goals, improving the quality of the interactions among the members, building the cohesiveness of the group, or making individual competencies available to the group.

Teachers, by virtue of their role, have the greatest potential for leadership. However, to limit leadership functions in the classroom solely to the teacher would not present an accurate picture of classrooms. Most teachers have faced some active or passive resistance by students and realize that power does not solely reside in the ascribed role of the formal leader. Actually, leadership is performed by many members of a group, and, in the classroom, students can influence other students in many different ways. Some student influence, of course, can be in opposition to the goals of the school. A classroom with a positive social climate has leadership performed by many students and the teacher. The potential for influencing another person is an important facet of one's own feelings of self worth and satisfies the basic striving for power. In classrooms where only a few students are able to influence others, powerlessness and negative feelings about self and school are often the resulting feelings of those who have no power.

Most early research on classroom leadership emphasized the role of the teacher in influencing students; it assumed that the teacher is the most powerful participant in the classroom. In classic studies by Lewin, Lippitt, and White (1939), Anderson (1939), and Withall (1951), it was found that the climate of the group was related to the leadership behaviors of the teacher. In these studies the verbal behavior of teachers was studied and noted. Lewin, Lippitt, and White created the designations of *democratic, authoritarian,* and *laissez-faire* climates; Anderson used the concepts, *dominative* and *integrative;* and Withall used *teacher-centered* and *student-centered* climates. For the most part, these researchers focused on the teachers' behaviors rather than the actual group processes in the classroom. They shed light on the differential effects of teacher behavior but did not contribute understanding to the classroom group processes. However, the research was useful in showing that by being "democratic," "integrative," or "student-centered," teachers could disperse influence throughout the classroom group.

Naturally, the curious researcher questions the importance of dispersed influence in a group. Does it enhance the school's educational goals? What difference does shared influence make, if any, to students' feelings about themselves? We do know from research and experience that students' feelings of self-esteem and personal competence are related to their feelings of influence in relation to others. To be powerless is to be out of contact with others and, for students, feelings of powerlessness will diminish their concentration on academic work. Even the teacher who feels powerless will not remain an effective teacher very long. Students, of course, cannot make the choice to opt out of the classroom like teachers can. They are forced by law to remain in school and can find solace only in psychologically retreating from the classroom group. It is this psychological retreat that can be so very detrimental to achievement.

Several studies done in industry, in voluntary organizations, and in schools have demonstrated that the satisfaction of subordinates is related to their perception of the degree to which they can influence decision-making, as well as to the kind of influence their superior has over them (Tannenbaum 1968). Hornstein et al. (1968) found that relationships between superiors and subordinates in schools were much like those of other organizations. Teachers reported greatest satisfaction with their principal and the school district when they perceived that their principal and they themselves were mutually influential. This was especially true when they felt that their principal's influence emanated from his or her expertise. This same principal-teacher relationship was found to be associated with the perception of higher satisfaction on the part of students.

We believe that these findings hold also for the classroom group; a positive classroom climate is one in which the leadership functions are well distributed and where all participants can feel power and self-worth in accomplishing academic tasks and in working together.

Attraction

Human beings need close friends to feel secure and comfortable; they strive to be loved or at least to be personally related to others. Without affiliation, feelings of loneliness, worthlessness, and anxiety arise preventing the maximum use of their potentials. If a classroom is organized so that the students feel liked and respected, they will be more likely to behave in a manner which makes them deserving of the liking and respect of others. Likewise, when the classroom environment is filled with anxiety, hostility, and self-doubt, the students will behave in unconstructive and unproductive ways, thus perpetuating a negative climate.

Research by Richard Schmuck (1966) showed that classroom groups with *diffuse* friendship patterns exhibited more positive climate than classrooms which were *centrally* structured. The two types of structures were distinguished as follows:

> Centrally structured peer groups are characterized by a large number of pupils who agree in selecting only a small cluster of their classmates as pupils they like. Along with this narrow focus on a small number of pupils, many other pupils are neglected entirely. Diffusely structured peer groups, on the other hand, are distinguished by a more equal distribution of liking choices; by no distinct subgroups whose members receive a large proportion of preferences; and by fewer entirely neglected pupils (1966, p. 341).

The research indicated that the classroom group's structuring of liking patterns had decided effects on the individual students. Students were more accurate, for instance, in estimating their own status in the centrally-structured groups and in particular the low-status children were more aware of their low status. The greater accuracy in the centrally-structured classroom was interpreted in terms of the clarity of status positions. Almost every student knew who was liked and who was not liked. In such classes, there was an absence of generalized emotional support which might otherwise obscure a student's low status. The importance of these results is heightened by further findings that a student's perception of holding low status—more than the fact of actually having such status— was related to incomplete use of intellectual abilities and to holding negative attitudes toward self and toward the school.

Norms

Norms are shared expectations or attitudes about what are appropriate procedures and behaviors in the classroom. Students behave somewhat predictably largely because of their adherence to norms. Norms are strong stabilizers of behavior because the members of the classroom group monitor one another's behaviors. The strength of group norms in the classroom arises out of two kinds of forces: (1) forces within the individual to reduce conflict felt when personal actions are different from those held by others, and (2) forces induced by others who wish to influence the person's behavior.

Important norms in classrooms are those that exercise influence over the students' involvement in academic work and those that influence the quality of interpersonal relations between the members. Because there are so many individual differences in the classroom, it is important that norms be flexible and changeable. A positive classroom climate is one in which the range of tolerable behavior is broad and one in which there is a great deal of latitude for idiosyncracies.

Jackson (1960) showed that when a group has norms characterized by very narrow ranges of tolerable behavior, the likelihood of breaking a norm is very high, and consequently the probability of being punished is high. He pointed out that the range of tolerable behavior can be placed on a continuum, from very narrow to very broad. In a class where the normative ranges are broad, there is a tone of encouragement and flexibility rather than restraint and rigidity. When the range is narrow, it is likely that norms will be broken because the environment is threatening and restrictive.

Richard Schmuck (1966) showed a relationship between classroom liking structure, group norms, and cohesiveness. Classroom groups with diffuse liking patterns shared more positive norms about the teacher and doing schoolwork than did classrooms with centrally structured liking patterns. The message typically communicated by teachers in classrooms with positive social climate supported the norms of, "I am here to help you," "It is important for us to understand one another," and "Let's work together as a group." The classrooms which were diffusely structured were also typified by broad ranges of behavior; students and the teacher were able to "do their own thing," provided it was consonant with learning and did not interfere with others.

Communication

Communication, both verbal and nonverbal, is the vehicle by which group processes in the classroom occur. Without communication there could be no classroom and yet it is one of the least understood features of classroom climate. Even although much research has been done on verbal communication, it has not been linked very well to classroom climate.

Flanders wrote, "The chances are greater than 60% that you will hear someone talking if you are present in a classroom." He went on to show that the great majority of time the person who is talking is the teacher. Most research following up on the development of Flanders' Interaction Analysis system has focused on the verbal behaviors of teacher-student interaction in the classroom. Although most verbal communication exists between teacher and students, communication also exists between student and student. We maintain that peer group communication as well as teacher-student communication is critical for understanding the totality of a classroom.

Unfortunately, little direct research has been done on student-student communication patterns. Not only is verbal communication important but hushed whispers, nods, winks, chuckles, and touches also communicate a great deal between students. In our opinion patterns of peer group interaction are directly related to the classroom climate. Classrooms in which members hesitate and are reticent in speaking with each other are classrooms which have minimal amounts of involvement and intimacy. Many classrooms are constrained environments where students do not feel free to touch one another psychologically; empathy is almost nonexistent and the teacher does over 80 percent of the talking. In contrast, communication in a classroom with positive social climate involves high amounts of dialogue and communication between members; instructions or directions would emanate not only from the teacher but from the students as well. Communication would be lively, feelings of involvement would be high, and several hushed but meaningful conversations might be going on simultaneously.

Cohesiveness

The cohesiveness concept is concerned with the feelings that class members have about the classroom group. A measure of cohesiveness is achieved by summing up all of the individual's feelings about the group. It differs from attraction; its emphasis is upon the individual's relation to the group as a whole rather than upon relations with individuals, subgroups, or the teacher.

Research in industrial organizations has demonstrated the importance of cohesiveness to morale and productivity. Cohesiveness is correlated with the productivity of a group, provided the norms are supportive of production. Cohesive groups are more goal-directed than noncohesive groups, and as long as the goals of the individuals are in line with productivity, cohesiveness is a facilitating factor. Classroom groups which have strong goals have satisfied students. Moreover, students who know what is expected of them and who are involved and close to their peers in pursuing educational goals are more satisfied than students in classrooms that are disorganized and fragmented.

Both Muldon (1955) and Richard Schmuck (1966) showed that cohesiveness in classroom groups was related to the friendship structure. Classrooms with more dispersed liking structures were more cohesive. Moreover, classroom groups which could clearly point to the popular and unpopular members had less cohesiveness and did not work as a total group. When there was a more diffuse liking structure there was also a classroom with clear goals and an appreciation for individual diversity. A cohesive classroom group will enhance the positive climate of the group.

Sometimes peer group cohesiveness can work against the academic goals of the school when the norms held by the peer group are negative or unsupportive of involvement in academic work. Cohesive peer groups with strong norms opposed to the teacher and school can undermine the development of a climate for learning. In such classrooms, the teacher will have to work hard in developing new norms for behavior.

Sequential Stages of Development

A classroom group develops through stages in a systematic fashion just as an individual develops. Although classrooms differ from each other, there are some common stages of development. Classroom groups can also become arrested at one stage of development, just like a neurotic individual.

There appear to be at least four different stages that classroom groups move through as they develop. The initial period of testing to discover those behaviors that are acceptable and functional occurs during the first part of the school year. Class members and the teacher are striving to find their place in the group and to feel included during this first phase. There are subsequent feelings of disharmony, argumentation, conflict, and overt disunity as the students and teacher struggle to test their relative influence in the group and to see what the tolerance is in the group for unique behaviors. During this second phase, leadership emerges and norms are established. The third stage deals with goals—both the goals of individual students as well as of the group—which often are antagonistic to each other. Finally, the fourth stage of growth occurs when members of the class are clear on the goals of the group and the roles they are to perform. During this stage, the group is best able to function productively on academic work, either individually or in groups.

We believe the climate of a classroom is enhanced when members are free to discuss their stage of development as a group. We will provide examples of exercises and procedures classroom groups may use at different stages. The important aspect is awareness of "where we are" as a group in relation to "what we are doing" and "where we are going." Healthy classroom groups attempt to establish where they are developmentally and what they have to do to move to the next, more mature stage of development.

The School Organization

Although classrooms are relatively autonomous as related to one another, a schools' organizational characteristics can influence the group processes within it. *A schools' organization* refers to those processes through which all the subsystems work together, including the curriculum and other academic resources, formal and informal relationships among staff and between faculty and students, as well as community and other outside forces. School organizations are living, complex social systems which are continually adapting to changes within themselves or to forces from without.

Five salient characteristics of school organizations can directly affect classroom group processes: (1) The trust and openness between members of the faculty can set the emotional tone of many teacher-student interactions; (2) communication skills employed by the adults in the school are often similar to the sorts of interpersonal communications present in classrooms; (3) feelings of influence that teachers have in relation to school decision-making are associated with the amount of influence the teachers allow students to exert in the classroom; (4) the principal's behavior in relation to the staff can serve as a model for the sorts of leadership exerted by teachers within the classroom; and (5) the prevailing norms of the faculty with regard to a philosophy about human nature can influence the ways teachers interact with students within the classrooms.

To the extent that the above propositions are valid, interventions to improve the school's organizational processes could have beneficial effects on interpersonal relations in the classrooms. *Organization development* is one method of consultation for schools that is designed to take action on the organizational characteristics. The theory and techniques of organization development in schools have been documented in books by Schmuck and Miles (1971), Schmuck, Runkel, Saturen, Martell, and Derr (1972), and Owen (1974). A recent text by the authors of this book, *A Humanistic Psychology of Education: Making the School Everybody's House* contains an evaluation of how organization development procedures can be used to help teachers humanize the relationships in their own classrooms.

Organization development can be defined as a planned and sustained consultative effort to apply behavioral science for system improvement by the use of reflexive, self-analytic methods. Our research and experience indicates that organization development can bring about enduring changes in the interaction among staff members and between the faculty and students. These changes, in turn, often become reflected in the classroom processes. Of these processes we believe that *supportive interpersonal expectations, shared leadership, dispersed friendships, norms of helpfulness, open communication,* and *peer group cohesiveness* will endure and grow best within school organizations that have a healthy, self-renewing staff climate.

References

Amidon, E., and Hunter, E. *Improving Teaching*. New York: Holt, Rinehart & Winston, 1966.

Anderson, H. H. "The Measurement of Domination and of Socially Integrative Behavior in Teachers' Contacts with Children." *Child Development* 10 (1939): 73-89.

Argyris, C. *Intervention Theory and Method: A Behavioral Science View*. Reading, Mass.: Addison-Wesley, 1972.

Backman, E. W., and Secord, P. F. *A Social Psychological View of Education*. New York: Harcourt, Brace & World, 1968.

Bany, M., and Johnson, L. *Classroom Group Behavior*. New York: Macmillan Co., 1964.

Bradford, L.; Gibb, J.; and Benne, K., eds. *T-Group Theory and Laboratory Method*. New York: John Wiley and Sons, 1964.

Brown, M., and Precious, N. *The Integrated Day in the Primary School*. New York: Agathon Press, Inc., 1968.

Cartwright, D., and Zander, A. *Group Dynamics: Research and Theory*. Evanston, Ill.: Row, Peterson, 1953 and 1960; New York: Harper & Row, Publishers, 1969.

Chesler, J. "Innovative Governance Structures in Secondary Schools." *Journal of Applied Behavioral Science* 9, nos. 2 and 3, (1973):261-80.

Chesler, M., and Fox, R. *Role-Playing Methods in the Classroom*. Chicago: Science Research Associates, Inc. 1966.

Claiborn, W. "Expectancy Effects in the Classroom: A Failure to Replicate." *Journal of Educational Psychology* 60 (1969):377-83.

Dennison, G. *The Lives of Children*. New York: Random House, 1969.

Doyle, W.; Hancock, G.; and Kifer, E. "Teachers' Perceptions: Do They Make a Difference?" Paper presented at annual meeting of the American Educational Research Association, 1971.

Dyer, W. G. *Modern Theory and Method in Group Training*. New York: Van Nostrand Reinhold Co., 1972.

Fox, R.; Luszki, M.; and Schmuck, R. *Diagnosing Classroom Learning Environments*. Chicago: Science Research Associates, 1966.

Getzels, J. W. "A Social Psychology of Education." In *The Handbook of Social Psychology*, edited by G. Lindzey and E. Aronson. Reading, Mass.: Addison-Wesley, Vol. 5. 1969. Pp. 459-537.

Glidewell, J. C.; Kantor, M.; Smith, L. M.; and Stringer, L. "Classroom Socialization and Social Structure." In *Review of Child Development Research*, edited by M. Hoffman and L. Hoffman. New York: Russell Sage Foundation, 1966. Pp. 221-57.

Golembiewski, R. *The Small Group*. Chicago: University of Chicago Press, 1961.

Good, T., and Brophy, J. *Looking at Classrooms*. New York: Harper & Row, Publishers, 1973.

Guskin, A. E., and Guskin, S. L. *A Social Psychology of Education*. Reading, Mass.: Addison-Wesley, 1970.

Hare, A. P. *Handbook of Small Group Research*. New York: Free Press, 1962.

Hare, A. P.; Borgatta, E. F.; and Bales, R. F. *Small Groups: Studies in Social Interaction*. New York: Alfred A. Knopf, 1955 and 1965.

Henry, N., ed. *The Dynamics of Instructional Groups*. 59th Yearbook, part 2. Chicago: National Society for the Study of Education, 1960.

Herndon, J. *How to Survive in Your Native Land.* New York: Simon and Schuster, 1971.

Hornstein, H.; Callahan, D. M.; Fische, E.; and Benedict, B. A. "Influence and Satisfaction in Organizations: A Replication." *Sociology of Education* 41, no. 4 (1968):pp. 380-89.

Jackson, J. M. "Structural Characteristics of Norms." In *The Dynamics of Instructional Groups.* 59th Yearbook, part 2, edited by N. Henry. Chicago: National Society for the Study of Education, 1960. (See also the same article reprinted in *The Role Orientation: Readings in Theory and Application,* edited by R. J. Thomas and B. J. Biddle. New York: John Wiley & Sons, 1966; or as revised and abridged in *Current Studies in Social Psychology,* edited by I. D. Steiner and M. Fishbein. New York: Holt, Rinehart & Winston, 1965.)

Johnson, D. W. *The Social Psychology of Education.* New York: Holt, Rinehart & Winston, 1970.

Katz, D., and Kahn, R. *The Social Psychology of Organizations.* New York: John Wiley and Sons, 1966.

Kohl, H. R. *The Open Classroom: A Practical Guide to a New Way of Teaching.* New York: A New York Review Book, 1969.

Kozol, J. *Death at an Early Age.* Boston: Houghton Mifflin Co., 1967.

———. *Free Schools.* New York: Houghton Mifflin Co., 1972.

Lewin, K.; Lippitt, R.; and White, R. "Patterns of Aggressive Behavior in Experimentally Created 'Social Climates.'" *Journal of Social Psychology* 10 (1939):271-99.

Lieberman, M. A.; Yalom, I.; and Miles, M. *Encounter Groups: First Facts.* New York: Basic Books, Inc., 1973.

Likert, R. *New Patterns of Management.* New York: McGraw-Hill Book Co., 1961.

Lippitt, R.; Fox, R.; and Schmuck, R. *Pupil-Teacher Adjustment and Mutual Adaptation in Creating Classroom Learning Environments.* Final Report. U.S. Office of Education, Cooperative Research Project, no. 1167. Washington, D. C., 1964.

Luft, J. *Group Processes: An Introduction to Group Dynamics.* Palo Alto, Calif. National Press Books, 1963 and 1970.

March, J., and Simon, H. *Organizations.* New York: John Wiley and Sons, 1958.

McGrath, J., and Altman, I. *Small Group Research.* New York: Holt, Rinehart & Winston, 1966.

Miles, M. B. *Learning to Work in Groups.* New York: Bureau of Publications, Teachers College, Columbia University, 1959.

Muldoon, J. F. "The Concentration of Liked and Disliked Members in Groups and the Relationship of the Concentration to Group Cohesiveness." *Sociometry* 18 (1955):73-81.

Napier, R. W., and Gershenfeld, M. *Groups: Theory and Experience.* Boston: Houghton Mifflin Co., 1973.

Olmstead, M. *The Small Group.* New York: Random House, 1959.

Owen, R. *Administering Change in Schools.* Englewood Cliffs, N. J.: Prentice-Hall, Inc. 1974.

Palardy, J. "What Teachers Believe—What Children Achieve." *Elementary School Journal* 69 (1969):370-74.

Postman, N., and Weingartner, C. *The Soft Revolution.* New York: Delacorte Press, 1971.

Raven, B. *Bibliography of Publications Relating to the Small Group.* Technical Report, No. 1, Office of Naval Research. Washington, D. C., 1959.

Render, G.; Moon, C.; and Treffinger, D. "Directory of Organizations and Periodicals on Alternative Education." *Journal of Creative Behavior* 7 (1973): 54-66.

Schein, E., and Bennis, W. *Personal and Organizational Change Through Group Methods.* New York: John Wiley and Sons, 1965.

Schmuck, R. A. "Some Aspects of Classroom Social Climate." *Psychology in the Schools* 3 (1966):59-65.

Schmuck, R. A.; Chesler, M.; and Lippitt, R. *Problem Solving to Improve Classroom Learning.* Chicago: Science Research Associates, Inc., 1966.

Schmuck, R. A., and Miles, M. *Organization Development in Schools.* Palo Alto, Calif.: National Press Books, 1971.

Schmuck, R. A., and Runkel, P. *Organizational Training for a School Faculty.* Eugene, Ore.: Center for the Advanced Study of Educational Administration, 1970.

Schmuck, R. A.; Runkel, P.; Saturen, S.; Martell, R.; and Derr, B. *Handbook of Organization Development in Schools.* Palo Alto, Calif. National Press Books, 1972.

Schmuck, R. A., and Schmuck, P. A. *A Humanistic Psychology of Education: Making the School Everybody's House.* Palo Alto, Calif.: National Press Books, 1974.

Shepherd, C. *Small Groups.* San Francisco: Chandler Publishing Co., 1964.

Silberman, C. *Crisis in the Classroom.* New York: Random House, 1970.

Tannenbaum, A. S. *Control in Organizations.* New York: McGraw-Hill Book Co., 1968.

Thelen, H. A. *Dynamics of Groups at Work.* Chicago: University of Chicago Press, 1954.

———. *Education and the Human Quest.* New York: Harper & Brothers, 1960.

Trow, W.; Zander, A.; Morse, W.; and Jenkins, D. "Psychology of Group Behaviors: The Class as a Group." *Journal of Educational Psychology* 41 (1950): 322-38.

Withall, J. "The Development of a Climate Index." *Journal of Educational Research* 45 (1951):93-99.

CHAPTER 3

Expectations

At the heart of all classroom group processes are the personal expectations that each participant—teacher and students—holds for the ebb and flow of interaction with others. These expectations grow out of the individual's own personality structure as well as his or her general images of what school is like, and out of specific reactions perceived to be coming from classmates. In this chapter we will first describe the psychodynamics of personal motive structures and expectations in the classroom. We will then describe how individuals develop expectations about others. Next, we will look at how perceptions, motives, and expectations get played out in interactions with others through what we call the circular interpersonal process of interaction. Finally, we will explore the social psychological dynamics involved in the self-fulfilling prophecy, popularly known as the "Pygmalion effect," paying particular attention to the expectations that teachers have for student performance.

Achievement, Power, and Affiliation

We think of students as constantly growing and developing. As one concept or skill is learned they set forth new objectives and new levels of aspiration. Their master motive seems to be a constant striving for self-esteem and self-respect. Such personal striving takes place in at least three important domains: (1) the striving for *achievement,* also labeled as competency, efficacy, and curiosity; (2) the striving for *power* or influence in relation to others; and (3) the striving for *affiliation* and affection. Thus, the basic psychological questions are: What can I accomplish? How can I exert my will? Who will go with me? Typical emotions resulting from frustrations of these motives as noted in our observations of classrooms are feelings of inferiority, worthlessness, being put down, loneliness, betrayal, lack of interest, and dullness. Incompetence, powerlessness, and rejection are, in other words, the most serious psychological problems within the classroom.

These next few chapters concentrate on the three above-mentioned motives. This chapter is concerned primarily with the first—striving for achievement. Chapter 4 focuses on leadership and deals with the striving for power and influence, while Chapter 5 concentrates on the striving for affiliation and affection. The subsequent chapter on norms will deal with all three motives as they take form in the group culture. Norms are shared expectations for interpersonal behavior and thus supply the basic matrix in which individuals can fulfill their psychological interests.

The Striving for Competence

Motivational theories and research have played predominant roles in the development of psychology as a science of human behavior. Early in the history of psychology, concepts such as instincts and other human inborn attributes dominated the thinking about the strivings of mankind. Next, the pleasure and pain principle of hedonistic philosophy replaced the earlier concepts of instincts. Man was viewed as acting to increase pleasure and to avoid or decrease pain. Later, a number of notable psychologists such as Guthrie, Hull, and Tolman provided concise and measurable ideas that could be tested within the animal laboratory. Although these ideas were precise and objective, they were so narrowly conceived that they were in general not applicable to understanding complex situations. The high point in the history of psychological work on motivation came, from our point of view, in a classical article by White (1959).

In his very comprehensive and insightful article, White developed a motivational theory which we find especially useful and sensible and which bears on the achievement motive. White referred to this motive as the "motive for competency." He argued that behavioral energy comes largely from the feeling of efficacy in accomodating to the environment. Moreover, he saw human behavior as basically social psychological. In other words, human striving for achievement exists primarily in relation to someone, or some group, or some environmental situation. Such striving does *not* emanate just from an inborn attribute. It develops through social learning and through coping with challenges and this coping, in turn, brings social rewards with it. Basically, the environment responds well and it feels good inside when we behave competently!

To act competently requires that the individual has a realistic and objective view of the immediate environment. Pepitone (1964) referred to the search for accurate knowledge about the external world as the need for *cognitive validation*. The need for cognitive validation develops along with the striving for competence. The individual learns how to attend to particular environmental cues and how to "read the world" in relation to his or her own coping skills. The psychodynamics of cognitive validation commence at a very early age as the infant establishes mental pictures and unconscious predictions about the world. Through simple conditioning, footsteps come to be associated with food, and arms with caring. Later, more complex cognitive pictures are painted about the mother's feelings—about her affection and her anger. As life accumulates in complexity and difficulty, it becomes necessary to rely to a greater extent on one's readings of the environment based on previous experiences. People would not exist very long—at least exist normally— if every social situation were completely new and completely unpredictable. To attain maturity means, in part, that we have a variety of psychological skills for coping competently with changing situations.

But the six-year-old has not, of course, attained such competency. Consider a child's first school experience! For many children, especially those who have had little experience outside of their nuclear family, the unknown nature and unpredictability of the classroom can be frightening and even traumatic. For many children, the anxiety is so great in relation to the first days at school that a syndrome known as "school phobia" has been noted by psychologists as a common phenomenon. Of course, most youngsters who manifest a school phobia during the first days of the first grade will be able to cope with classroom interactions after they have developed some clear expectations about what life will be like in school, with the teacher, and with classmates. Even some teachers experience a certain amount of anxiety and stress when they are faced with a new class in a new neighborhood. Indeed, it is generally frightening for any person to think of entering a scene where past experiences may not hold true. Under such circumstances the human striving for competency is heightened; the behavior we see represents how the individual has learned to act competently in strange and new circumstances.

Expectations and Interpersonal Relations

The complexities involved in relating competently with the physical world seem small compared with the depths of meaning and feelings that arise out of relationships with other people. Expectations are a natural part of interpersonal relations. For our own security and cognitive clarity, we normally make subconscious predictions about how a particular interpersonal interchange will transpire. Indeed, a great deal of our relationships with others take on an almost game-like quality; there are rules to follow and we establish regularized routines quickly in many of our relationships. Most people follow the rules and put themselves into the regularized routines most of the time.

Indeed, we have tended to establish so many interpersonal games and to follow routinely so many rules that a major problem of contemporary urban society is the erosion of genuine interpersonal closeness and authenticity. We interact all too often as partners in a role configuration—as wife, husband, child, teacher, student, and administrator—leaving out of our relationships any recognition of the fact that we all are individuals. We have thereby made it increasingly difficult to establish interpersonal intimacy and empathy. The rise and strength of the encounter group movement during the past twenty-five years attest to the fact that many people are searching for avenues back into relationships that are less game-like and more authentic. Unfortunately, many people have become encounter group zealots—striving to achieve depth and meaning in virtually all human interchanges. We believe that such intensity of experience cannot easily occur in every relationship that human beings have —it would be exhausting and dysfunctional. Hopefully, we can learn to use interpersonal skills for playing out the rules of the game effectively sometimes, and to break down the game-like barriers for achieving closeness and empathy at other times.

In most formal role relationships we usually play out the rules of the game. We expect particular behaviors from the supermarket clerk, others from the plumber, and still others from the physician. Moreover, generally we expect the same sorts of behaviors from all clerks, all plumbers, and all physicians. Of course, as we get to know each of them as individuals we gradually expand our pool of expectations about them. We come to expect certain idiosyncracies from each clerk, each plumber, and each physician. We come to expect a joke from the clerk at the corner store, or a sour face from that plumber who fixed our shower, or a special kind of greating from the family doctor. And we might become mildly upset if the three do not act in ways we come to expect.

There also are formal role relationships within the school. Particular behaviors are expected from persons playing various roles in the building; the secretary in the office performs functions and behaves quite differently from the principal; and the custodian differs from the aides. Even on the first meeting of a class in which the teacher and students are strangers to one another, certain expectations already exist because the classroom context carries meanings even without interpersonal interaction. These nomothetic features of classroom life soon give way to some extent, however, as the teacher and students get to know one another. The students soon develop pictures of how the teacher will behave in certain situations; the teacher learns to count on particular students for the correct answer; students learn which of their peers will be helpful to them and which ones will stay away from them; and all members will begin to establish expectations about the students who will create trouble, those who will study hard, and those who will help the group to laugh. Thus, the development of both nomothetic and idiographic expectations about interpersonal behavior in the classroom is natural and inevitable.

Expectations Include an Assessment

Expectations about interpersonal relations involve more psychological content than just cognitive predictions. They also involve making assessments of other people along evaluative dimensions. In other words, interpersonal expectations are made up of both thoughts and feelings. Obviously, the teacher assesses the student who is expected to do exemplary work differently from the student who is expected to be a troublemaker. Likewise, students will assess peers they expect to be congenial differently from those they expect to be moody or aggressive.

Evaluation as a part of interpersonal expectations emerges in bold relief when one's expectations are not met. The parents who expect their child to act in a well-mannered fashion in a restaurant are disappointed when the child does not live up to their expectations; and a teacher who expects students to work independently will become upset when students act in a disorderly fashion during a study period. The student will feel rejected and angry when his trusted friend puts him down publicly by revealing something confidential.

Colloquially, the term "expect" often is used to mean "holding hopes or aspirations." When parents say, "We expect you to have good table manners," they may in fact be hoping the child will have good manners but actually predict no such thing. If they simply predicted good table manners, they would not be motivated to communicate a reminder to the child. The teacher who "expects" students to study independently may also appoint a monitor to watch over the students during study time. The presence of a monitor may communicate to the students that the teacher expects them to goof off. In other words, the monitor communicates merely by walking up and down the aisles that the teacher predicts trouble during independent study.

We believe that interpersonal predictions can have an even stronger effect on group processes in the classroom than interpersonal hopes and aspirations. In this chapter, we will *not* use the concept of expectations to mean hopes or aspirations. Instead, we will use it to mean those working predictions that are used in relating with others in the classroom. When such expectations are not supported, feelings will inevitably interact with the cognitive predictions.

Expectations Are Communicated

Expectations as interpersonal predictions are communicated in various direct and indirect ways. Consider, for example, a student who has seriously broken a school rule for the first time and is called to the principal's office. If the principal says something like, "I'm surprised and disappointed in your behavior; explain to me how this happened," a different interpersonal stage has been set between the principal and the student than if the principal says, "This is intolerable, but I'm not surprised; I'm going to make sure that you are not in a position to do this again." The first communication from the principal establishes that the principal did not predict that the student would have behaved the way he or she did, while the second communication establishes that the principal does believe that the misbehavior will continue unless strong measures are taken.

There are other more indirect ways of communicating one's predictions about other people. For example, the teacher who has an important observer visiting within the classroom may choose to call on those students whom she predicts will be able to perform well. Her interest in showing off a bright and capable class will not be missed by the students even if it is missed by the observer. In another example, students making choices for a baseball team will, in the doing, convey their assessments of another student's baseball skills to the entire group. In still another, a student indirectly communicates his predictions about interpersonal rapport by approaching one classmate for academic help rather than another.

It is important to point out here that interpersonal predictions are often incorrect. The teacher may actually call on the wrong students to get the correct answers; the students may not choose the very best baseball players first; and the student may not choose the most skillful helper in a given academic area. Nevertheless, these behaviors communicate interpersonal expectations that can have impact in creating the reality they predict.

Finn (1972, p. 390) has defined expectations usefully from our point of view. He wrote that expectations are evaluations—whether conscious or unconscious—that one person forms of another (or of himself) which lead the evaluator to treat the person evaluated as though the assessment were valid. The person doing the expecting typically anticipates that the other person will act in a manner consistent with the assessment.

Self-Expectations

No less crucial to an understanding of group processes within the classroom are the expectations that each participant has for his own behavior. Although self expectations develop within specific social situations, they also are influenced strongly by the general picture of self brought into the situation. We all make predictions of how well or poorly we will do in a given situation based in part on our feelings of security and self confidence in general.

Consider the youngster who was called to the principal's office. If he had an image of himself as a troublemaker, even though he never had broken a serious school rule, he may have thought to himself, "Here I go again!" On the other hand, the student who views himself as a conscientious, rule-abiding member of the school will view the interaction with the principal quite differently. Likewise, the student who knows he is skillful in baseball may not care if he's chosen near the end and the student who has many friends may not be frustrated by not being chosen as an academic helper.

Sometimes the images we hold of ourselves are so firmly set that our self-expectations are realized even though the objective facts may be quite different. Eric Berne (1972), as part of his work on transactional analysis, has developed the concept of life-script to explain the power of self-expectations. Life-scripts are firmly grounded in self-expectations. For example, the "born loser" confirms his lack of effectiveness again and again. He always loses and in fact seems able to perceive a loss even when he actually is on the winning side. For most people, feedback can be used to reassess competencies and to move to a new level of self-expectations. For the loser, however, favorable feedback can be twisted and tangled until it fits the negative image he has of himself.

Self-Expectations and Achievement

We believe that students, for the most part, strive to be competent and that the ways in which they will behave to prove their competency are strongly influenced by their self-expectations for personal success. Students with low confidence in their own abilities will behave differently than students who have high self confidence. And the classroom group is used often as a testing ground for the student's self-expectations. A student who believes that an excellent job has been done on an assignment and who receives a similar evaluation from the teacher will feel bolstered by the classroom experience. If a low evaluation had been received, the dissonance would have motivated that student to reassess capabilities and to expect a somewhat lower level of personal performance on subsequent occasions.

Research has shown that classroom performance can be altered by changes in students' self images. Benjamin (1950) first asked forty-eight senior high school students to rank themselves on their own intelligence level. Next, he administered an intelligence test, after which he presented false information to each student about his or her performance. For half of the students, Benjamin presented scores that were one level above what the students expected, and for the other half, scores below actual student predictions were presented. Finally, Benjamin administered another form of the same intelligence test. A majority of scores for the second test changed in the direction of the falsely reported ranks; students who thought they did better than they had expected performed better on the second test and students who thought they did poorer than they had expected actually did do poorer on the second test.

In other research Sears (1940) showed that a student's level of aspiration is influenced by his or her past experiences in the area of success and failure within the classroom. She tested a sample of upper elementary students on their arithmetic and reading performance, making estimates of the time each student took to complete a page of work. Those students who experienced failure on these tests set their levels of aspiration at unrealistically high or unrealistically low levels. These unrealistic students had a high fear of failure, lacked self-confidence, and viewed themselves as losers. Either they set up each situation so that they would most certainly succeed and be able to dismiss their success to themselves by saying "anyone can do that!" or they set goals that they could not possibly achieve, once again proving to themselves that they were incompetent. Those students who set realistic goals were the ones who had experienced successes in the past. They chose levels of aspiration that were challenging but which offered high probabilities of success nonetheless.

In more recent research DeCharms (1971, 1972) theorized that students differ according to the extent that they act as "pawns," and as "origins." Pawns are students who possess very little self-confidence. They feel that someone or something else is in control over them and they do not often make deliberate choices about the direction of their lives. An origin, on the other hand, is a student who directs his or her own life.

Origins are confident that they can make choices on their own and can planfully pursue their own interests. DeCharms has applied these theoretical notions to classroom situations.

In his research, DeCharms looked at two important hypotheses bearing on his theory about student pawns and origins. First, he posited that student pawns and origins are created out of the expectations that other key people hold for them. Second, he posited that a relationship exists between origin-like student behavior and successful academic achievement. He conducted a three-year intervention and evaluation program in an urban school district to test these hypotheses, collecting data from fifth graders and following these same students during their sixth and seventh grades.

Simultaneously to collecting data from fifth graders about their pawn-origin orientations, DeCharms was training sixth and seventh grade teachers on how to help students develop more origin-like behavior. The teachers were trained to use exercises for bolstering the self-concept, procedures for stimulating achievement striving, and were taught concepts bearing on the pawn-origin concept. DeCharms' evaluation data showed that in the experimental groups the teachers did change their classroom behaviors and that the students in these same groups gained in academic achievement and in origin-like behaviors as compared with control groups. DeCharms showed, in other words, that a student's expectations about his or her own behavior can be crucial to what happens in the student's striving for academic achievement and that a teacher can have significant influence on the expectations that a student develops about himself or herself.

How Expectations Develop

Developing expectations about how other people will behave in particular circumstances is a very natural, human phenomenon. Without predictions and assessments of others, in fact, life would be overly complex, perhaps even chaotic. We have attempted to show that the most obvious and direct way of obtaining expectations of others is through repetitive interaction with them. At the same time, there are other less direct avenues for developing interpersonal expectations as when people fill such roles as clerk, physician, or plumber. In schools, teachers and students use many ways to develop assessments of others. We believe that four means of developing interpersonal expectations are used most frequently in school settings. These are the gathering of information about others; the stereotypes of social class, minority group membership, and sex; the force of a social situation in which the other is placed; and the ways a person is assumed to act because of his or her role in a group. Let us explore each of these.

Expectations Through Gathering of Information

Many teachers routinely receive formal information about their students. School records typically describe each student's psychological history in terms of grades, I.Q. scores, and achievement test scores; some cumulative school records include scores on personality inventories and notes of anecdotes or impressions prepared by former teachers. Conscientious teachers seek out these kinds of data and use them to plan their instructional program. The reason for such deliberate planning is obvious, especially in special skill courses involving reading and math. Students who are performing below an expected standard for their chronological age will, of course, require special instruction.

Some teachers also use other diagnostic techniques to obtain information about their students. These include attitude inventories, sociometric tests, student essays, discussions about goals and aspirations, or special diagnostic tests focused on specific academic areas. Such attempts at diagnosing classroom learning environments and the attitudes of the students can help move teacher and students closer together and can facilitate collaboration and emotional support in the peer group.

Unfortunately, data about students are often misused by teachers. Information about students' previous intellectual performances and their personality characteristics can predispose teachers to expect the students to continue to perform as they have in the past. And these teachers' expectations, in turn, can influence the sorts of interactions that take place between teacher and students. There are teachers, for example, who use reading achievement scores to set up permanent reading groups, thus building psychological boundaries between students. Often such grouping is implemented on the basis of a single test. Even first grade teachers who have very little data on children at their disposal still use informal and intuitive means to estimate their students' I.Q.s before any testing takes place. Doyle, Hancock, and Kifer (1971) asked first grade teachers to estimate their students' I.Q.s before formal testing. Then, later in the school year, they found that those students whose I.Q.s had been overestimated by the teacher had achieved more in reading than would have been predicted from an I.Q. score. Conversely, those students whose I.Q.s had been underestimated achieved less. Furthermore, the research showed that teachers who generally underestimated the I.Q.s for their entire class had students who were achieving less at the end of the school year compared with the students of teachers who had done more over-estimating.

The student who has been labeled as a troublemaker or behavior problem carries those labels with him from teacher to teacher. Such students sometimes are confronted on the very first day of class with a statement from the teacher such as, "You can be rest assured I will not allow you to get away with any misbehavior here!" Or, the teacher might comment; "I've heard about you; for starters, you can sit right here by my desk so I can keep my eye on you." Typically, such troublemakers are boys, thus giving rise to the teacher stereotype that boys will require more control than girls. Some boys begin to act out the stereotype because the teachers expect them to create some disturbances.

Likewise, students gather information about teachers from which they develop expectations. Of course, the information retrieval process is not so formal as that of cumulative records. Information about teachers usually gets passed on through the informal "grapevine." It has been our experience that teachers seem reticent to acknowledge the fact that students pass on information about teachers and that students very quickly form favorable and unfavorable expectations about particular teachers. But the process of sharing expectations about teachers within the student peer group is very real. Students say, "He's hard," "She's strict," "He's nice," "She's interesting," "He's having trouble at home, so he doesn't demand much," and "She dislikes the principal," etc. In a few open schools that we know about, information about teachers has been organized and disseminated formally. It is seen as legitimate and useful to talk about the attributes of the staff. Some of these schools have booklets that describe courses and teachers. Other schools, described by Shaw (1973), have built formal procedures for getting student evaluations of teachers to the teachers as a means of improving instruction. Information about teachers or students can be valuable and useful provided it is descriptive and not just evaluative.

Expectations Through Cultural Stereotypes

Like all of us, students and teachers are continually bombarded by images of the sociological categories that exist in the culture. Such images are transmitted through television, newspapers, radio, and books as well as through discussions of social events with family and friends and through participation in the neighborhood with civic groups and other organizations. This transmission process, often referred to as acculturation, involves the internalization of stereotypes. A stereotype involves assumptions and beliefs about a category of people that are assigned to every member of that category. So, for example, "redheads have tempers," "electricians are skinny," "plumbers are fat," or "southerners are bigots." Such thinking is natural and becomes detrimental when we do not allow new information to change the stereotypes. Three kinds of cultural stereotypes that are prominent (and often detrimental to healthy classroom interaction) in our society involve the categories of social class, minority group membership, and sex.

Frequently, teachers establish firm expectations about a group of students because of the socioeconomic level of the neighborhood in which the students live. In one study, Rist (1970) documented how first grade teachers perpetuated a social class hierarchy within the classroom by assigning students to reading groups according to their socioeconomic background. Unknowingly the teachers placed middle class children in higher level reading groups than the lower class children. A study conducted by Finn (1972) revealed that teachers of suburban schools held higher expectations for the academic performances of their students than teachers of urban schools. Finn asked 300 fifth-grade teachers to evaluate some essays written by students. The essays were accompanied by fictional data on the sex, race, intelligence level, and achievement test scores. The urban teachers paid special attention to the fictional information on intelligence and achievement in evaluating the quality of the essays. The suburban teachers, in contrast, were less influenced by the fictional data. Finn wrote, "In the urban school, the expectations held by the teachers for pupils of differing ability and achievement were so strong as to pervade their evaluations of the pupil's actual performance (p. 403)." His conclusion was that the urban teachers had built an image of urban students as being socioeconomically deprived and expected them to have low intelligence and achievement levels.

In another study focusing on the problem of social class and discrimination in the schools, Martell (1971) discussed a legal brief that had been prepared by a community group in Toronto maintaining that the Toronto school district had discriminated against students from low-income families. Apparently with good intentions, students of low-income families were being placed in "opportunity classes" which were seen by everyone as the "bottom stream of the educational ladder." The community group's survey (included within the legal brief) showed that

"if . . . you're classified . . . 'sheet metal worker' . . . your child has 18.5 [times] the chance of ending up in one of these bottom streams as the child of an accountant, engineer, or lawyer! The figure jumps to 40 times the chance if you are on workman's compensation or retired and to 43.5 for unemployed and 67 times the chance for welfare or mother's allowance (p. 11)."

Acknowledging the fact that lower class children did indeed have more academic problems than their middle class counterparts, the community group asked that their children be granted adequate educational facilities and resources without the cultural stigma of being "dumb" and "deprived." The group exhorted the school to emphasize the positive resources of children from lower class and minority group backgrounds and to measure success and resourcefulness in the school more broadly than before.

Of all the cultural stereotypes that pervade American society, none is so destructive as the stereotypes of racial and ethnic group differences. In our society the visible minority groups—Afro-Americans, Mexican-Americans, Native-Americans, and Asian-Americans — are continually faced with and must cope with pervasive stereotypes about themselves. Along with obvious discrimination in jobs, housing, and education, the damage of cultural stereotyping is heightened by informal relationships in organizations and informal groupings. And, of course, the sort of social phenomenon described by Finn in which teachers hold different expectations for minority group youngsters is too often true.

Our consciousness has also been alerted recently to the stereotyping of the sexes. In one study of first grade teachers, Palardy (1969) asked the teachers to indicate whether, among first-graders, boys could learn to read as fast as girls. For those teachers who did not expect a difference in reading performance between the sexes, there was not any difference by the end of the year. Conversely, those teachers who expected the girls to learn to read faster than the boys did typically fulfill their predictions. Other sorts of stereotypes having to do with personality attributes and behavioral characteristics are, of course, also communicated within classrooms and schools.

Expectations Through Social Situations

The cultural meanings inherent in particular social situations also can be important in developing interpersonal expectations. In a clever research project by Rosenhan (1973), eight stooges were admitted to a mental hospital after feigning the hearing of voices. After admission, all eight behaved naturally. They presented accurate stories about their backgrounds, personal interests, and social norms. All eight were admitted with the diagnosis of schizophrenia and released subsequently with the label of schizophrenia in remission.

While in the hospital, perfectly normal behaviors and interests on the part of the eight healthy stooges were interpreted by the hospital staff as part of the schizophrenic syndrome. Although the staff remained detached, impersonal, and sometimes cruel toward the eight, all of the stooges believed that staff members were not operating out of malice or incompetence. Rosenhan concluded that the staff's perceptions and behaviors were influenced more by the culture associated with the hospital situation than by malicious dispositions. In a different, more benign environment, the staff members' reactions no doubt would have been more supportive and effective. The main point of the research was that the labeling of someone as schizophrenic within a hospital situation overdetermines others' reactions to that person.

Professional personnel within schools often interact with students in particular social situations that give rise to interpersonal expectations. The vice-principal in charge of discipline may assume right off that a student walking into the office has done something wrong. School psychologists who are asked to test a child may quickly assume that the child has a serious problem for which they must find an appropriate diagnostic label. And remedial reading teachers may expect the students they receive to have serious reading disabilities. In all of these social situations, expectations may significantly bias the sort of interaction that would take place.

A teacher who taught a special classroom of mentally retarded students in a junior high school, had reason to believe that many of them could perform quite well in a regular class, even though most of the students had been in the special class for several years. After careful mental testing, done at her insistence, she discovered that less than half actually were retarded. Many of the youngsters needed special help; many were from lower class and minority group backgrounds. Most of the children were not, however, technically retarded. The teacher experienced great difficulty in trying to persuade the school's administrators that new alternatives were called for; she had even more difficulty in convincing the students that they were indeed *not* mentally retarded.

Expectations Through Taking a Role

Over a period of time all groups—families and classrooms included— develop a regular pattern of interpersonal behavior. This regularized interpersonal pattern can be referred to as the group's informal role structure. In some families, for example, one child may take on the role of mediator while another performs more often as the scapegoat. Indeed, some learning problems that students have can be traced to a role they are playing out within their families. In many classrooms, student roles emerge early and remain the same throughout the year. Some students are pegged early as helpers, clowns, wise guys, and troublemakers. Often interpersonal expectations become so firm and consensual that individual students find it difficult to get support for making changes in their behaviors.

The Circular Interpersonal Process

In interpersonal exchanges between two people, expectations about the other person interact psychologically with self-expectation to give rise to the behavior. These two kinds of expectations, about the other and about the self, grow out of previous encounters with the other and through other indirect avenues such as information, cultural stereotypes, social situations, and expected role functions.

Two examples of common interpersonal exchanges in classrooms may be instructive. Students who view themselves as competent, secure, and helpful typically will behave in friendly, supportive, and enhancing ways. Other students will perceive this friendliness and helpfulness and in turn convey their own satisfaction with the others' behaviors. The first-mentioned students are reinforced for their behavior. Later, if they do not behave in these expected ways there may be surprise and even disappointment shown. Others will think, "I wonder what is wrong with them today?"

Conversely, troublemaking students become engaged in a much different sort of behavioral cycle. Teachers often have defined for themselves who the troublemakers are and quickly curtail behaviors from the troublemakers that they would normally allow from others. The teachers usually argue that, "the troublemaker doesn't know when to stop, so I have to do it." Yet, troublemaking students come to rely on the teacher to control their behavior and thus expect to be controlled.

When two people interact over a long period of time, their relationship becomes rather stable and predictable. Lippitt (1962) has referred to this stable and predictable interpersonal exchange as the *circular interpersonal process*. As you can see in Figure 1, the two most important factors in the initiation of any behavior are the attitudes and expectations one has of the self as well as the attitudes and expectations one holds for the other.

Figure 3.1 shows, in boxes 1 and 2, the psychological processes and behaviors of person A. Attitudes about the self and others, as well as the expectations that A holds for the behaviors of others, influence A's intention to act, and in turn influence the way A behaves in relation to others. Each aspect of A's behavior is shown as arising out of these psychological processes.

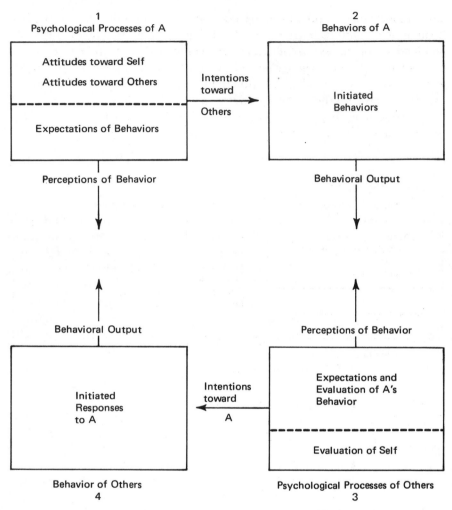

FIGURE 3.1 / *Circular Interpersonal Process.*

To complete the circle, psychological processes and behaviors of others are depicted in boxes 3 and 4. The others' perceptions of A's behavior influence their expectations and assessments of A and themselves. These help to shape the others' intentions which, in turn, become actualized in behavioral output. A perceives these behaviors, and the circle is completed.

An example of a positive and supportive cycle of interpersonal relations is shown in Figure 3.2. Student A has a positive feeling about self and about others, and has received liking responses from others, thus feeling secure in their presence. A's behaviors toward others represent a blend of openness, helpfulness, and congeniality. As others perceive A's behaviors, their expectations of A as a warm, supportive person are confirmed; A is viewed as nonthreatening and as enhancing the others' positive views of themselves. Others are thereby free to interact with A without fear of losing security or self-esteem. Their responses are positive and supportive toward A; and A, in turn, receives reinforcing

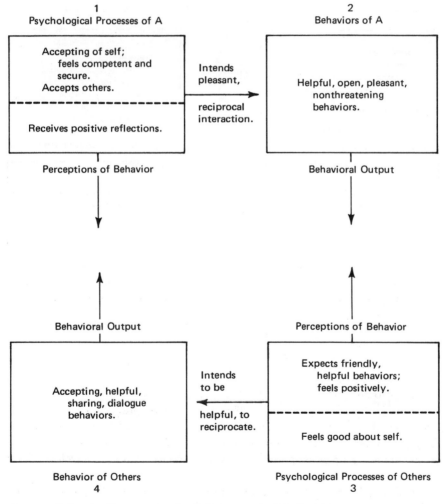

FIGURE 3.2 / *Positive Cycle of Interpersonal Relations.*

evidence of personal likability. Thus, person A and associates support each other in a mutually friendly and respectful interchange.

Figure 3.3 describes a negative cycle of interpersonal relations, one which is significantly more unsupportive than the one shown in Figure 3.2. Student A has ambivalent feelings about self and about others, and has adopted a defensive interpersonal orientation because of rejection or isolation in the past. A student with a psychological pattern characterized by low self-esteem, insecurity, and feelings of incompetence might

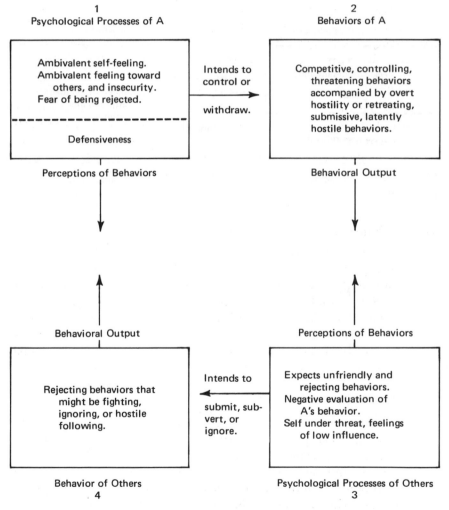

FIGURE 3.3 / *Negative Cycle of Interpersonal Relations.*

behave in one of at least two very different ways. One person could attempt to control others in order to establish self as being worthy; an absence of affiliation for such persons can lead to a grab for power. Another person might withdraw from others and become an isolate so as not to face their rejection. Such people often retreat submissively, accepting others' attempts to influence them while still harboring latent hostility toward them. Both patterns of behavior—domination or withdrawal—would likely be viewed as unfriendly and unhelpful and the communication of these perceptions will confirm A's self expectation of being unfriendly, unhelpful, and rejected.

The expectations about a student's behavior that are set may become so firm that even as a student attempts behavioral changes others will not perceive the changes. Expectations can influence perceptions to such a degree that incoming information is biased and distorted. Thus, a student involved within a negative interpersonal cycle might try to act in a friendly fashion. The student might, for example, tap another student softly on the shoulder to indicate liking or to indicate agreement nonverbally, but such physical behavior might be perceived as hitting or acting smart or as trying to start an argument. Negative cycles of interpersonal relations can become especially vicious when even neutral and benign behaviors are viewed as negative and as confirming original expectations.

Teacher Expectations and Student Performance

Through circular interpersonal processes such as those described above, teachers' expectations for students affect their interaction with the students and at the same time affect the psychological reactions of the students. Recent studies in the social psychology of classroom interaction have sought to establish the validity of this general hypothesis and to go beyond it by pinpointing how the teacher's expectations relate to the quality of the circular interpersonal process and how different qualities of interpersonal interaction relate to student academic performance.

The Self-Fulfilling Prophecy

An early pioneer in American sociology, W. I. Thomas, set forth a postulate basic to social psychology: "If men define situations as real, they are real in their consequences." Later, Robert Merton (1949) elaborated on Thomas's postulate in his classical text by introducing the self-fulfilling prophecy. Merton argued that public predictions or prophecies of a situation can become an integral part of the situation and thus affect subsequent developments. The self-fulfilling prophecy is, at the outset, an invalid definition of the situation evoking a new cluster of behaviors which makes the originally false conception come true. An attempt to show how the self-fulfilling prophecy is at work in the classroom was made by Rosenthal and Jacobson (1968).

The title of their book, *Pygmalion in the Classroom* made reference to Bernard Shaw's story of how an unschooled young woman from the slums was transformed into a "fair lady." In their research, Rosenthal and Jacobson presented false information to a sample of teachers about their students. The experimenters told the experimental teachers that some of their youngsters tested out as "academic spurters"—they would show great progress in their academic achievement during the school year. Other youngsters were given no special designation by the experimenters. In actuality, tests of academic potentiality were never actually administered, and the students who were described as "spurters" were chosen randomly. Data collected after the year of schooling showed that the "spurters" made more significant gains in intelligence test scores, reading test scores, and in the teachers' ratings about their personal and social adjustment than their nonlabeled peers.

Several reviewers of *Pygmalion in the Classroom* severely criticized the research methods employed in the study. For example, Thorndike (1968) and Snow (1969) questioned the presumed reliability of the I.Q. measures pointing out that some of the premeasures of intelligence were incredibly low. These and other critics also criticized the use of teachers as data collectors, the accuracy of the data, and the resulting analyses. Critics pointed out that the data as presented in the tables and appendix caused questions to be raised as to the interpretations made by Rosenthal and Jacobson. Rosenthal (1973), by himself, responded to the critics by showing that as many as 84 out of 242 studies had replicated aspects of the original Pygmalion research, giving substantial corroboration to the original findings. Rosenthal argued that only 12 studies, not 84, would be expected to support the Pygmalion hypotheses by chance. Finn (1972) and Brophy and Good (1972) offered very useful and reasonable reviews of the Pygmalion studies, pointing to the many methodological problems inherent in this sort of research on the circular interpersonal process. Both reviews concluded that the research on the self-fulfilling prophecy in the classroom leaves little doubt that the expectations of teachers have important and real effects on students. However, both reviewers also concluded that the impact of these expectation effects probably are not so strong as the Pygmalion zealots would have us believe. Nevertheless, one must conclude that the making of a "fair lady" is observable and measurable in the classroom.

The Quality of Teacher-Student Interaction

In the Rosenthal and Jacobson study no data was collected on interpersonal interaction between teacher and spurters. The Pygmalion effects were established by noting statistical variations between what the experimental teachers were told about their students (analogous to teachers' reading cumulative student records) and how the students changed in their performance on mental tests. What might occur in terms of social processes between teacher expectations and student academic performance has been studied by Brophy and Good (1970). Indeed, they established a new and, from our point of view, improved methodological direction in research on the self-fulfilling prophecy.

Brophy and Good put special emphasis on the quality of teacher-student interaction within the context of studying Pygmalion effects. They did not look at mental test scores nor did they attempt to manipulate the teachers' expectations. Instead, they asked four teachers about their current expectations for different students—expectations that were formed naturally—and then very carefully studied the circular interpersonal processes themselves.

Brophy and Good asked the four teachers to rank all of their current students according to intellectual ability. Then observers plotted the sorts of circular interpersonal processes that occurred in the four classrooms. The data indicated that those students whom the teachers labeled as having very high ability received more praise, more coaching and help in forming ideas, and more time in answering questions than those students whom they labeled as having low ability. In the case of the students who were designated as having low ability, the teachers were more critical, accepted poorer quality answers, and were less likely to praise good performance even when quality performance did occur. The research indicated that the teachers waited longer for the "high-ability" students to answer difficult questions than they did for the "low-ability" students to answer, just the reverse of what most teachers would consider to be sound pedagogy.

In a partial replication of the Brophy-Good research, Rubovits and Maehr (1971) studied neophyte student teachers. The student teachers were told that their students were either from the "gifted track" or the "regular track" of the schools they attended. Like the findings of the Brophy and Good study, the teachers paid attention to and praised the "gifted students" more than they did the "regular students."

Using these and other studies, Rosenthal (1973) discussed four social psychological mechanisms by which teachers communicate expectations for student performance. The first is *climate;* high expectations for another's behavior give rise to a climate of warmth, attention, and emotional support. Second is *feedback;* teachers give more encouragement and praise to students for whom they have high expectations. Third is the sort of *input* that teachers give to students for whom they have high expectations; they rephrase questions, give helpful hints to answers, and give more information to students they believe know an answer than to "low-ability" students. Finally, the fourth social psychological mechanism involves the teacher's encouragement for the *output* of student responses; teachers wait longer for answers from "high-ability" students than from their "low-ability" peers.

Although competent teaching involves helping students move a step beyond where they are presently, the Pygmalion research indicates that many teachers follow this rule of thumb only for those students for whom they have high expectations. Many teachers do not encourage or demand high performance from students who they believe have low ability. Apparently for most teachers their bias in favor of high-ability youngsters is unconscious. If teachers are to be instrumental in helping each student perform optimally, one of the essential understandings they must have concerns their own expectations for students. Through introspection, teachers may be able to note how they are unwittingly behaving in discriminatory ways within the classroom. It is hoped that they can become aware of the natural tendency to focus more on the students who are doing well and to pursue a consistent course of appropriate and equitable support and encouragement for all students.

We know that giving appropriate and equitable support to all students is not easy. We know too that as parents we often have influenced our daughter and son to behave in favorable and unfavorable ways because of our expectations for their behavior. We know that as teachers we often have behaved inappropriately because of our expectations. It's because of our own frustrations over trying to conquer the subtle power of interpersonal expectations that we like to think back on a very successful teaching experience that one of us had.

It was Patricia Schmuck's experience while she was teaching a group of boys with severe learning disabilities. Her initial impression was how unlovable the boys were. They had been academic failures and their self-concepts were very negative. They were often boisterous, uncooperative, and just plain obnoxious. While she found it easy to see what was wrong with the boys, it was very difficult nonetheless for her to find their redeeming attributes. Needless to say she started the school year by not expecting much academic performance and by expecting a great deal of difficulty.

In an attempt to overcome her own negative expectations, it was decided that she should seek to discover at least one attribute of each boy that was likable and hopefully resourceful. She did find strengths and admirable qualities in each boy that were hidden under many layers of defensiveness and aggressiveness. She employed some of the action ideas found at the end of this chapter and several that are described in later chapters of this book. Her eye was on developing a comfortable climate, on using as much positive feedback as possible, on attending to any nonverbal cues of confusion from the boys, and on sticking with them to clarify questions, procedures, and assignments. That year and that class of partially disturbed boys turned out to be one of her most satisfying teaching experiences and added a great deal of real, existential experience to what is being written about in this book. Once she had discovered something favorable about each student she was liberated from a tendency to coddle or apologize or make allowances for the students. She felt free to expect and demand adequate academic performances. In her own mind, she felt free to say honestly to each student, "You will do this assignment because I know that you really can do it—I am here to help and support you as you do the assignment!" In most instances, the Pygmalion effect worked and the boys were transformed into "admirable gentlemen."

Student Performance

The power of the self-fulfilling prophecy is very real to us. We believe the essence of the Rosenthal-Jacobson findings even though we question the simplicity of those findings. We believe—and some research supports this belief—that teachers have an influence on achievement, sociometric position, self-esteem, and satisfaction of students. At the same time, not all teachers have such power and even very powerful teachers do not influence all their students in the same ways. Certainly the influence of the students' families and of their neighborhood peer groups cannot be discounted. Even in the classroom, the teacher's expectations and resulting behaviors are mediated by the interpersonal norms and relationships in the peer group. We believe therefore that student performance is influenced simultaneously by the teacher, by the peer group, and by the family. Teachers' expectations for student achievement are very important but they represent only one phase of the multiple circular interpersonal processes that are occurring in the lives of the students.

Implications for Teachers

The following summary statements capture the key implications of the contents of this chapter for teachers.

—It is psychologically functional to develop expectations for the behaviors of students. These expectations normally include an evaluative assessment of the students.

—It is important to be aware of the expectations held for each individual student as well as for groups of students.

—Our expectations for how the student will behave influence the ways in which we behave in relation to the student.

—It is important to introspect and to obtain feedback about the ways in which we are behaving toward each student. It is also important to use many diverse sources of information for understanding what each student is like.

—Our interaction with students becomes stable and regularized over time.

—It is important to be ready to modify our expectations and behaviors toward students upon receiving new information.

—Our continual treatment of students can influence those students to behave in ways we expect them to behave.

—It is important to know about and to be able to implement action plans for breaking into negative circular interpersonal processes.

Action Ideas for Change

The following classroom practices were carried out by teachers in an attempt to reduce the detrimental effects of interpersonal expectations in the classroom.

CONFRONTING NEGATIVE CYCLES OF INTERPERSONAL RELATIONS. A junior high teacher working with a difficult group of youngsters introduced the diagram of circular interpersonal process (shown in Figure 3.1) as an instructional device. She discussed how people can become involved in negative cycles, using some of the contents of Figure 3.3. Next the teacher asked the students to enact some dramatic vignettes that she had developed to depict the ways in which negative cycles get going. She developed several scripts using ideas from Chesler and Fox (1966) in which each character's intentions and expectations were made clear to the students. It was up to the students to behave as they imagined the characters would have behaved. After the students had become accustomed to discussing interpersonal difficulties (after about three weeks), the teacher used real classroom events both in planned lessons and on the spot. All vicious cycles were not eliminated but they typically were ended rather quickly because of this curriculum. Although this teacher worked with this kind of curriculum for only the last four months of school, she planned to use it at the beginning of the following school year.

RAISING PEER'S EXPECTATIONS OF ISOLATED STUDENTS. A sixth grade teacher wanted to bring several isolated youngsters more squarely into the classroom peer group. After corroborating his suspicions of their isolation with a sociometric inventory, the teacher asked another teacher to collaborate in finding ways of bringing the three isolates into the group. Because all three students were rather good at school work, they were asked to serve as tutors in the other teacher's class for one hour every other day. Along with these three, several other less isolated children were also asked to serve as tutors. These six students in all were granted preferential treatment and thus could hardly go unnoticed by their classroom peers. The teacher also went to special lengths to praise and encourage the three isolates during regular class time. It should be noted, parenthetically, that these isolates did not display overt behavior problems; they were simply being ignored by their peers. After five months the teacher gave another sociometric inventory from which he discovered that the isolates were being chosen by several classmates. They had not become "stars" but they had made headway in gaining some acceptance from classmates.

COMBINING STUDENT AND TEACHER EXPECTATIONS FOR LEARNING. The expectations of students and teachers for learning can be combined by building contracts for learning cooperatively. Through collaborative discussions, students and teachers come to some agreement about what is to be learned, how it will be learned, and how long the learning process will take. We will illustrate such "contract-building" with two school situations: one plan was designed and implemented by a high school math teacher while the second was developed by a teacher of a self-contained third grade class.

The high school math teacher decided upon the basic concepts and skills (enumerated for the students as the competency requirements) to be learned over a particular period of time (usually two to three weeks) along with a system of accountability (most often a written test; sometimes an oral exam and sometimes a project). The teacher presented the students with several alternative means to take in learning to perform the competencies within the alotted time. Some options were: working collaboratively with several peers; using old workbooks and ditto sheets (new programmed materials were not available); working with a student teacher in a small group; or working in a large lecture-type session with the teacher. At the beginning of each period of work, the teacher would present the competencies to be mastered. Students would then decide how they would attempt to master the competencies and would present a written contract (indicating the means and schedule) to the teacher. The teacher offered conferences for those students who he saw could not handle the contract-building. Competency tests could be taken at any time and no limits were placed on how many times they could be taken. Many students would finish the competency requirements early. For these students, a supply of learning games were available. In fact, one war game lasted so long that a previously underachieving student worked for long periods of time outside of class to complete his competency requirements so that he could return to the game.

A third grade teacher used learning contracts in a more general way. Each day students were asked to write down how they would spend their time on the next day. At the very beginning of the year, the students planned for only one hour, then for half a day, and finally for the whole day. By the end of the year, many students were writing out week-long plans. The teacher also asked the students to each put down one new major learning objective for themselves each week. These objectives were as varied as learning the multiplication tables, learning not to interrupt, making a new friend, finishing a report, or making a spaceship. On Friday of each week, the students met in small groups to review their progress. These discussions with peers were especially helpful in giving new ideas to students who were having difficulty building and completing contracts.

References

Benjamin, J. "Changes in Relation to Influences Upon Self-Conceptualization." *Journal of Abnormal and Social Psychology.* 45 (1950):573-80.

Berne, E. *What Do You Say After You Say Hello: The Psychology of Human Destiny.* New York: Grove Press, 1972.

Brophy, J., and Good, T. "Teachers' Communication of Differential Expectations for Children's Classroom Performance: Some Behavioral Data." *Journal of Educational Psychology* 61 (1970):365-74.

———. "Teacher Expectations: Beyond the Pygmalion Controversy." *Phi Delta Kappan* 54 (1972):276-78.

Chesler, M., and Fox, R. *Role-Playing Methods in the Classroom.* Chicago: Science Research Associates, 1966.

DeCharms, R. "Personal Causation Training in the Schools." *Journal of Applied Social Psychology* 2, no. 2 (1972):95-113.

Doyle, W.; Hancock, G.; and Kifer, E. "Teachers' Perceptions: Do They Make a Difference?" Paper presented at annual meeting of the American Educational Research Association. 1971.

Finn, J. "Expectations and the Educational Environment." *Review of Educational Research* 42, no. 3 (1972):387-410.

Lippitt, R. "Unplanned Maintenance and Planned Change in the Group Work Process." in *Social Work Practice.* New York: Columbia University Press, 1962.

Martell, G. "Class Bias in Toronto Schools: The Park School Community Council Brief." *This Magazine is About Schools* 5, no. 4 (1971):7-35.

Merton, R. *Social Theory and Social Structure*. New York: Free Press, 1949.

Pepitone, A. *Attraction and Hostility*. New York: Atherton Press, 1964.

Palardy, J. M. "What Teachers Believe, What Children Achieve." *Elementary School Journal*, April 1969, pp. 370-74.

Rist, R. "Student Social Class and Teacher Expectations: The Self-Fulfilling Prophecy in Ghetto Education." *Harvard Educational Review* 40 (1970):411-51.

Rosenhan, D. L. "On Being Sane in Insane Places." *Science* 179 (1973):250-58.

Rosenthal, R. "The Pygmalion Effect Lives." *Psychology Today* 7, no. 4 (1973): 56-63.

Rosenthal, R., and Jacobson, L. *Pygmalion in the Classroom*. New York: Holt, Rinehart & Winston, 1968.

Rubovits, P. C., and Maehr, M. L. "Pygmalion Analyzed: Toward an Explanation of the Rosenthal-Jacobson Findings." *Journal of Personality and Social Psychology* 19 (1971):197-204.

Sears, P. "Levels of Aspiration of Academically Successful and Unsuccessful Children." *Journal of Abnormal and Social Psychology* 35 (1940):498-536.

Shaw, J. S. "Students Evaluate Teachers and It Works." *Nation's Schools* 91, no. 4 (1973):49-53.

Snow, R. E. "Unfinished Pygmalion." *Contemporary Psychology* 14 (1969): 197-99.

Thorndike, R. "Review of Rosenthal and Jacobson, *Pgymalion in the Classroom*." *American Educational Research Journal* 5 (1968).

White, R. W. "Motivation Reconsidered: The Concept of Competence." *Psychological Review* 66 (1959):297-333.

CHAPTER 4

Leadership

The human striving to wield influence in relation to important others is basic. It enters into classroom life whenever the quality of leadership is demonstrated by the teacher or by students. Although leadership has been studied more frequently than any other topic in this book, research on it has yielded diverse—even contradictory—findings. Nevertheless, despite this confusion about leadership, we believe the execution of influence in the classroom is one of the most significant group processes to shape the interpersonal climate. In this chapter, the focus is on group dynamics studies which help us understand the relationships between leadership and classroom climate.

Leadership generally has been conceptualized from two different perspectives, as a property of either an individual or of a group. From the individual point of view, leadership is analyzed in terms of the personality or social background characteristics of the leader. Historically, this position has been emphasized more, but it has had definite limitations. Generally, the research has not led to consistent results about the traits or behaviors of great leaders. The ability to lead successfully appears to involve more than just a single set of personality characteristics. For example, research on the personality traits of "successful" teachers has not led to any consistent findings (Ryans, 1960). Indeed, effective teachers appear to have a full array of traits with no particular personality pattern standing out.

The second perspective places emphasis on interaction within a group and appears to be more useful. Here leadership involves such variables as social prestige, the holding of legitimate authority, the performance of duties in a role, and the emotional relationship between leader and followers. The significant point about this perspective is its emphasis on the transactional interchange between the person exerting leadership and those who accept the influence. This view includes the social structure of the group and leadership is an *interpersonal event* in relation to that structure; it is not simply a personal style, intentions, or skills of an individual.

This second approach has been labeled "functional leadership"; leadership behaviors are defined in terms of needed group functions. Leadership is viewed as the performance of acts which help a group achieve its preferred outcomes and it is a dynamic process that exists between members of the classroom group. Such a view frees us from the concept that only teachers exert leadership in the classroom. Students also perform group functions; sometimes these behaviors facilitate classroom learning and other times they impede it. In fact it appears that students wield great amounts of classroom leadership. This becomes most obvious when students are victorious in a struggle with the authorities of the school.

In our analysis of classroom leadership, we wish to step beyond the perspective of functional leadership as being wielded only by the teacher, and to look at leadership as the influence processes within a classroom. Emphasis is on interpersonal influence—whether involved with academic concerns or not—within the group. Leadership is behavior which influences others in the classroom group to follow. Sometimes such behaviors are employed by the teacher, at other times by students; sometimes they may facilitate reaching educational goals, at other times they may impede the achievement of those goals. Of course the major concern here is with promoting leadership behaviors which facilitate the achievement of academic objectives. To this end functional leadership will be described first, followed by a discussion of the bases of power that are prominent in the classroom. Later there will be a discussion of the ways in which classroom members can use goal-directed influence (defined here as behavior that helps the group move toward valued educational goals).

Functional Leadership

Class members can influence one another in many different ways, but two general categories of group functions, task and social emotional, have been described as necessary for group effectiveness (Benne and Sheats 1948). Task functions help accomplish the work-oriented, subject-matter requirements of the classroom, while social emotional functions help the group maintain its internal cohesion and interpersonal feelings. Examples of task functions are the initiation of ideas, the seeking out and giving of information, clarifying or elaborating, summarizing, or checking to see if others in the class understand the curriculum. Examples of social emotional functions are the encouragment of others, the expression of feelings in class, harmonizing, compromising, seeing to it that silent members get a chance to speak, and the application of standards to the class's functioning. Ideally, most, if not all, students should be able to perform both task and social emotional functions. Generally, however, they do not. The teacher, in most classrooms, usually performs both sets of functions. Furthermore, in most classes, only a few students perform any particular group functions and quite often the ones the students perform are of the social emotional category rather than task functions.

Functional leadership emphasizes the transactional nature of group process in the classroom. The meaning of any leadership act or the execution of any group function arises out of the interpersonal relationships between class members as well as the nature of the acts themselves. The class member who is disliked or viewed as incompetent will not be successful in executing a group function even if his or her behaviors are appropriate and competent. Similarly, the influence of a student who is well liked will also be ineffective if that student either chooses to perform a group function at the wrong time, or fails to perform the function competently.

Classroom leadership involves interpersonal relationships and behavioral skills; it requires competent behaviors in relation to others—the meaning of any behavior being dependent upon the nature of the relationship between the members. The teacher who is interested in helping students improve their performance of the functions of leadership needs to be concerned with not only the students' behavioral repertoires for performing such acts but also the quality of the interpersonal relations and norms that determine the significance of behaviors.

Bases of Influence

An analysis of the bases of interpersonal influence is helpful for an understanding of leadership in the classroom. French and Raven (1959) have developed a useful set of categories concerning the bases of influence. The set includes *expert* power (extent of knowledge that a person is viewed as possessing), *referent* power (extent of identification or closeness that others perceive in relation to a person), *legitimate* power (stemming from internalized values that others have in relation to the accepted right of a person to be influential), *reward* power (extent to which a person is viewed as having ability to give rewards), and *coercive* power (extent to which a person is viewed as being able to punish others). According to research by Hornstein et al. (1968), teachers want to work under a principal who employs expert or referent power, but not under one who imposes legitimate or coercive power. We suspect that much the same is true for students in relation to their teacher.

These five bases of influence can be observed in a classroom by looking at *teacher authority* and *student power*. A teacher's legitimate power position is not achieved by dint of personal effort; a teacher has authority by virtue of values communicated to the students and their parents by the larger community outside the classroom. The school as a formal organization and the community through the elected school board designate the teacher as the legitimate and official authority in the classroom. Moreover, state laws usually grant the teacher certain powers to wield control and often set duties of a custodial nature upon the teacher. This legitimate authority of the teacher has three bases of interpersonal influence associated with it: legitimate, reward, and coercive powers. Research indicates that these are the least effective of the five bases of power for exerting interpersonal influence, yet we can not deny that teachers have power in the classroom. The major issue, then, is *not* that teachers have authority invested in their position, but rather *how* that authority is exerted interpersonally. Several studies support the supposition that successfully influential teachers develop *referent* or *expert* bases of power with their students.

In their classic study of leadership, White and Lippitt (1960) studied three types of leader behavior in boys' clubs. Each leader's authority position was rooted in legitimate influence, but there was a difference in the way each such power position was played out in interaction with the boys. The autocratic leader's power was based mostly on legitimacy with dependence on coercion, and to some extent on his rewarding the students. He made virtually all of the group's decisions; he gave specific directions as to what the work was to be and how it would be accomplished. The autocratic leader kept and used all of the legitimate power that was vested in him. The democratic leader, in contrast, based his power more on the boys' identifying with him, and to some extent on his expertise. He distributed power throughout the group to a considerable extent by asking the boys to perform many of the group's functions; for example, asking the students to decide among alternatives and then informing them of the various materials they might use as they set out to work. In short, the democratic leader used his authority position to distribute influence among the younger members of the group. The laissez-faire leader, at the other extreme, abdicated his authority and performed no leadership behavior. The only basis of power that he retained was that of legitimacy.

The behaviors of the students were strikingly different under the three types of leadership. Boys with the laissez-faire leaders experienced the most stress; they were disorganized, frustrated, and produced little if any work. Groups with autocratic leaders produced quantitatively more, but democratic groups were qualitatively better in their performance. The most outstanding difference between these two latter types of groups, however, was not in their productivity but rather in the interpersonal relations between the leader and members, and among the members themselves. Hostility, competitiveness, and high dependency marked the autocratic groups; openness, friendly communication, and independence typified the democratically-led groups.

The groups also differed in the matter of who did the performing of group influence functions. In the laissez-faire groups, very few influence functions were carried out by anyone. The designated laissez-faire leader exerted influence only rarely to keep the group stable. In the autocratic groups, influence resided almost solely in the assigned leader. He carried out mostly task functions, executing very few social emotional acts. In the democratic groups, both the designated leader and the members performed task behaviors that led to getting the work done and prompted social emotional behaviors which helped in maintaining a high quality of interpersonal relations within the group.

Another relevant piece of classroom research on the bases of influence was done by Kounin and Gump (1958) who studied ways in which teachers use their authority to discipline students. They were concerned with the social effects of a teacher's coercive power over one student for his misbehavior, on the rest of the class; they called the resulting social phenomenon in the peer group the "ripple effect." The research indicated that the most effective way for a teacher to use coercive power was to be very specific and clear about issuing instructions, or in the making of a disciplinary intervention. For example, when a teacher demanded, "Eric, put down the truck and go to the painting table," in contrast to simply, "Eric, stop that," the probabilities were quite good that Eric would conform and that other students who observed the more specific demand would show a higher degree of conformity with teacher requests subsequently. On the other hand, the research disclosed that harsh, punitive, and nonspecific techniques usually led to immediate changes in the behaviors of the misbehaving student but that such disciplinary tactics backfired because observing students would subsequently be more disruptive. In terms of the bases of influence, Kounin and Gump's research showed that teachers' coercive power is increased if they also have referent power. Teachers who are attempting to discipline students have greatest leverage when the students are attracted to them and in some sense identify with them (Kounin 1970).

Teachers enter the classroom with certain bases of power ascribed to them. Students typically view teachers as having legitimate authority and coercive power, and as holding the possibilities for reward. The actual leadership of teachers appears to be enhanced if they distribute group functions to the students, encourage independence, stimulate open communication, and attempt to become attractive to the students. Holding on tightly to authority and only occasionally allowing students to influence the class often leads to high dependency as well as resistance and interpersonal tension and friction. In short, the teacher should attempt to establish interpersonal influence relationships with students based on referent and expert power to go along with the legitimate, reward, and coercive bases of power. Even though students do not hold legitimate authority, they do have significant power in the classroom. They can get their peers to do things by rewarding them with smiles, gifts, or other inducements; they can also be influential by coercing peers through threats of physical punishment or exclusion. Some students are influential because they are charismatic, i.e., others find them attractive and can identify with them. Still others are able to get their peers to follow them because they are viewed as experts.

Several studies have systematically and empirically explored the characteristics of students with high power in formal group and classroom setting (Polansky, Lippitt, and Redl 1950; and Gold 1958). This research generally showed that the influential students possessed attributes that were valued by members of the peer group. Students who held positions of high power were good at doing things (expert power) and had a cluster of highly valued personal characteristics (referent power) such as strength, good looks, friendliness and helpfulness in interpersonal relations. Moreover, the actions of powerful students were observed more closely by their peers than the actions of others in the classroom. Thus, they could either measurably enhance or inhibit effective classroom group dynamics by their actions.

The teacher who is able to help influential students feel involved in the classroom will have an easier time influencing the entire group than a teacher who is in conflict with the high power students. Research on the "ripple effect" by Kounin, Gump, and Ryan (1961) indicated that the ripples of disturbance in the class were greatest when students with high power were the targets of the teacher's disciplinary actions. The entire class showed tension and behavioral disturbances when the high power students showed defiance toward the teacher's requests. Conversely, detrimental and disturbing ripple effects were barely discernible when low power students were the targets of a teacher's discipline.

The bases of teacher power are especially undermined in the classroom when overt conflict occurs with high power students. Since quite often the power of students is based on their being identification figures who are attractive (referent power) and teacher power is based only on legitimacy, high power students have more influence over the peer group than the teacher does. When teachers face overt conflict situations in the classroom, they cannot achieve influence and increase student learning by simply resorting to their legitimate authority or by using punishment. Coercion may gain short term, overt compliance, but punitive actions reduce the students' longer term interest and lessen the likelihood of reaching educational goals. Direct, open encounters between students and teacher—encounters recognizing the *right* of students to have some power over their own classroom procedures—can be used as a means for developing plans and procedures acceptable to both parties. The teacher who learns the skill of sharing decision making with students will generally achieve some degree of referent power and will in fact have fewer instances of overt power struggles.

Knowing about the issues of power in the classroom—who has power and how it is used—are highly important for an understanding of classroom climate. Students who feel powerful and influential are happy, effective, and curious. Teachers who feel interpersonally influential with students can relate closely to students while also providing clear and direct leadership in pursuit of academic subjects. Class members with some degree of influence feel secure and useful in the classroom. But students who feel powerless possess poor images of themselves; they feel negative about school and do not perform at levels consonant with their abilities. Powerlessness induces anxiety; the classroom becomes a threatening and insecure place. A classroom with a positive social climate is one in which all students see themselves as having some influence. Although shared power and influence is difficult to establish in a classroom, a teacher can begin by distributing part of the legitimate power to students and by arranging for students to participate actively in classroom leadership positions. At the end of this chapter we suggest several plans for action a teacher may use to disperse influence in the classroom.

Attempting Leadership

A theory of motivation developed by Atkinson and Feather (1966) is useful for organizing some of the psychological factors involved in attempting leadership in the classroom. The two proposed that the tendency to act is determined by a motive force, an expectancy factor, and an incentive value of acting, all put together in a multiplicative relationship. According to this theory, the tendency to attempt leadership would be a function of a person's motive for power multiplied by an expectation of success in leading, multiplied by an incentive for accomplishment.

The motive force for power is viewed as a drive for influencing others which stems from a relatively stable aspect of personality. It is related to such personality needs as control, achievement, and affiliation. Of course individuals differ in their drives for control or power. We would expect students with strong needs for control, achievement, and affiliation to make bids for leadership provided they have some expectation of succeeding, and that an external incentive exists for gaining leadership.

Hemphill (1961) reviewed four studies that supported the expectancy-of-success and incentive-value parts of this theory. Expectancy involves the belief that one can be successful when attempting leadership. Hemphill showed that persons who previously had been successful subsequently attempted leadership more often than before, and also that persons who viewed themselves as being expert in the discussion attempted leadership more often than did those who saw themselves as being less expert. Incentive value is a reward for actually being successful in leading. In another experiment reported in the same article, Hemphill varied the amounts of reward for completing a group task and found that members of groups with high incentive attempted more leadership than persons in low-incentive groups.

We would expect that students who have previously been influential in the classroom would continue to attempt leadership again and again. Moreover, the confident students who think of themselves as knowing a lot about a topic will attempt more leadership than others, even though their perceptions of their own expertise may be quite inaccurate. When rewards are available for exerting influence such as being laughed with, applauded, followed, or even elected to an office, students will be more likely to attempt to influence their peers.

The tendency to attempt leadership can also be influenced by interpersonal and situational factors. Hemphill showed that support and acceptance of a person's ideas encouraged that person to attempt leadership more often. Moreover, Hamblin (1958) found that situations in which all group members face a common crisis induce more leadership attempts. Groups that are developing or changing show higher incidences of attempted leadership than static groups. These findings have direct implications for classrooms.

All students probably have psychological fantasies about attempting to influence others. For instance, perhaps Susan wants the class to take a field trip to a museum and she believes it is a good idea. Will she speak out? Will she attempt to sway others in the group? Will she try to exert leadership? It depends on her motives, her expectations, and her perceptions of the incentives. Her motives may include a strong desire to travel and to visit the museum in hopes of learning something new (achievement), she may simply want to be near a girl friend (affiliation), or she may wish to exert her influence over others in the group (control). Her talking out and attempting influence will depend on the presence of some of these motives along with her expectations and perceptions of incentives. If her previous experiences in the group in making suggestions were positive, she will want more to attempt influence; and if she perceives the teacher as wanting to go to the museum and feels that the teacher will like her suggestion, she will have some incentive to attempt leadership. However, if her suggestions have been met with negative responses and if she sees valued peers as being opposed to the museum trip, she may hesitate in stating her wishes. She would have little desire to "stick her neck out" and risk being rejected and rebuffed by her peers.

Even if Susan's expectation for success and incentive value were low for attempting influence, she might try if certain group circumstances prevail. If there is a general climate for accepting ideas from many people, Susan might speak out. If the group's membership had changed greatly and expectations are still unclear, she might risk making the suggestion. If the group's decision-making process is open and there are expectations to hear from everyone before making decisions, she would probably speak out. In brief, Susan will attempt to influence the group provided encouragement for such influence on the part of peers and the teacher is considerable, or she has some motive to satisfy, or she expects to be successful, and particularly if she sees some reward forthcoming for trying.

Students such as Susan usually find their way into some niche in the classroom power structure. The power structures of most classrooms tend to remain stable throughout the year (Lippitt and Gold 1958). Moreover, Glidewell (1964) indicates that one can accurately predict a student's power position in the classroom from year to year. Even though change in the power structure is possible, it seldom has been shown to be self-sustaining. The reasons for such stability appear to lie in the expectations in the group for what particular students will be like. Also, students have their own internalized expectancy structure regulating their own behavior. The dual force of the social structure and the individual's psychological makeup account for a great deal of the stability of power structures in the classroom.

The teacher should be aware that change in the classroom power structure cannot be effected simply by attempting to bring about a change in some of the individual students. Attempts at helping low power students learn skills that would enable them to wield interpersonal influence may meet with some short-term success, but only cultural changes in the climate of the entire group would assure major changes in classroom leadership patterns.

Lilly (1971) experimented with improving the social acceptance of unpopular, low achieving elementary students by having them participate in a special movie-making project. They worked with popular peers and were given permission to leave the regular classroom to engage in this highly valued project. The treatment was successful in improving the acceptance of the low status peers—but for only a short time. Using the same measures, given six weeks after the treatment, Lilly found that the gains did not endure. Changing the interpersonal environment of a classroom group requires keen diagnosis, positive action and continual and persistent efforts over a long period of time.

A teacher wishing to improve the leadership capabilities of a student should observe several aspects of a student's behavior to diagnose whether he or she feels powerful and secure enough to attempt leadership. When classroom work is going on, the teacher might see (1) who gives ideas and suggestions in classroom discussions, (2) who voices opinions that are different from the teacher and other students, and (3) who takes the initiative or performs their own work independently without checking with the teacher.

When peers are in formal interaction around classroom work, especially working in small groups, the teacher might observe (1) who tries to put ideas across to get them implemented, (2) who suggests things to study or how to do work, (3) who suggests ways of presenting the products of the group to the teacher or class, and (4) who offers help and advice to other students.

When there is informal interaction with peers, the teacher might make observations on (1) who tells others of good movies, records, or things to do outside of school that other students would enjoy, (2) who organizes activities, either in subgroups or with individuals, at recess or lunch, and (3) who offers to help other students with problems they are facing either in or out of school.

Such observations can be made in a variety of ways. They can be carried out when students are doing classroom work, when they are involved in formal interaction with peers in the classroom, and when they are relating informally with peers. They can be made on an un-planned basis, whenever the teacher has time and interest. The teacher can also set up brief periods of five or ten minutes of observation during different parts of the day. Such observation periods ought to be carried out during different activities, e.g., classroom discussions, highly structured individual work time, or more loosely structured work in small groups. The teacher might make use of a student teacher, aide, parent or small group of students to set up larger blocks of time for observation. Finally, the teacher might concentrate on just a very few students at one time to observe their leadership attempts.

Many behaviors might be observed; the important point is to look beneath superficial events to interpersonal influence in all areas of the school. Peer-group influence processes are subtle and often hidden. Teachers interested in understanding the power structure of the classroom peer group will have to use tools to sharpen their observations and to focus their listening (Fox, Luszski and Schmuck 1966).

Interpersonal Influence

Interpersonal influence involves directing a class's actions in either constructive or destructive directions. It may emerge informally or be imposed. Emergent influence occurs when the acceptance of power is based on the consent of followers; imposed influence is based on superior authority as defined by group roles and norms. In the classroom the teacher has imposed influence by virtue of legitimate authority, while students, if they are to acquire power, generally gain emergent influence.

Hollander (1961) has described the essential bases of a person's emerging with interpersonal influence as adhering to group norms and as being seen as competent and approachable. In the classroom, the students who have emergent influence initially behave in ways that confirm other students' expectations about how class members ought to behave. Then the student accumulates what Hollander refers to as "idiosyncracy credits." Idiosyncracy credits are those actions which are seen as contributing to the group's task while also living up to interpersonal expectations. The accumulation of credits requires that the student accurately estimates opinions of other students in the class. In other research on emergent influence, Bugental and Lehner (1958) found that emergent leaders are superior to others in judging the group's opinions on familiar and relevant issues. Hamblin (1958) showed that persons who gain influence may lose it if they are unable to maintain some attractiveness for others and to continue to be seen as competent. His research leads to the conclusion that the basis of emergent influence in the classroom peer group will often be either referent or expert power. Kirscht and others (1959) discovered that emergent leaders reinforce and maintain their positions by giving and asking for suggestions, as well as by summing up and integrating the comments of others.

Research studies indicate a number of characteristics of persons who wield imposed influence—characteristics which shed light on teacher behaviors. Persons who have imposed influence seem to differ, but only slightly, from those who emerge as leaders. For instance, both types wield influence successfully, especially when they possess empathic ability. Empathic ability, the ability to understand what others are feeling, is a skill of very great importance to the classroom teacher. Imposed leaders influence successfully when they reward members actively (Spector and Suttell 1957), when these rewards are given frequently (Bennis et al. 1958), and when they allow the members to participate actively (Hare 1953). Sometimes even dominating, authoritarian leadership can be influential. Berkowitz (1953) showed that some members of groups did not object to dominating leadership when they knew that they could also participate and, at times, take the initiative.

We believe that the successful authoritarian teachers also communicate some sense of openness and accessibility to their students. Such direct teachers often are respected by their students. But even though the highly respected authoritarian teacher exerts successful influence, and may even lead students effectively through the maze of academic learning, we should also be aware of other outcomes. It is likely that the actions of such teachers also encourage high dependency, high competition among students, feelings of some powerlessness, and at times feelings of being alienated from the subject matter.

As we described above, interpersonal influence can be used to accomplish constructive or destructive ends. The teacher who encourages high amounts of dependency or competition through influence behaviors often is reaping debilitating outcomes for students. Likewise, students can often exert influence for unproductive ends. For example, Polansky, Lippitt, and Redl (1950) studied campers' influence attempts—those kinds of influence about which teachers have nightmares. Even though the powerful youths in this study had severe emotional problems, their behaviors were not unlike those that might occur in average classrooms. Students with high emergent influence initiated lewd songs, threw food in the lunch room, and generally disobeyed rules of the camp. Other less powerful students tended to imitate and follow them. The counselors were powerless to stop the misbehaviors. In most classrooms, teachers have experienced students seizing power and leading the class, however momentarily, in such games as "drop your pencil every five minutes," "sharpen your pencil—everyone—at 3:00 P.M.," or perhaps "everybody cough at 2:15 P.M."

With the possibility of such disruptions occurring in any classroom, it is important for the teacher to diagnose the power structure in the peer group and to work in concert with it rather than trying to run counter to it. Early in the school year teachers should look for cues that will help them predict which students will emerge as informal leaders. Generally, safe predictions can be made by following certain guidelines. Students who will emerge as classroom leaders usually possess fairly high self-esteem, are secure, intelligent, articulate (perhaps even verbose), flexible, low in anxiety, and they often possess a high tolerance for ambiguity. Quite often they will also be risk-takers. Their followers, on the other hand, will tend to be characterized by self-doubt, insecurity, lack of insight, quietness, an element of rigidity, having high anxiety, and manifesting a low tolerance for ambiguity. These characteristics of the followers undergird their propensity to be easily persuaded by others.

Goal-Directed Influence

Goal-directed influence requires both interpersonal influence and movement toward some valued outcomes. Such influence which has also been labeled effective leadership by Bass (1960) is based on more than simply interpersonal influence; it is measured by the effectiveness of the influence behaviors in achieving classroom goals of academic learning and positive personal development.

Many teachers can exert imposed influence successfully but do not wield goal-directed influence in the way the term is being used here. One particular teacher, as one example, had taught second grade for many years. Her teaching methods were highly controlled. She was dictatorial, used a traditional curriculum, and ran a very well-controlled class in which the students did what they were told. She was very highly respected by parents, teachers, students, and by us. She encouraged her students to do good work and she had successful teaching experiences with students who were unable to work well with other teachers. She was, in many senses, a successful teacher and, by only observing the immediate classroom processes, one would consider her as having goal-directed influence as well. After all, the students were learning and they felt good about it. What more could one ask for?

The major problem with that kind of influence was what happened to her students as they passed into the third grade. They had learned subject-matter, but they were unable to take initiative to learn something on their own. They had learned from the book that was studied, but were unable to search out new vistas of learning independently. They had learned to work quietly alone in their seats and to speak respectfully to adults, but they had not learned how to work effectively in small groups. They had worked hard through competition, but they had not learned how to cooperate. Even though they had respect for the rights of others, they did not know how to express their feelings to others and they were afraid to state openly their frustrations and anxieties to the teacher.

Goal-directed influence in the classroom should include concerns about both academic learning and the development of autonomous, self-initiating students. Furthermore, we believe that a focus on both task and social emotional group functions would be helpful in realizing goal-directed influence. If the teacher's leadership is shared so that many class members are performing both task and social emotional functions, then goal-directed leadership, as we are discussing it, will more likely be realized. It seems especially important that leadership in the classroom be dispersed to achieve a positive social climate. Research has shown that classroom groups with diffuse power structures—in which most students have some degree of power over some other student—have a better than average number of students with high self-esteem who are working up to their intelligence levels. Classrooms in which only a few students have influence have a greater percentage of students who evaluate themselves negatively and who are not working up to their potential.

Our action research in schools indicates that, although classroom power structures are tenacious and difficult to change, they can be changed and a greater dispersion of leadership can be achieved. Increased sharing of goal-directed leadership can be encouraged through the teacher's working on the total group's orientations to influence. The teacher can encourage and reward attempts at leadership on the part of the less powerful students. Teachers can keep the group open for decision making and for the expressions of feelings. Teachers can reward for students' goal-oriented acts even though, at times, the students' leadership may be ill-conceived and poorly executed.

Flexible Leadership

Since goal-directed influence requires accurate diagnosis of changing situations as well as the ability to enlist appropriate member behaviors, it inevitably must be flexible to be effective. In some kinds of situations, direct leadership acts and close supervision will be appropriate; at other times standing back and doing very little will prove to be the more effective leadership. We will discuss briefly two classes of situations that have been researched and that commonly occur in classrooms; situations of working alone or interdependently, and situations in which goals are clear or those in which goals are unclear.

In research on industrial work groups, Dubin (1965) studied production that could be carried out by a single worker and contrasted it with production that required the interdependent actions of several workers. The first kind of work, termed "unit production," is typified by the cabinet maker; the second kind of work, "continuous production," is found in the typical assembly line. Dubin found that less direct supervision was effective in relation to unit production, while more direct supervision was effective for continuous production. An analogy from Dubin's findings to learning activities fits the classroom. The effectiveness of direct supervision by the teacher will be low when students are working alone, but the stimulation of a very active and confrontative teacher leadership will be more effective when learning activities are being carried out in small groups of students.

In another series of research studies, Shaw and Blum (1966) found direct leadership to be quite effective when group goals and tasks were well understood and agreed upon. Conversely, they found that when goals and tasks were unclear a more indirect style of leadership was superior. In the classroom, when most everyone is ready to "get going" and is clear about goals and tasks, direct leadership will be accepted, even wanted. With the direction of action being clear, stimulation from a direct leader will be encouraging and facilitative. On the other hand, in confusing learning situations students' tasks will be made easier by their being able to ask questions and to enter into two-way communication with their teachers. Thus, more of a discussion style of leadership which involves a number of questions and answers is appropriate when students are not sure about where they are going and what they are doing.

Practical Issues for Classroom Leadership: Control and Responsibility

Sharing power with students is one of the most difficult instructional issues for teachers. Those teachers who are sincerely interested in improving some of the unhealthy interpersonal dynamics within their classrooms often are reticent to give up their legitimate authority for fear that, "If I let the kids decide, they'll run wild. I will lose all control." Such worried teachers incorrectly assume that sharing influence with students is the same as their abdicating authority and responsibility. But shared leadership does *not* involve the abdication of teacher power and responsibility within the classroom. It rather extends influence to students so that they can learn how to control their own behaviors and how to enter into collaborative decision making.

These views have been echoed by Ms. Lois Bergin, a fourth grade teacher who used ideas appearing in the previous edition of this book to share leadership with her students. Ms. Bergin wrote:

> The first big step to change came when the children and I together laid out our problems and began to attack them. . . . I learned to share power with the children to an extent I had never thought possible.

Ms. Bergin went on to explain how she employed several of the action ideas for change described at the end of this chapter. Through these practices she gave students more opportunity to initiate their ideas and to decide more on how they would carry out some of their academic assignments. Gradually, Ms. Bergin gave up some of her prerogatives, providing students with more and more control over their own learning goals and procedures. She said it well:

> A class that was once so uncontrolled that we could accomplish little has come through several developmental stages. A class once seated individually for best teacher control is now divided into groups of four who work together. The children use self-control when they are capable of it; when they aren't, I use their control.

Individual Control and Responsibility

Teachers who hold on to all power and responsibility for student learning and behavior may well have orderly, quiet and even pleasant classrooms—provided the students as a group aren't "uncontrollable." In contrast, teachers who share leadership with their students will often *not* have such neat and orderly classrooms—problems which occur will quickly come into the open and the routines of classroom life will be disrupted frequently by discussions on immediate interpersonal concerns. But teachers of the latter type will be allowing their students to learn about self-control and individual responsibility; they must expect, in turn, that the students will have some trouble with learning to control their own behavior just as they sometimes have trouble understanding a mathematical concept. What students learn about their own abilities to control their behavior and to be responsible for themselves can also have direct implications for their academic work. Self-control and self-responsibility are not only concerns about discipline; these issues are integrally involved in the behaviors toward the pursuit of academic objectives.

Dweck and Rapucci (1973), in a study of "learned helplessness" in fifth graders, found that children who quickly gave up on academic tasks also took less personal responsibility for their behavior compared with those students who completed most tasks. The former group had learned to be "helpless"; they relied on forces outside themselves rather than on their own initiative. This research complements the work of DeCharms (1972) previously discussed (Chap. 3), who, as will be recalled, argues that students learn to act as pawns (helpless) or to act as origins (self-initiators) from the ways they are taught by their teachers. Teachers who received special training in facilitating more origin-like student behavior afterwards established classrooms in which a greater percentage of the students could be classified as origins than could be so classified in the rooms of teachers who did not receive the training. They learned how to help students set their own goals, pursue those goals in their own ways, and take personal responsibility for their classroom actions. In addition while the students were acting more origin-like, they also were improving in their academic achievement.

It seems clear to us that teachers who wish to teach their students self-control, responsibility, and origin-like behavior must come to grips with the ways in which power and leadership are put into effect in the classroom. High teacher control does not facilitate self-initiative among students. Teachers cannot retain absolute power over academic goals and procedures and at the same time teach students to be self-controlling and responsible for their own behaviors.

Group Control and Responsibility

Behavioral control and responsibility in classrooms are cultural as well as individual issues. In some classes expectations shared in the peer group about what behavior is appropriate may be in opposition to the goals of the teacher and may hinder academic learning. Such a classroom group may be described by adults as "uncontrollable"; it probably will be viewed by many students, however, as having a regular interpersonal pattern. A vivid illustration was described by Ms. Bergin:

> The group of children I met in September was beyond anything I could ever have imagined. They are too many; but more than that they have too many problems. Some have withdrawn tendencies but most are very aggressive, keeping the classroom in almost constant turmoil with their disruptive behavior.

They are hostile, noisy, explosive, excitable. They seem unable to listen or to follow directions. They fight, kick, bicker, shout, stick pins and pencil points into each other. Their habit of tattling must be the worst on record. There are cliques, loners, outcasts, liars, extortionists. They seem to hate each other, themselves, and me. They're full of headaches, toothaches and stomach aches. Many are underfed, underclothed, and underloved. There are not nearly enough corners in the room to accommodate all the problem children, nor enough children who make good buffers to separate the rest.

Our room looks like a disaster area: more than half the desks have big shirt-tails of messy papers hanging out; pencils and crayons can't be found because they are rolling down the aisles; the children cannot hit the waste can. It is rather like living in the city dump.

Ms. Bergin began by changing the expectations of the peer group by collaborating with the students in "laying out the problems" and attacking them. She also faced the risk—and joy—of sharing power. She had to give up some of her own plans through the process of negotiation with the student's ideas. She changed some of her expectations for what was "proper" to do within a classroom. She later wrote:

I think I am actually "putting up" with more, but am more comfortable and relaxed than I was last year when I had a group of children that was as trouble-free as any I'd ever worked with.

Like Ms. Bergin, all teachers face a number of decisions about how much they will share leadership with their students. Because of the legitimate power vested in the teaching role, teachers can decide just what type of leader they will be. They, of course, should expect that their best intentions may not always come to fruition because of the powerful influences inherent in the culture of the student peer group. But even though the peer group can wield significant influence, the teacher's choices about the sharing of leadership will usually have important implications for how the dynamics of the classroom group will be played out.

Implications for Teachers

The following statements summarize the key implications of this chapter's contents for teachers.

- —All human beings want to feel some influence in relation to important others.
- —Leadership is interpersonal influence; it is *not* the characteristic of an individual.
- —Because of their legitimate status, teachers hold the most potential power in the classroom for executing leadership.

—Functional leadership involves interpersonal influence in relation to group tasks and social-emotional concerns.

—Students' attempts for classroom leadership are a function of their personal motives for power, their expectation for success, and the external incentives they perceive.

—Students frequently attempt leadership in classrooms with positive social climates.

—Influence attempts in the classroom can facilitate or hinder academic learning. Goal-directed influence of either teacher or students—by definition—facilitates learning.

—A teacher's leadership will have a significant impact on the climate of the classroom.

—The influence structure of a classroom group can be changed. Teachers should take the initiative in working toward a dispersed influence structure.

—Students will feel influential and learn to be self-controlling and responsible for their own behavior when they are helped to share classroom leadership with the teacher.

Action Ideas for Change

The following plans for improving the dynamics of leadership in the classroom were developed by public school teachers as part of several action research projects.

Encouraging Students with Interpersonal Influence to Pursue Constructive Goals: A Steering Committee

The goal of this practice was to improve the climate for learning in a classroom by helping students with high influence in the peer group to use it constructively. The teacher diagnosed the class as having a preponderance of antilearning, antischool attitudes which were held by high-power students. The hindering influence of these students was leading to continual conflict between the teacher and a large part of the classroom peer group.

The teacher used sociometric questionnaires to measure formally the peer group influence structure (Fox, Luszki, and Schmuck 1966). Next, a six-member steering committee was appointed. It consisted of the most popular and influential students in the class. The teacher worked with the committee every day for one week at lunch time, training the members to understand and to use the task and social-emotional group functions. After one week of training in group processes, the steering committee met twice each week to discuss problems, goals, and possible rules for classroom behavior and work. The teacher participated as a member in the discussions.

After about one month of such deliberations, the steering committee presented plans to the class in the form of a panel report. The plans were then discussed by the entire class. Following this, the steering committee was reconstituted, and thereafter continuously changed its membership every two weeks by class election, until all class members had served. The class decided to change only three steering committee members every two weeks so there would be continuous overlap of membership.

The steering committee became more autonomous and self-regulating as the year went on. One member at each meeting was designated as an "observer" to make comments toward the end of the session on how the committee had worked together. The teacher also gave steering committee members additional powers as the year progressed. They were asked to discuss, to draw up plans, and to make decisions about the curriculum and instructional procedures in the class. After about three months of operation, the teacher asked the students to evaluate what they were doing. They developed brief questionnaires which they administered to their peers. Following the evaluation, still other changes were made in the operation of the steering committee. For example, the committee remained intact for three weeks instead of two because of the time it took for each newly constituted group to work well together.

This procedure is excellent for developing leadership skills and for dispersing student power and responsibility in the classroom. In this class, and in several others that tried the steering committee, there were significant changes in the negative and cynical orientations of the students. Several of these classes moved from drab, hostile environments to ones of excitement, curiosity, activity, and warmth. However, even though this procedure can be powerful for a classroom group's development, it is also very difficult to execute successfully.

The teacher who wishes to implement a classroom steering committee must relinquish power honestly and with patience. The teacher must clearly designate the powers given to students. For instance, if the steering committee wants to decide about grading procedures and the teacher wishes to maintain this prerogative, a discussion about grading should be ruled out of order. The teacher should *not* allow the committee to discuss a topic in hopes that its members will eventually agree with the teacher's position. Such hidden manipulation often backfires and leads to mistrust between teacher and students. We believe that the teacher should limit the boundaries of decision-making at the beginning of the year and broaden them gradually as students learn more skills and more trust is developed. The major theme of the steering committee is the opportunity it provides for students to determine their fate in the classroom. Just making it a rubber stamp for a teacher's authority would be a mistake.

Training Students in Goal-Directed Leadership

The goal of this practice was to improve the quality of group work in the classroom by dispersing leadership throughout the peer group. The two teachers involved—one an elementary teacher, the other secondary—were concerned that only a very few students were executing task and social-emotional functions. The elementary school teacher developed the following observation form for use with his students. The secondary teacher made use of the task and social-emotional group functions as follows.

The training commenced in each classroom with the teacher leading a discussion about each point on the observation sheets. Then the teacher asked for six volunteers to form a discussion group, with the rest of the class as audience. The group was given a real problem to discuss, one that was relevant to the group processes of their classroom, for example, "Why do so few people participate in class discussion?" or "Why don't more people in our class try to help one another to learn?" These discussion groups were given a limited time period to talk (usually about ten minutes in the elementary classrooms and twenty minutes in the secondary classrooms).

While the group discussions were taking place, the remainder of the class used their observation sheets, marking down the initials of a student whenever he performed one of the leadership functions. Next, the class discussed their observations and attempted to see what use could be made of the observation forms in other class situations. One variation on the use of the sheets, suggested by a secondary student, was that each one try to designate (prior to a group discussion) what functions he would especially wish to perform during the subsequent discussion. Then later, observers could see if he had been able to achieve his objectives. After using these sheets for several weeks, the teachers used them about twice each month in conjunction with regular class sessions.

Some precautions should be taken, especially with elementary students. In the beginning phases, the teacher may have to stop after each function is performed to ask the observers, "What happened there?" "What did you check?" Guidance such as this will be needed often at the start, but can gradually be reduced as the class becomes more comfortable with the observations.

OBSERVATION SHEET FOR GOAL-DIRECTED LEADERSHIP
(Elementary)

TASK JOBS	INITIALS OF STUDENTS			
	Time 1	Time 2	Time 3	Time 4
GIVING IDEAS:				
GETTING IDEAS:				
USING SOMEONE'S IDEA:				

PEOPLE JOBS				
BEING NICE				
SAYING HOW YOU FEEL				
LETTING OTHERS TALK				

FIGURE 4.1 / *Observation Sheet for Goal-Directed Leadership (elementary).*

Giving Students an Opportunity to Teach Their Own Lesson Plans

The goals of this action idea were to establish more power for students in implementing the curriculum and to help them develop leadership skills by way of formally leading the class. The teacher involved in this innovation diagnosed the class as having low involvement in academic work. The teacher also hoped to find some time to work with a small group who needed special attention; and therefore, wanted the rest of the class to be led by someone else.

The teacher started the practice by dividing the class into subgroups of six or seven students each. Each group was told that it would work together for one hour daily to study designated topics. The concepts to be learned were listed. Each group was told that every student would be expected to be the leader of a group for one week of the term. The teacher described the responsibilities of the leaders and asked each group to select its first leader.

These initial leaders were asked to draw up lesson plans for one week. A lesson-plan format was presented by the teacher. The teacher met with

OBSERVATION SHEET FOR GOAL-DIRECTED LEADERSHIP

(Secondary)

Task Functions	Time				
	1	2	3	4	5
1. Initiating: proposing tasks or goals; defining a group problem; suggesting a procedure for solving a problem; suggesting other ideas for consideration.					
2. Information or opinion seeking: requesting facts on the problem; seeking relevant information; asking for suggestions and ideas.					
3. Information or opinion giving: offering facts; providing relevant information; stating a belief; giving suggestions or ideas.					
4. Clarifying or elaborating: interpreting or reflecting ideas or suggestions; clearing up confusion; indicating alternatives and issues before the group; giving examples.					
5. Summarizing: pulling related ideas together; restating suggestions after the group has discussed them.					
6. Consensus testing: sending up "trial balloons" to see if group is nearing a conclusion; checking with group to see how much agreement has been reached.					
Social Emotional Functions					
7. Encouraging: being friendly, warm and responsive to others; accepting others and their contributions; listening; showing regard for others by giving them an opportunity or recognition.					
8. Expressing group feelings: sensing feeling, mood, relationships within the group; sharing his own feelings with other members.					
9. Harmonizing: attempting to reconcile disagreements; reducing tension through "pouring oil on troubled waters"; getting people to explore their differences.					
10. Compromising: offering to compromise his own position, ideas, or status; admitting error; disciplining himself to help maintain the group.					
11. Gate-keeping: seeing that others have a chance to speak; keeping the discussion a group discussion rather than a 1-, 2-, or 3-way conversation.					
12. Setting standards: expressing standards that will help group to achieve; applying standards in evaluating group functioning and production.					

FIGURE 4.2 / *Observation Sheet for Goal-Directed Leadership (secondary).*

the leaders during lunch one day and went over their plans. Some leadership skills were discussed, and each leader was able to meet individually with the teacher if there was a need for additional help. The leaders were given total responsibility for teaching and evaluating for their one week. Their week was completed after they had supplied the teacher with written reports on the progress of their group.

Cross-Age Tutoring

In this procedure an older student was paired with a younger student for the purpose of tutoring the younger in some academic area. The actual behaviors of the older students varied considerably; in some instances a younger student was taken to the library and read to, and in some instances a younger student was assigned for specific lessons to be taught, such as reading or arithmetic.

Most of the teachers who have used cross-age tutoring find that the older student gains most from the tutoring relationship; older students, for example, who have trouble with reading may well be assigned to a beginning reader; or, as another example, an older student who has problems in math may benefit from teaching a younger student simple mathematical skills. Patricia Schmuck used cross-age tutoring with a group of junior-high age boys who had severe reading disabilities; their reading skills as well as their understanding of personal problems were greatly enhanced through tutoring younger students in reading.

References

Atkinson, J., and Feather, N. *A Theory of Achievement Motivation.* New York: John Wiley & Sons, 1966.

Bass, B. *Leadership, Psychology and Organizational Behavior.* New York: Harper & Brothers, 1960.

Benne, K., and Sheets, P. "Functional Roles of Group Members." *Journal of Social Issues* 4 (1948):41-49.

Bennis, W.; Berkowitz, N.; Affinito, M.; and Malone, M. "Authority, Power, and the Ability to Influence." *Human Relations* 11 (1958):143-55.

Berkowitz, L. "Sharing Leadership in Small Decision-Making Groups." *Journal of Abnormal and Social Psychology* 48 (1953):231-38.

Bugental, D., and Lehner, G. "Accuracy of Self-Perception and Group Perception as Related to Two Leadership Roles." *Journal of Abnormal and Social Psychology* 56 (1958):396-98.

DeCharms, R. "Personal Causation Training in the Schools." *Journal of Applied Social Psychology* 2 (1972):295-313.

Dubin, R.; Homans, C.; Mann, F.; and Miller, D. *Leadership and Productivity: Some Facts of Industrial Life.* San Francisco: Chandler Publishing Co., 1965.

Dweck, C. S., and Repucci, N. D. "Learned Helplessness and Reinforcement Responsibility in Children." *Journal of Personality and Social Psychology* 25, no. 1 (1973):109-16.

Fox, R.; Luszki, M.; and Schmuck, R. *Diagnosing Classroom Learning Environments.* Chicago: Science Research Associates, 1966.

French, J., and Raven, B. "The Bases of Social Power." In *Studies in Social Power,* edited by D. Cartwright. Ann Arbor, Mich.: Institute for Social Research, 1959.

Glidewell, J. C. "Unpublished data, reference file #884." Clayton, Mo.: St. Louis County Health Department, 1964.

Gold, M. "Power in the Classroom." *Sociometry* 21 (1958):50-60.

Hamblin, R. "Leadership and Crises." *Sociometry* 21 (1958):322-35.

Hare, P. A. "Small Group Discussions with Participating and Supervision Leadership." *Journal of Abnormal and Social Psychology* 48 (1953):273-75.

Hemphill, J. "Why People Attempt to Lead." In *Leadership and Interpersonal Behavior,* edited by L. Petrullo, and B. Bass. New York: Holt, Rinehart & Winston, Inc., 1961. Pp. 201-15.

Hollander, R. P. "Some Effects of Perceived Status on Responses to Innovative Behavior." *Social Psychology* 63 (1961):247-50.

Hornstein, H.; Callahan, D. M.; Fisch, E.; and Benedict, B. A. "Influence and Satisfaction in Organizations: A Replication." *Sociology of Education* 41, no. 4 (1968):380-89.

Kirscht, J. F. et al. "Some Factors in the Selection of Leaders by Members of Small Groups." *Journal of Abnormal and Social Psychology* 58 (1959): 406-8.

Kounin, J. S. *Discipline and Group Management in Classrooms.* New York: Holt, Rinehart & Winston, Inc., 1970.

Kounin, J. S., and Gump, P. V. "The Ripple Effect in Discipline." *Elementary School Journal* 59 (1958):158-62.

Kounin, J. S.; Gump, P. V.; and Ryan, J. J., III. "Explorations in Classroom Management." *Journal of Teacher Education* 12 (1961):235-46.

Lilly, M. S. "Improving Social Acceptance of Low Sociometric Status, Low Achieving Students." *Exceptional Children,* January 1971, pp. 341-47.

Lippitt, R., and Gold, M. "Classroom Social Structure as a Mental Health Problem." *Journal of Social Issues* 15 (1959):40-58.

Polansky, N.; Lippitt, R.; and Redl, F. "An Investigation of Behavioral Contagion in Groups." *Human Relations* 3 (1950):319-48.

Ryans, D. G. *Characteristics of Teachers: Their Description, Comparison, and Appraisal.* Washington, D. C.: American Council on Education, 1960.

Shaw, M., and Blum, J. M. "Effects of Leadership Style Upon Group Performance as a Function of Task Structure." *Journal of Personality and Social Psychology* 3 (1966):328-42.

Spector, P., and Suttell, B. J. *An Experimental Comparison of the Effectiveness of Three Patterns of Leadership Behavior.* American Institute for Research, 1957.

White, R., and Lippitt, R. *Autocracy and Democracy.* New York: Harper & Brothers, 1960.

CHAPTER 5

Attraction

Small groups of all kinds are replete with feelings that influence their task performances. Soldiers perform less satisfactorily in their combat units when interpersonal relations are unsupportive; industrial work groups perform more successfully when workers "on the line" relate favorably to one another; and a person's suggestions in a problem-solving group are accepted or rejected partly on the basis of their degree of popularity with other group members. Classroom groups are similar; they have a hidden world of attraction and hostility among peers that influences the academic performances of the individual students. Students with some support from friendly peers use their intellectual potentials more completely than do their fellow students who are rejected by the peer group.

Despite the obvious importance of friendship patterns in the classroom, some teachers still maintain that they are employed to teach content and that they should not be concerned with students' positions, insofar as their being liked is concerned, within the peer group. We think such a point of view is naive; it grossly oversimplifies the social psychological realities of the classroom. Teaching and learning involve an interpersonal process, and when that process is underway it is complicated and affected by the many relations among the students, and between the students and the teacher. The teacher's style and the curriculum, the students' feelings about themselves and their academic abilities, and the nature of the interpersonal relations in the classroom group all are major influences on this teaching-learning process.

Antecedents to Liking

A large amount of research has been done on the characteristics of liked and disliked students. Much of it has been carefully reviewed by Glidewell et al. (1966), and we have relied heavily on that review. Although there is a great deal of research on this topic, much of it is incomplete, and almost all of it is correlated in nature. The typical study shows correlations between certain personal attributes and liking status in the classroom. From such findings we are unable to draw causal inferences, except when an obviously static antecedent condition, such as the physical attributes of a student, is studied. Nonetheless, much of the research is valuable in helping to sketch a picture of the kinds of students who are most likely to be attractive and those who will most likely be unfortunate recipients of hostility.

Physical Attributes

Physical appearance, although often considered a superficial variable, is an initial factor in making friends, choosing dating partners, and in selecting marital partners. Walster et al. (1966) showed that a college male's liking or not liking his date and his wanting or not wanting to date her again were largely determined by her physical attractiveness, as judged by disinterested observers. Gold (1958) discovered that physical attributes were considered to be valued resources by elementary students. Terms denoting attractive physical appearance such as "pretty," "good-looking," "dresses well," "looks nice," as well as terms denoting skillful use of the body such as "participates in sports well," "is coordinated," and "can do things well," were offered by students as highly valued resources and as reasons for liking other students.

Unfortunately, it also appears to be true that persons with obvious physical limitations are not easily accepted by others. Students with severe physical handicaps, as well as those with peculiar psychomotor disabilities, often are not chosen as friends by students. Moreover, even very minor physical drawbacks, such as a lack of coordination in playing ball, or in jumping rope, or being unable to run very fast, may lead to peer group rejection. Such prejudices seem to arise toward the disabled and those with limiting physical abilities because they are at the low end of the scale in American society that places high value on youthfulness, physical prowess, and beauty. Students simply copy the norms of the adult society in this regard.

Social Behavior

Although physical attributes have a significant impact on liking patterns, the social behaviors of students appear to be much more important. Social behaviors refer to acts carried out in relation to other people.

Lippitt and Gold (1959) did extensive research on the social behavior of liked and disliked students. They found that students who were rated as attractive by their peers exhibited interpersonal behavior that was enhancing, supportive, and helpful to others, rather than threatening and hostile. Rejected students expressed more negative affect toward others and behaved in actively aggressive or passively hostile ways. Their highly attractive counterparts were friendly, empathic, and outgoing.

Lippitt and Gold went on to show differences between the sexes as to which social behaviors were related to liking. Aggressive hostility, physical abuses, and overt defiance were associated with boys who were disliked by their peers. For girls, passive dependency and social immaturity were associated with rejection. Both overt aggression on the part of boys and passive dependency on the part of girls made others in the class feel uncomfortable and insecure.

The findings from Lippitt and Gold's research are most applicable to classrooms with predominantly middle-class students. Aggression, physical fighting, and high amounts of dependency run counter to middle-class values and expectations. Lower-class settings are sometimes quite different. Pope (1953) showed that, in predominantly low socioeconomic settings, the students who were often held in highest esteem by their peers were the ones who were belligerent and nonconforming. Pope pointed out that such defiant students were not necessarily liked, but that they were respected. In the same vein, students who conformed to classroom regulations often were rejected by peers.

The prevailing social class structure of the school makes a difference in the kinds of social behavior that will be liked or disliked by the students. Pope found that boys in lower-class schools valued physical strength and prowess, loyalty, and friendliness whereas Lippitt and Gold found that boys in the middle class valued coordinated skills, activity, and competition. Boys in both social classes valued friendliness, but its expression was much more physical in the lower class than in the middle class. No such striking differences between the social classes existed for the girls; in both social classes they valued social skills and cooperation. The middle-class girls did, however, place greater value on buoyancy and activity.

In schools with mixed populations of middle- and lower-class students, the norms of the middle class typically prevail. The social behaviors of middle-class students are usually more appropriate for the demands of the school and, therefore, the middle-class students tend to receive rewards and to achieve success more easily than do the lower-class students. In one study Cook (1945) showed that the middle-class students in a school with both middle- and lower-class students received more nominations from their peers on such things as best dressed, best liked, most fun, and real leaders. Even after an intensive program of change which sought to increase social interaction among students and to democratize classrooms, Cook's findings showed that a social class stratification of friendships still prevailed. Students of higher social class levels were being chosen more often for a variety of attractive attributes than the students of lower-class origins. Unfortunately, an awareness of social class differences gains importance as the student gets older; high school students generally are well aware of such differences, and their preferences for relating with others are influenced by these perceived differences.

Intelligence

Scores on intelligence tests have been found to correlate positively with acceptance in the classroom; the correlations tend to be small, but associations between intelligence and liking are especially high at the extreme ends of the intelligence range. Mentally retarded students in normal classrooms often are the most rejected by the peer group. Jordon (1961) has argued that the mentally retarded might just as well be segregated in their own schools because they are already so completely isolated and rejected in normal classrooms. Torrance (1963), studying the highly intelligent students, found that social acceptance was high for intelligent students who were also conformists, but that acceptance was not so high for bright students who were also creative. The highly intelligent, creative students were viewed as being odd and different; they received low acceptance ratings by both their peers and teachers.

The studies by both Jordan and Torrance suggest that the critical antecedent factor for acceptance is not intelligence alone, but rather an assortment of social behaviors that are concomitant with high intelligence. It is likely that mentally retarded students often behave in socially inappropriate ways. They do not have a sense of timing, they are often clumsy and poorly coordinated; they may not even know the jargon of the peer group, especially when it changes rapidly from month to month. In a similar way, highly creative students often will behave in divergent and unexpected ways. Nonconformity, especially when it is unexpected, is uncomfortable and threatening to others.

Little relationship between achievement and liking appears to pertain in the early primary grades, but the relationship does become significant in about the fifth grade and continues to get stronger into high school (Buswell 1951). R. Schmuck's research has shown that students who are rejected by their peers do not achieve at a level that would be expected in relation to their intelligence (1963). A large discrepancy exists between the intelligence and performance levels, especially of upper-elementary students who are rejected. Rejected students experience alienation from the learning environment, have reduced self-esteem as students, and are unable to concentrate for long periods of time on cognitive tasks. Acceptance by the peer group, on the other hand, increases a student's self-esteem and facilitates working up to potential. This relationship between liking and using one's potential is correlational, and its causal direction is, therefore, unknown. We believe that either direction of causation is clearly possible and that both are occurring every day in our schools. Students who enter a classroom under-achieving may manifest fear and confusion in relation to peers and thereby find themselves being rejected. Other students may reduce their likeability by initially doing unkind things to others. Subsequently, they are unable to perform well on their studies because of the anxiety they feel in being rejected.

Mental Health

Acceptance in the peer group is related to the general psychological well-being of the individual student. Numerous studies which have made use of teachers' ratings, personality tests, and student nomination devices to assess mental health have shown significant correlations between rejection by peers on the one hand and high anxiety, maladjustment, primitive defense mechanisms, hostility, and instability on the other. This relationship between liking in the peer group and mental health appears to be monotonic, that is, the greater the severity of the student's psychological disturbance, the greater the likelihood that such a student will be rejected. Students who frequently lose contact with reality and who daydream in the classroom respond inappropriately because they are listening to their inner selves instead of tuning in on external social situations. Autistic students need special teaching; unfortunately, however, they generally need more help than even the most accomplished regular teacher can provide.

Most students who might be labeled as "mental health problems" are not so extreme as to require special teaching. Their behaviors are often inappropriate and their ability to concentrate is often spasmodic but such students can be helped in a regular classroom provided the climate is supportive and nonthreatening. Unfortunately, the label "emotionally disturbed" is too often used as a rationalization for teaching failures. Some teachers justify ineffective teaching behaviors by pointing out that many of their students are disturbed; such disturbances naturally are viewed as developing out of inadequate family experiences, rather than out of a hostile and uncomfortable classroom climate. In one training event the teachers began to cope effectively with the behaviors of students whom they had previously labeled as "disturbed" (R. Schmuck 1968). After training they referred to them as energetic, active or lively. A more constructive orientation for a teacher is to view many deviant behaviors of students, at least initially, as divergent, creative, and, perhaps, as uniquely individual. Moreover, such behaviors often can become more constructive if they are responded to as arising out of restlessness, anxiety, and energy, rather than as being "crazy" or weird.

Personal Resources as Antecedents to Liking

Research on the characteristics of liked and disliked students indicates that the former often are physically attractive, have well-coordinated motor skills, are outgoing and socially effective, are intellectually competent, and are mentally healthy. Some differences between social classes have also been noted; for example, lower-class boys in predominantly lower-class schools gain acceptance by being more defiant and physically aggressive. Students are often rejected for one or more reasons, such as (1) being limited in their physical ability, (2) having difficulties in relating socially to others, (3) having intellectual limitations, (4) having mental health difficulties. In many classrooms, the social behaviors of lower-class students lead to their being rejected because their overt aggression or passive dependency run counter to middle-class values.

These findings can be understood on the basis of a theory developed by Lippitt et al. (1952) and explained by Gold (1958). The theory states that all students possess properties which are defined as personal characteristics. Physical attributes, personality characteristics, and intelligence are examples of personal properties. These properties are converted into *resources* when they are valued by the group. Since different students and classroom groups value different things, a property of a student which is a resource in one social context may not be a resource in another. Similarly, as the same classroom group faces various situations or developmental stages, different properties of class members may be valued or re-evaluated. This theory links the concept of resource with the concept of liking by assuming that a resource has the function of inducing those who value it to be attracted by one who possesses it. Gold states that this is an economic theory essentially. "On the one hand, we have someone who possesses something the other wants or wishes to avoid; on the other hand, we have someone who wants or wishes to avoid it," and the outcome is attraction. Gold goes on to state:

> But we find immediately that we must further qualify our concept of resource. For it is not enough in the economic scheme of things for a property to be valued that we consider it a resource; it must also be something that can be given. Even more, there must be the expectation that it might be given. For example, it is not enough that the property of money is valued in order that it be a resource. The person who has the money must be able and willing to give it away. Simultaneously, it is not enough for someone to be capable of being warm and friendly; he must be able to bestow this warmth and friendliness on another if it is to be considered a resource in the relationship.

This theory emphasizes the dynamic characteristics of an interpersonal exchange of resources as the basis for likeability in the classroom. We concur that it is the interpersonal expressions or the social behaviors as they are emitted that most importantly lead to being liked or disliked. The following section shows how classroom liking patterns are perpetuated once they are put into motion.

The Circular Interpersonal Process

In Chapter 3 we explained the Circular Interpersonal Process; it is also a useful way to describe the liking patterns in a classroom based on enhancing or resisting the exchange of personal resources. Students who see themselves as competent in physical skills or in academic ability may attempt to actualize their resources by offering to help someone with less skill (transmit some of their resource), or by using their physical prowess to force someone to do what they want them to do (convert resources into personal power). In the former case, they likely will become attractive; in the latter they will probably become disliked. Students in need of help on their schoolwork may initiate an effort to use the resources they perceive a classmate as having by asking for help. The resources of being liked can be analyzed in terms of the actualization efforts initiated by the possessors of the resource to express friendly feelings toward others, or to exert influence over those that are attractive to them.

These interpersonal processes involving the exchange of resources become stable and predictable in most classrooms and can be conceptualized using the model of the circular interpersonal process. The circular process is helpful for providing an understanding of how friendships remain stable over time. It includes attitudes toward the self and others; how these get expressed behaviorally, and reactions of the others involved in the interaction.

As noted in Chapter 3, expectations play a major role in circular interpersonal processes. For example—even as a student involved negatively may attempt to change behaviors, it will be difficult for others to notice the changes because they believe so strongly that he or she will behave negatively and with hostility. Often one's expectations influence his or her perceptions so that the incoming information received is biased. Thus, a student involved in a negative cycle might try to act friendly, by sometimes tapping a fellow student softly on the back, or by nonverbally agreeing with another, but because the others' expectations are so strong, the student may be viewed as hitting or as acting smart and as trying to perpetuate an argument. Negative cycles of interpersonal relations become vicious when even benign behaviors are seen as negative and as confirming original expectations.

Some Bases of Attraction

We have stated that each person has motives to be influential, competent, and attractive. The last of these is especially important to the developing youngster. Indeed, interpersonal attraction and hostility are primary forms of social behavior. Students' valuations of themselves play a significant part in how attractive they are to their peers. But the psychodynamics are considerably more complex than this. Four salient and relevant theories from social psychology can shed light on classroom liking processes.

Cognitive Validation Theory

Pepitone (1964), a major proponent of cognitive validation theory, argued that persons have a drive for veridicality, that is, seeing reality as it really is. According to Pepitone, each of us wishes to read the external world correctly and to behave in appropriate social ways because such reality-oriented behavior will facilitate effective survival. Bizarre, inappropriate, autistic behavior is maladaptive because it satisfies only internal needs without connection to the external social world. Over a period of time, such maladaptive behavior will become destructive; consequently, we strive to adjust to the world around us by trying to tune in on reality.

Pepitone states:

> The validation motive is the need for an individual to maintain a cognitive structure which correctly maps physical and social reality concerning the

value of himself and others along some dimension. Generally implied by this formulation is that whenever an estimate of his own worth deviates from estimates of objective valuation in a given respect, the individual will tend to change his cognitive structure so that such valuations are more in line with reality. (p. 50)

Thus, persons seek to know and to check and recheck their attitudes by mapping them against what is outside. If a part of the real world tells them that they are worthy and have value, they will then be attracted to that part of reality. If, on the other hand, interpersonal events show persons that they are worthless and without value, they will feel hostile. Thus attraction and hostility get built up out of the messages about one's self that a person receives from others.

Pepitone did a number of experiments to test aspects of this theory, and to seek the bases of attraction and hostility. His key hypothesis was that interpersonal attraction emanates from others' rewarding expressions which serve to enhance one's *status* and *security*. In very simple terms, Pepitone argued that persons are attracted to those who assign them a position of high status or who help them to feel secure. Persons tend to feel hostile toward those who demean them in the eyes of others or of themselves.

Pepitone designed a series of laboratory experiments to test the roles played by status and security in the interpersonal attraction process. In one experiment, subjects were interviewed by an actor performing as a braggart who made invidious comparisons between himself and the subjects in order to demean the subjects. For example, while looking at his own stylish wearing apparel, the interviewer would ask, "Do you always come to appointments dressed as you are now?" Under such conditions, most of the subjects became angry and highly hostile toward the interviewer.

Next Pepitone was interested in learning about conditions under which boastfulness would or would not arouse hostility. In a second experiment on the effects of boastfulness, researchers presented a taped recording of a highly technical discussion involving industrial development in Liberia. One group participant on the tape was extremely omniscient; he knew all the problems and presented solutions for each of them in highly technical, wordy language. The omniscient participant was introduced differently to three experimental groups; first, as a student (low status), then as an official in the State Department (high status), and finally as a world-renowned expert (super status). Subjects were most hostile toward the participant when they thought that he was a student and least hostile when they thought that he was a world-renowned expert.

Pepitone argued that interpersonal attraction involves checking one's perceptions against reality. When a person's expressed opinion of self agrees with the professional status, we tend to agree with the valuations of high self worth and to be attracted to the person. If there is some discrepancy, however, such as a student acting as though he or she is omniscient, that person's statements appear to be inconsistent with reality and we tend to feel hostile toward the person due to these mannerisms.

In another experiment on self-evaluation, subjects were made to feel that they had violated a norm. As members of a fictitious College Disciplinary Committee, they were induced by stooges to deal with a misbehaving student harshly. Later, they discovered that the student was under psychiatric care and that they had dealt inappropriately in their condemnations. In the end, the subjects essentially had two choices, either to deny that they had violated a norm (thus maintaining self-esteem) or to re-evaluate and devalue their reactions (thus diminishing their self-esteem). Pepitone found that most subjects would take all available opportunities to maintain their self-esteem. The subjects looked to authorities, projected blame on others, rationalized their own behavior, and defended what they had done as the only way. Wherever "outs" were available, such as a letter from the misbehaving student's psychiatrist saying that the student "had not been putting forth effort to improve," subjects tended to defend their behavior, thereby keeping evaluations of themselves high. But when all "outs" were eliminated, the subjects did tend to re-evaluate themselves and did begin to express dissatisfaction with their own behavior. Reality pressures could be made strong enough so that the subjects were compelled to see that their actions were inappropriate.

These experiments support Pepitone's idea that we strive to assess ourselves and others against social reality. Moreover, they indicate that two facets of the real world, *status* and *security*, key into attraction and hostility in interpersonal relations. These findings have direct implications for the classroom. Students react to one another in terms of their expectations of the others' behaviors. They tend to evaluate themselves in terms of the enhancement or reduction of their own status in the eyes of peers and the security they feel in knowing that they responded appropriately to social reality. Those peers who enhance the students' status and security needs are liked by the students, while peers who behave in ways that are threatening to the students' status and security needs are disliked by the students.

Balance Theory

Balance theory assumes that when behavioral systems are in states of imbalance, forces arise to restore balance such as in the case of the students in Pepitone's Disciplinary Committee. Imbalance occurs between two people when they are attracted to each other but hold divergent attitudes. Price (1961) showed that when two people like each other very much but hold different attitudes about others, they feel uneasy and strive to reduce the disagreement.

Research on balance theory (Zajonc 1960) has focused either on twosomes or one person's thoughts concerning his or her relationship with another, but we believe that the theory can also contribute to an understanding of classroom liking relationships.

It differs from cognitive validation theory in its emphasis on internal consistency within the psyche. Whereas validation theory leads to an analysis of the social inputs from the environment, balance theory focuses on the need to organize thoughts, beliefs, attitudes, and behavior in a psychologically consistent manner. Such striving for consistency often veils irrationality and autism. Allport (1954) presents the following examples of balance from his studies of prejudice:

Mister X: The trouble with Jews is that they only take care of their own group.
Mister Y: But the record of the Community Chest shows that they give more generously than non-Jews.
Mister X: That shows that they are always trying to buy favors and intrude in Christian affairs. They think of nothing but money; that is why there are so many Jewish bankers.
Mister Y: But a recent study shows that the percent of Jews in banking is proportionally much smaller than the percent of non-Jews.
Mister X: That's just it. They don't go in for respectable business. They would rather run night clubs.

Balance theory argues that persons tend to like those people who agree with them and to like especially those who hold similar attitudes and values. Conversely, persons are not attracted to those whose values are quite different from their own and may feel hostile toward people who confront or upset their well-organized images of the world. Balance theory emphasizes the need to achieve psychological consistency among one's cognitions and attitudes, as well as a social balance between one's view of reality and the views of those with whom one interacts.

Newcomb (1961) did extensive field research on balance theory. Twice he offered free rent for a semester to seventeen students who agreed to be observed or interviewed each week. His overall findings substantiated balance theory—those students who agreed on a variety of attitudes were attracted to one another and such attraction strengthened as students learned of an increase in the number of attitudes that they shared.

Likewise, in the classroom, students continuously check one another's beliefs and attitudes. Liking takes place between those who share similar attitudes and values. Also, the development of a close friendship increases the probability that the friends will find more and more ways in which they are similar. Once this process gets going it tends to reinforce itself as in the manner of the circular interpersonal process.

Self-Esteem Theory

In contrast to balance theory which plays up the importance of internal consistency within the human psyche, proponents of self-esteem theory argue that enhancing one's self-esteem is a more powerful desire than achieving cognitive balance. A key hypothesis in self-esteem theory is that people are attracted to those who give them favorable feedback and not attracted to those who demean them, regardless of whether or not the feedback is consistent with the recipient's views of themselves. The theoretical position of cognitive balance would lead us to predict that persons with low self-esteem would react favorably to negative evaluations—since such inputs would be consistent with their own self-image.

Jones (1973), an advocate of self-esteem theory, has argued that balance theory does not often hold under conditions of favorable and unfavorable feedback. He wrote that the unhappy self derogator seems to glow when praised and glare when censured even more than his self-confident counterpart (p. 197). He poetically states the importance of self-esteem for understanding the attraction process by rewriting a so-called "knot" presented by Laing (1970). Whereas, Laing wrote: "I am good—you love me—therefore you are good"; and "I am bad—you love me—therefore you are bad," Jones rewrites the second part: "I am bad—you love me—therefore you are truly beautiful." And Jones' research supports his point.

Although Jones may be correct where the particular topic of love is concerned, both the balance and the self-esteem theories are useful for understanding attraction in the classroom. Depending on the social psychological circumstances, one theory or the other will take precedence in explaining interpersonal attraction. Favorable feedback always occurs within an interpersonal context that has a history and a cluster of contemporaneous impinging forces. Jones discusses, for example, two climate conditions in which the desire to enhance one's self worth may be temporarily suspended in favor of either cognitive validation or cognitive balance. The first condition occurs when the consequences of favorable evaluation are perceived by the individual as being unrealistic; the favorable inputs are viewed as being undesirable for the recipient over the long term. The second condition takes place when the motivation behind the favorable feedback is distrusted by the recipient.

Let us discuss the former condition first as it might occur within the classroom. The classroom is replete with feedback in the form of interpersonal evaluation. Students are frequently evaluated formally on their school work by teachers, and are even more frequently evaluated informally about their interpersonal reactions by their peers. For students who want very much to become competent in an academic subject or a psychomotor skill, or in their personal interactions, feedback from others will be essential to keep them on a "learning track." Unrealistically positive feedback will not be helpful in overcoming tough obstacles during the learning process. As Nyberg (1971) has indicated, learning is both "tender and tough." Only through honest feedback that is "right-on" will a student be able to learn new competencies. Students who begin to notice that particular kinds of favorable feedback are not helpful to them in achieving their own goals will not be attracted to the giver of that kind of feedback. In this circumstance, the desire for self-worth is delayed for future gratification and tough feedback is valued as being instrumental to higher levels of self-esteem.

The second condition, discussed by Jones, has to do with the motivational basis of the approving feedback. Students wish to think of themselves as having some control over their own fate (Coleman 1966). When they see that their own behavior has prompted approving feedback, they view themselves as being the cause of the favorable response and are attracted to the giver. However, if a teacher praises everyone indiscriminately, a student receiving such praise will not feel personally responsible. After all—the student rationalizes—our teacher says that to everyone. This process can be explained by balance theory. The student is attracted to the giver of both favorable feedback and unfavorable feedback when the student views the cause of either type of feedback as emanating from his or her own behavior. The psychological balance involved is rewarding because either kind of feedback fits the reality of the student. In other words, authenticity may be more interpersonally enhancing of attraction than perceived dishonesty.

Need Complementarity Theory

This theory states that persons become attractive to one another as their psychological needs are gratified in an interlocking, complementary manner. It focuses upon the exchange of personality needs through interpersonal transactions and thereby differs in emphasis from the other three theories which place greater emphasis on either the social forces outside relationships or the internal, psychic dynamics of the individuals involved in the interaction.

In an empirical study of the need complementarity theory, Winch et al. (1955) discovered that marital partners often chose each other to satisfy complementary needs, e.g., assertive persons tended to marry receptive persons, and dominant individuals sought out submissive ones. Schutz (1958) made use of this sort of formulation in his theory of interpersonal relations. He argued that persons relate in terms of inclusion, control, and affection needs. Attraction occurs between two persons when they each satisfy the other's needs in these areas, e.g., a person with a strong need to express control will be attracted to another who wants to be controlled.

Need complementarity is also the basis for some of the friendships that form in classrooms. Students who want to be very affectionate will like peers who need to receive a lot of affection. Students who want very much to be included in games and activities will like peers who strongly wish to include them. Students who are dependent and anxious about their status in the group may like peers who show them what to do and who exert a good deal of leadership.

Classroom Liking Patterns

Friendship formation in the classroom develops in systematic ways. Physical appearance and proximity trigger off the friendship. Students who strike each other as attractive as well as those who initially sit close to each other commence interaction. Then, provided there are no significant threats made to the students' common needs for status and security, communication between the students will continue. The discovery of common attitudes, values, and interests deepen the relationship and encourage informal meetings outside the classroom. The favorable reactions from others enhance one's self worth and one reacts positively. The presence of complementarity and interlocking personality needs buttress the relationship and help to maintain it. Our best guess about the development of interpersonal attraction in the classroom involves a series of "filtering factors" with proximity, physical attraction, and social status similarities operating early; granting status and security by favorable approval to the other next; discovering consensus on values and interests somewhat later; and need complementarity still later, always through the enhancement of self-esteem by getting and giving favorable reactions to others. A mismatch at any point in this development could cause the friendship to be dissolved.

Distinct sex differences also exist in classroom liking patterns. Boys appear to be psychologically influenced more by having low influence or power in the class than girls. Girls, in contrast, are affected more by having low liking status (Van Egmond 1960). In attempting to isolate variables affecting the academic performance of boys and girls, Schmuck and Van Egmond (1965) found that girls were significantly influenced by their position in the peer group, their satisfaction with the teacher, and their level of perceived parental support. Boys, on the other hand, were influenced only by the peer group and teacher and not significantly by their parents.

At the group level, classroom liking patterns have been described in terms of peer group sociometric structure. The senior author (R. Schmuck 1963) described two types of sociometric structures: (1) centrally structured groups, characterized by a narrow focus of interpersonal acceptance and rejection, and (2) diffusely structured groups, characterized by a wide range of positive and negative choices with little or no focus of interpersonal acceptance and rejection upon a few members. In centrally structured groups, a large number of students agreed in selecting a small cluster of their classmates as highly accepted or rejected. Diffusely structured groups, on the other hand, were *not* typified by small clusters of highly accepted and highly rejected students, i.e., there were no distinct subgroups whose members received most of the sociometric choices.

The research indicated that students were more accurate in estimating their liking status in centrally structured groups than in diffusely structured groups. The theoretical bases for this finding originated with Gestalt perceptual theory on the one hand (Kohler 1947), and group dynamics theory on the other (Cartwright and Zander 1969). The assumption from Gestalt theory was that at least one significant determinant of perceptual veridicality lies in the structure determinant of perceptual veridicality lies in the structure of the distal stimulus object, i.e., its "good form," clarity, symmetry, distinctiveness, etc. Centrally structured compared with diffusely structured peer groups represented clearer and more distinct social stimuli for individual students. From group dynamics, studies on communication nets and group structure (Leavitt 1951) indicated that task leadership was recognized more quickly and easily in centrally structured groups. Social emotional status could also be expected to be more easily recognized in groups with centrally structured liking patterns.

Validation, balance, and self-esteem theories are useful for understanding the effects of different sociometric group structures. Validation theory says that students will strive to assess themselves in the eyes of their peers by trying to find out their position in the classroom liking structure. If the sociometric structure is so ordered that only a few students are clearly the most liked, then it should be relatively easy for a student to determine his or her place in the peer group.

The perceptions of students in centrally structured classes are in close agreement with the actual structure. With a striving for psychological balance at work, a sense of rejection by others leads to negative opinions about one's self worth which, in turn, leads to a perception of the classroom as a threatening environment. And, according to the self-esteem theorists rejection by others would usually lead to frustrations in enhancing self worth and a disliking for those who are negative. Even though the need for validation is strong for students in diffusely structured classes, the status patterning is unclear. A student receives about the same number of positive choices as his peers; more students view themselves as highly liked or at least as secure. In diffusely structured classrooms the students' high cognized positions encourage high self-esteem which helps them perform well in academic learning. The classroom is not a threat and they feel a sense of security and status.

Effects of Classroom Liking Patterns on Academic Performance

Richard Schmuck's research (1966) further indicated that a student's perceived sociometric position within the classroom had implications for the accomplishment of that student's academic work. Those students who were accurate when estimating their position in the liking structure and who were negatively placed in that structure were lower utilizers of academic abilities and had less positive attitudes toward self and school than students who were accurate and positively placed. Moreover, students who thought of themselves as being liked, as they did quite often in diffusely structured classrooms, were using their abilities more highly and had more positive attitudes toward self and school, even though objectively speaking they often had low classroom liking status. Finally, the research indicated that students who had very few friends outside the classroom group were more influenced by their liking status in the group than were students who had more nonclass friends.

These findings were corroborated in a recent study by Lewis and St. John (1974) which dealt with the achievement of black students within classrooms that had a majority of whites. In an effort to study the dynamics of racially integrated classrooms, Lewis and St. John set out to test the conception derived from the 1954 Supreme Court Decision that integrated school experiences would facilitate the achievement of black students. They collected extensive data from 154 black sixth-graders in 22 majority white classrooms in Boston. Their results showed that a rise in the achievement of blacks depended on two factors: (1) Norms stressing achievement in the classrooms; and (2) acceptance of black students into the classroom peer group. This second factor was shown to be especially important. The mere presence of academically achieving white students was not sufficient to raise achievement levels of black students. The performance of blacks was strongly influenced by their being accepted as friends by white students.

We believe that a student's attractiveness to his or her peers is a very important variable within the matrix of forces facilitating or inhibiting achievement. Students who receive unfavorable and negative feedback from their peers are put in a threatening environment for many hours each day; their anxiety and insecurity reduces their self-esteem and their lack of adequate self worth, in turn, decreases their effort to succeed in academic work. A lack of peer acceptance undermines a student's self confidence and debilitates his or her motivation to persist in the face of tough academic obstacles.

Teacher Behavior and Classroom Liking Patterns

Naturally, teachers' attitudes toward their students also are fraught with affect. Teachers tend to like those students who are attractive to peers, who exhibit positive feelings toward other people, and who adjust to the school's demands. On the other hand, teachers tend to dislike students who create disturbances and who keep other students from attending to school work.

Girls, in general, have more compatible relationships with their teachers than boys. Boys more often than girls are disliked by teachers. Teachers have been found to give most negative feedback to boys with low status in the peer group liking structure especially. Lippitt and Gold (1959) showed that teachers often paid closer attention to the social behavior than the academic performance of low peer status boys and that the low status boys received more overt rebuke and criticism than other students. At the same time, teachers appeared to grant low peer status girls support and affection. These findings were accompanied by others to the effect that low status boys were aggressive and disruptive, while low status girls tended to be more dependent, passive, and affectionate.

Flanders and Havumaki (1960) showed experimentally how teachers' behaviors can influence the liking patterns in a classroom group. They asked teachers to respond positively and consistently to selected students and not to others. For a week, teachers interacted with and praised only students seated in odd-numbered seats; while in comparison groups, all students were encouraged to speak and the teachers' praise was directed to the whole class. Students in the odd-numbered seats, in the former situation, later received more peer-group sociometric choices than students in the even-numbered seats. In the comparison classrooms, the difference between sociometric choices of students in the odd- and even-numbered seats was insignificant. The peer choices were spread around more evenly, indicating greater general acceptance. Retish (1973) showed similarly that planned and systematic teacher reinforcement of rejected students resulted in the significant net gains of the sociometric statues of the targeted students.

Further research on classroom liking patterns indicated that teachers of more diffusely structured classrooms, compared with other teachers, attended to and talked with a larger variety of students per hour (R. Schmuck 1966). Teachers with centrally structured peer groups tended to call on fewer students for participation and seemed especially to neglect the slower, less involved students. Teachers with the most supportive peer groups tended to reward students with specific statements for helpful behaviors, and to control behavioral disturbances with general, group-oriented statements. Teachers with less positive liking patterns in their classrooms tended to reward individuals less often and to reprimand them publicly more often for breaking classroom rules.

Satisfaction with one's teacher is an important facilitative condition for a student's academic performance. Students are attracted to teachers who provide them with a boost of status in the peer group and who grant them security. Teachers who reward frequently and who do not rebuke or demean students in the eyes of their peers are attractive. Students who are satisfied with their teachers usually feel good about school, learning, and themselves. The continual rejection of an overtly aggressive student by both classroom peers and the teacher feeds the negative cycle of low self-esteem, unfriendly overtures to others, and poor performance in academic work.

Implications for Teachers

The following points summarize some of the most important implications of the contents of this chapter for teachers.

—All human beings strive to be attractive to someone else. Although the degree of affiliative motivation will differ from person to person, all people will look for some friendship in most groups.

—Friendship relationships within the classroom cannot be separated from teaching and learning; they are integral to instructional transactions between teachers and students and among students.

—Affiliative interactions take the form often of circular interpersonal processes. Favorable feedback begets favorable responses while unfavorable feedback begets unfavorable responses.

—Critical feedback is acceptable and can enhance friendships when it is viewed as realistic, authentic, and motivated by helpful intentions.

—Students who view themselves as being disliked or ignored by their peers often have difficulty in performing up to their academic potential.

—The instructional behaviors of teachers can have a significant impact on the peer group friendship patterns that develop in the classroom.

Action Ideas for Change

Some of the practices that follow are descriptions of what teachers did to stop vicious cycles of negativism. These plans were not easy to implement; they required courageous risk-taking, patience, and endurance.

Improving the Acceptance of Rejected Students

The goal of this practice was to attempt an improvement of the peer group environment for rejected students by training the class to empathize and to take the role of the other.

The teacher started by administering a sociometric questionnaire to determine which students had high and which had low liking status in the group (Fox, Luszki, and Schmuck 1900). She commenced the training by working first with a group of low status students, next with a group of high status students, and finally she finished the design by working with the whole class. She used a chair to stand for a fictitious person. The chair was placed in front of the group and given human characteristics. Low status students were asked to sit in the chair and to express behaviors that they thought would "turn other people off." The high status students were asked to sit in the chair and to express understanding, acceptance, and inclusion of others. Both groups discussed the behaviors and talked about their relevance to the classroom. After such training had gone on in separate groups for about one month, the entire class met to role-play classroom situations of acceptance and exclusion.

In the evaluation of the practice, the teacher said that considerable amounts of interpersonal strain had been reduced among many of the students.

Strength Building Exercise

The goal of this practice was to build the self-esteem of individual students by the sharing of positive characteristics of everyone in the class. The teacher first led a discussion on the variety of personal traits of people—valuable traits—and on the importance of knowing who is good at what things in the classroom. Students were then given a large sheet of newsprint paper, were asked to put their names at the top, and to list in large letters what they considered to be their individual strengths. Every student was encouraged to have at least three important items on the list. These sheets were hung up around the room, and the students were asked to add strengths to other students' lists, strengths that they had perceived in the past. Each student was encouraged to add something to the other sheets. Later, the teacher mimeographed sheets about all the students' resources and discussed ways of using the strengths in the class. In most classrooms where this practice has been employed, the results have been to increase closeness among the students.

Encouraging Acceptance of New Members

The goal of this practice was to increase interaction among students in order to facilitate the building of friendships for many students. The teacher asked each member of the class to prepare a biography about another member. Next, the whole class worked on building an interview schedule to collect personal data from others. Then, each student was assigned another student. Interviews were carried out, and the biographies were prepared. A booklet of class biographies was put together, and every Friday the class used the booklet for one hour during their reading period. The practice helped facilitate a rapid acquaintance process, especially for students new to the school.

Building Academic Work Groups to Change Classroom Liking Patterns

The main goal of this practice was to change a centrally-structured liking pattern into a diffusely-structured pattern. The teacher organized small work groups to work on social studies projects. The groups were organized to include a heterogeneous mix of high, medium, and low status students. The groups were altered every month so that almost every student had a chance to work with every other student during the year. The teacher felt that this simple procedure increased the liking statuses of most of the students who initially were not attractive to their peers.

Role Playing

Role playing is a specialized technique that has been used in a variety of professions and settings (see especially Chesler and Fox 1966; Shaftel and Shaftel 1967). It could be applied to most of the contents of this book, but we have a special reason for commenting on it here. Inclusion-exclusion and acceptance-rejection are critical areas for human beings. Because they are so real and so pervasive, it is often difficult to "get hold" of the issue and to discuss such critical matters openly. Role playing is a technique that takes interpersonal attraction out of hidden areas and places it in an overt and public situation for analysis and understanding. The sequence in using it involves: (1) selecting the problem; (2) warming up; (3) setting the stage by explaining the situation, describing participant roles, and explaining audience roles; (4) enactment; (5) analysis and discussion; (6) evaluation; (7) reenactment of the role play; and (8) generalizing.

References

Allport, G. W. *The Nature of Prejudice.* Boston: Beacon Press, 1954.

Buswell, M. "The Relationship Between the Social Structure of the Classroom and the Academic Success of the Pupil." Ph.D. dissertation, University of Minnesota, 1951.

Cartwright, D., and Zander, A. *Group Dynamics.* Evanston, Ill.: Row, Peterson and Co., 1953 and 1960; New York: Harper & Row, Publishers, 1969.

Chesler, M., and Fox, R. *Role Playing Methods in the Classroom.* Chicago: Science Research Associates, 1966.

Coleman, J. et al. *Equality of Educational Opportunity.* Washington, D. C.: United States Government Printing Office, 1966.

Cook, L. A. "An Experimental Sociographic Study of a Stratified 10th Grade Class." *American Sociological Review* 10 (1945):250-61.

Flanders, N., and Havumaki, S. "The Effect of Teacher-Pupil Contacts Involving Praise on the Sociometric Choices of Students." *Journal of Educational Psychology* 51 (1960):65-68.

Glidewell, J. D.; Kantor, M.; Smith, L. M.; and Stringer, L. "Classroom Socialization and Social Structure." In *Review of Child Development Research,* edited by M. Hoffman and L. Hoffman. New York: Russell Sage Foundation, 1966. Pp. 221-57.

Gold, M. "Power in the Classroom." *Sociometry* 25 (1958):50-60.

Jordan, T. E. *The Mentally Retarded.* Columbus, Ohio: Charles E. Merrill Publishing Co., 1961.

Jones, S. "Self and Interpersonal Evaluations: Esteem Theories Versus Consistency Theories." *Psychological Bulletin* 79, no. 3 (1973):185-99.

Kohler, W. *Gestalt Psychology.* New York: Liveright, 1947.

Laing, R. D. *Knots.* New York: Pantheon, 1970.

Leavitt, H. J. "Some Effects of Certain Communication Patterns on Group Performance." *Journal of Abnormal and Social Psychology* 46 (1951):38-50.

Lewis, R., and St. John, N. "Contribution of Cross-Racial Friendship to Minority Group Achievement in Desegregated Classrooms." *Sociometry* 37, no. 1 (1974):79-91.

Lippitt, R., and Gold, M. "Classroom Social Structure as a Mental Health Problem." *Journal of Social Issues* 15 (1959):40-58.

Lippitt, R.; Polansky, N.; Redl, F.; and Rosen, S. "The Dynamics of Power." *Human Relations* 5 (1952):37-64.

Nyberg, D. *Tough and Tender Learning.* Palo Alto, Calif.: National Press Books, 1971.

Pepitone, A. *Attraction and Hostility.* New York: Atherton Press, Inc., 1964.

Pope, B. "Socioeconomic Contrasts in Children's Peer Culture Prestige Values." *Genetic Psychology Monograph* 48 (1953):157-220.

———. "Prestige Values in Contrasting Socioeconomic Groups of Children." *Psychiatry* 16 (1953):381-85.

Price, K. "Intensity of Attraction as a Condition in a Social Psychological Balance Theory." Ph.D. dissertation, University of Michigan, 1961.

Retish, P. M. "Changing the Status of Poorly Esteemed Students Through Teacher Reinforcement." *Journal of Applied Behavioral Science* 9 (1973): 44-50.

Schmuck, R. A. "Some Relationships of Peer Liking Patterns in the Classroom to Pupil Attitudes and Achievement." *School Review* 71 (1963):337-59.

———. "Some Aspects of Classroom Social Climate." *Psychology in the Schools* 3 (1966):59-65.

———. "Helping Teachers Improve Classroom Group Processes." *Journal of Applied Behavioral Science* 4 (1968):401-35. Reprinted in *Learning in Social Settings,* edited by M. Miles and W. W. Charters. Boston: Allyn and Bacon, Inc., 1970; and in *Organization Development in Schools,* edited by R. A. Schmuck, and M. Miles. Palo Alto: National Press Books, 1971.

Schmuck, R. A., and Van Egmond, E. "Sex Differences in the Relationship of Interpersonal Perceptions to Academic Performance." *Psychology in the Schools* 2 (1965):32-40.

Schutz, W. *FIRO: A Three Dimensional Theory of Interpersonal Behavior.* New York: Holt, Rinehart & Winston, Inc., 1958.

Shaftel, F., and Shaftel, G. *Role Playing for Social Values: Decision Making in the Social Studies.* Englewood Cliffs, N. J.: Prentice-Hall, Inc., 1967.

Torrance, E. P. *Education and the Creative Potential.* Minneapolis: University of Minnesota Press, 1963.

Van Egmond, E. "Social Interrelationship Skills and Effective Utilization of Intelligence in the Classroom. Ph.D. dissertation, University of Michigan, 1960.

Walster, E.; Aronson, V.; Abrahams, D.; and Rottman, L. "Importance of Physical Attractiveness in Dating Behavior." *Journal of Personality and Social Psychology* 4 (1966):508-16.

Winch, R.; Ktanses, T.; and Ktanses, V. "Empirical Elaboration of the Theory of Complementarity Needs in Mate Selection." *Journal of Abnormal and Social Psychology* 51 (1955):508-13.

Zajonc, R. "The Concepts of Balance, Congruity, and Dissonance." *Public Opinion Quarterly* 24 (1960):280-96.

CHAPTER 6

Norms

Norms influence interpersonal relationships by helping individuals to know what is expected of them and what they should expect from others. Group life is orderly and predictable partly because of norms which are shared expectations and attitudes about thoughts, feelings, and actions. Without such guideposts for individuals, group processes could be confusing and, at times, chaotic.

A definition of norms must emphasize *sharing;* thus, norms occur in groups and are not psychological processes alone. The psychological counterpart of a norm is an attitude—a predisposition to think, feel, and act in certain specific ways. Norms are individuals' attitudes that are shared in a group. The interpersonal and intrapersonal dynamics of expectations was discussed in Chapter 3. In this chapter we look at the *shared* expectations for group members. These shared expectations are part and parcel of norms. When a norm is present, most group participants know that their attitude is also held by others and that the others expect them to have the attitude and to behave accordingly.

Sociologists and anthropologists have been more interested in norms than psychologists have been. Sumner (1906) developed the concept of folkways to describe the normative culture of a society or community. Later, the Lynds (1937) and Warner and Lunt (1941) described the social classes of American communities as having quite different norms, thereby attempting to explain the differences in behaviors between middle- and lower-class persons. Still later, Cohen (1955) delineated the effects of norms on the delinquent activities of urban gangs and Whytes' (1943) participant observation of gangs supported the importance of norms. They showed that delinquent gangs hold high standards for themselves and exert a great amount of influence on their members to abide by norms. More recently, Angell (1958) described current crises in our large cities as a condition of unclear and unshared moral norms, Wax (1971) described the problems of Indian education centering on peer group norms while Hargreaves (1967) demonstrated the impact of such norms for school achievement. Norms have been categorized as either *static* or *dynamic*, depending on the extent of active interpersonal influence; and as either *formal* or *informal*, depending on how codified or traditional they are.

Static norms make up the basic, unconscious culture of groups. They are those norms with which persons abide without much interpersonal pressure being exerted. For example, the shared expectation that every student shall have his or her own textbook for a class is a formal, static norm in many schools. The principle of "one-student-one-book" is probably assumed within the policy handbook of the school district or even in the state laws. If never questioned by students, teachers, or members of the community, it will remain static.

Norms of greater interest to the teacher are dynamic and informal. In some classrooms, for instance, a norm exists which specifies that students should *not* help one another with schoolwork, especially when tests are being taken. If fellow students and the teacher take action to keep one another from sharing and discussing an assignment, they are actively supporting maintenance of the norm through their interpersonal influence. A contrasting norm may exist in other classrooms—that of helping one another on schoolwork and viewing it as a valuable activity. Such a norm probably would not be sustained without the active support of a large part of the class.

Figure 6.1 delineates these distinctions in more detail. A norm could at any time in its development be placed in any of these boxes. Generally speaking, norms develop first as dynamic and informal and become either static and informal or dynamic and formal. Static and formal norms are those that have existed for a long time and which are a basic part of the assumed classroom group processes. Schools and classrooms are replete with all four types of norms which influence the behaviors of teachers and students. Although norms are pervasive in educational settings, very little systematic research has been done on the ways in which they function. Much of the material in this chapter

	Formal	Informal
Static	Rules abided by without much discussion, e.g., a) no cheating b) asking permission to leave the room c) addressing teacher when seeking permission to change something in the room	Procedures and routines, e.g., a) how students enter the room b) who talks to whom for how long c) saying "Good morning," "Thank you," etc., to the teacher.
Dynamic	Rules in need of at least occasional enforcement, e.g., a) no talking during story time or individual study time b) turning work in on time c) using correct grammar in talking and writing	Interpersonal actions about which there is active monitoring, e.g., a) addressing teacher in a nasty fashion b) wearing hair quite differently than other students do c) acting abusively toward others

FIGURE 6.1 / *Types of Classroom Norms.*

represents extrapolations from social psychological theory and research on settings other than the school.

The Nature of Norms

Norms are group agreements that help to guide the psychological processes of the group members. They influence perception—how members view their physical and social worlds; cognition—how members think about things; evaluation—how they feel about things; and behavior—how the members overtly act. In the real world of a group it is difficult to separate perceptual, cognitive, evaluative and behavioral processes. Nevertheless, we will keep them separate to provide a clearer understanding of the complexities of norms in action.

Perceptual Norms

In perception, the person derives meaning from sensory experiences. Sometimes perception is a straightforward process in a group when persons agree with what they see; at other times, however, individual group members differ widely on the meaning they attribute to an experience. Furthermore, groups can have a decided effect on how individuals within the group perceive a sensory experience. A first grader's perceptions of his or her teacher may be quite positive. The child views the teacher as a beautiful, supportive, and gentle person. However, if the youngster's peers were to speak about the teacher in critical ways, describing the teacher as cruel, judgmental, and aggressive, the student might begin to look for different behaviors to come from the teacher. The student would begin to look for cues of negative attributes and most likely would perceive behaviors that would confirm the group's inputs. Through an interpersonal influence process, perceptual norms are formed and students are affected psychologically.

Sherif (1935) conducted an experiment to describe the dynamics of perceptual norms in which he used the "autokinetic phenomenon"—a stationary pinpoint of light which takes on the appearance of movement in a totally darkened room. Subjects were asked to estimate the light's movement for 100 separate trials at two-second exposures. Initially, one-half of the subjects worked alone and declared their estimates of movement, thereby establishing personal standards of perceptual judgment. During this phase of the experiment, subjects generally settled on a range of movement somewhere between two and ten inches. Next, subjects worked in groups of two to four in which one-half of them had already established a perceptual standard and one-half had had no experience with the autokinetic phenomenon. The subjects were asked to declare publicly their individual estimates. In this small group situation, all subjects developed group agreements even though agreement was not stressed by the experimenter. If the group norm centered on eight to ten inches of movement, those who had previously seen the light moving three or four inches veered in the direction of the group and vice versa. Variation between groups was greater than the variation between individuals within the same group, even though individuals of the same groups initially had quite divergent perceptual standards. To complete a sequence of research, Sherif asked the subjects again to make judgments of the light's movement alone. Most of them—even with no apparent pressure to conform—persisted in estimates of movement that had been established in their small groups. The ambiguity of the sensory data, along with the public sharing of estimates within the small group, encouraged the development of a perceptual norm. This norm continued to be influential even when subjects were alone, because for most it had become an internalized attitude, guiding perceptions in an ambiguous, confusing circumstance.

The classroom with its grand variety of sensory experiences has many ambiguous and unclear events. At the beginning of the school year, although teachers are an especially important figure for the development of perceptual norms because of their significant potential power, they also are an unknown. What will the teacher be like? Will the teacher be tough? Can the teacher be trusted to be kind? Can the teacher be believed or have a change of mind and be confusing? Students begin unconsciously to establish perceptual norms on the meanings of the teacher's actions. Frequently, students bring negative attitudes toward active and open participation in class discussion from previous experiences. These attitudes quickly become shared and solidify into perceptual norms, particularly if the teacher dominates and cuts off students as they begin to speak. Ambiguity and confusion may arise when a new teacher states a desire to hear what is really on the students' minds. Is it for real? Can the students trust the teacher not to punish them for being outspoken?

In our observations, perceptual norms of suspicion for teacher actions are so strong in classroom peer groups that participation levels often remain low, even as the teacher states the desire for participation to be different. Such norms are tenacious because students fear that what the teacher said was not what was really meant, and that fellow peers will not be supportive in collaboratively testing the teacher's earnestness. The persistence of norms of suspicion for authority can only be broken by the teacher's continuing to reiterate an interest in openness and by behaving congruently with the requests. Students may gradually become willing to take risks to test the teacher and the norm may gradually give way if they are successful. Of course, if the situation becomes unclear again, students will rely more on strong, powerful peer group members to help them clarify their perceptions.

Cognitive Norms

Cognitive norms involve the sharing of thought processes such as reasoning, remembering, analyzing, and anticipating, and these norms are crucial to classroom life. Books must be studied, not thrown around; other students should be respected, not ridiculed; teachers are for helping, not for controlling. The development of such shared understandings which give critical support for academic learning can generally be divided into two subcategories: (a) cognitive norms as classroom goals, and (b) cognitive norms about classroom learning itself.

Intellectual and emotional development of students occurs more effectively when formal educational goals and some of the cognitive norms of the peer group are consonant. Conflicts between the two lie at the core of many current tensions in schools. Schools in which the goals center on preparing students for effective jobs are in conflict with peer group expectations of immediate relevance and satisfaction. Classes for which the goals emphasize freeing students to make more choices are in conflict with peer group expectations that adults are supposed to make educational decisions. Schools which stress public displays of school spirit through football games and concerts may be in conflict with students' expectations that educational activities should focus on solving social ills.

Perhaps the most serious contemporary conflict between peer norms and school goals concerns students' role in decision making. Modern technology, more and more, allows for individualization of instructions. Class schedules and individual programs can be computerized to render numerous creative permutations, and curriculum materials can be made more diversified and individualized. Students themselves can be used to tutor and learn from one another. But cognitive norms in the peer group to support such a modern design often are not present. What the norms should be for supporting independent study time for either students or teachers are difficult to define. Questions arise: Should a group of students work independent of an adult? If so, what rules should be established? Old expectations do not work. Only through effective discussions and by arriving at public, group agreements can such norms be established.

Cognitive norms about classroom learning, key to an effective classroom, can be divided into norms about content learning and norms about the processes of learning. Content learning refers to curriculum packages that are deemed valuable for classroom study, while process learning refers to the procedures that teachers and students use to learn the curriculum. Students appear to pursue learning of the curriculum most energetically if they are involved along with the teacher in establishing cognitive norms about the process of learning. Focusing upon the learning process itself is one good way of helping students understand how to learn. Unfortunately many teachers assign too many laborious tasks that require recitation of facts. They teach the conclusions of a content field rather than the processes of inquiry relating to that field. Out of this conclusion kind of teaching, students learn about the subject rather than doing the subject. For example, they learn about social studies as though the problems of society were removed from life or they parrot back mathematics rather than capture the subject's basic idea of order.

One third grade teacher summed up a year of modifying cognitive norms about learning in this way, "I worked with the students until the Christmas vacation on ways in which to learn. During the winter, we learned a lot of things and, starting in the spring, I tried to prepare them for continuing to learn on their own, even if another teacher might stand in the way." It is likely that this teacher's efforts would have been futile unless the group norms actually were modified and unless a substantial part of the group moved on together into the fourth grade. Nevertheless attempts to establish cognitive norms that support inquiry and discussion about how the learning is taking place can increase students' abilities to learn independently and can, with the support of the next teacher, carry over.

Evaluative Norms

Evaluative norms involve high amounts of favorable or unfavorable feeling. To be cruel to another student may be very bad in one class or highly respected and positively rewarded in another. In contemporary youth culture, to wear old clothes is "in," the Beatles are still great, Elvis Presley was square but is now part of the nostalgia craze, powerful authorities often are bad, and smoking pot can either be very good or very bad depending upon the group. Evaluative norms typically are dynamic, and should not be confused with cognitive norms which become static and about which there is little intense feeling. That the students rush out-of-doors in a scramble at recess may not be liked by the teacher, but it is expected, and after a time taken for granted. It is a cognitive norm. There are no active attempts to embarrass those who rush out. But evaluative norms are working when a student swears at the teacher or uses the teacher's first name, and criticism is received from the teacher or communicated by looks of disgust and criticism from peers.

Especially with evaluative norms, teachers should attempt to develop norms that support individual diversity and uniqueness—not only because this is valuable in itself, but also because learning for individuals seems to go better when they feel supported by the group. Overly rigid evaluations about hair length, dress, appearance, and behavior by the teacher or the peer group can lead to alienation and feelings of low self-respect on the part of some students. As with cognitive norms, it is important that evaluative norms are shared and discussed throughout the school year so that students can become clear on the definitions of good taste in the classroom. Should students chew gum in class? Should they talk and share during a work assignment? Should they interrupt the teacher to ask questions? Should students decide as to how certain lessons will be taught? These and other concerns can be discussed by the entire group. Active attempts should be made by the teacher to confront peer group evaluative norms that tend to restrict and isolate others from participating effectively in the group.

Behavioral Norms

A person's behavior is influenced by his or her perceptions, cognitions, and evaluations as well as circumstances in the external situation. Behavioral norms operate, on the one hand, to guide a person's actions through a complex psychological process involving perceptual, cognitive, and evaluative norms simultaneously—or on the other hand through cues and pressures to conform dictated by others in the social environment. The latter type, external conformity, does not involve the sharing of internalized processes of other norms but, rather, involves behaviorally subscribing to other persons when they are present.

Asch (1952) conducted an experiment to explore the effects of group pressure on behavioral conformity which pointed to the difference between behavioral norms and perceptual or cognitive norms. Fifty groups, each consisting of eight male college students, were asked to match the length of a line presented on a board, with one of three lines and to declare their judgments on twelve different trials. All of the members of each group, except the subject, had been instructed by the experimenter to give the wrong answer. The subject faced a situation in which his or her senses were in contradiction to the reports of all other group members. One-third of Asch's subjects, which he labeled yielders, conformed to the group's wrong answers about one-half of the time. According to interviews, very few of the yielders distorted their perceptions; almost all gave in in order not to stand out and be different. They could not understand the apparent contradiction but were unwilling to be unique and risk rejection in front of the others.

Asch's experiment sheds light on the dynamics of behavioral conformity in schools. Often students have not internalized peer group norms so that their perceptions, cognitions, or feelings have been modified. They conform to the expectations of others in order not to appear different and risk being rejected. The norms of the peer group become the student's personal standards, but only superficially. Once the student is outside the presence of peers, his or her behavior is no longer influenced by them. Similarly, teachers are aware that many students who appear to have internalized positive intellectual values are merely conforming behaviorally while in the teacher's presence. Their work is done on time, but they just get by. Their classroom behavior is seldom objectionable, and their apparent attitude toward school is passively accepting. They have not internalized values of involvement, academic interest, and curiosity, nor do they deviate behaviorally from those values a great deal. Even some defiant students conform in ways that do not run deeply into their personalities. They might deviate from adult expectations by going along with hostile peers while not feeling deeply counterdependent. Their behaviors are guided by deviant peer group members out of a desire for acceptance but without holding internalized feelings of destructiveness.

Some teachers find it useful to differentiate between perceptual, cognitive, and evaluative norms on the one hand, and behavioral norms on the other, since the latter are easier to modify. Behavioral norms can be modified through open, public communication with the relevant members of the class. The teacher can encourage the class to discuss circumstances in which superficial allegiance to behavioral pressures kept them from being effective. Since sharedness is the essence of normativeness, the teacher who wishes to modify particular behavioral norms should hold the discussion with the entire group. A classroom group can share the student's views of various classroom behaviors and the meanings they have attached to them if it hopes to establish helpful, influential perceptual norms. It might share "where it is going" (goals) and "how it plans to get there" (learning processes) if it hopes to establish influential cognitive norms. And it might share the deep feelings that members have about one another's behaviors in order to shape agreements about new evaluative norms.

Sometimes students' behaviors are influenced by misreadings of shared attitudes in the peer group. A special condition, called *pluralistic ignorance*, occurs when incorrect estimates of others' expectations influence a student's behavior without a true norm existing. In such instances students are influenced by what they think others think, even though their perceptions of the others are erroneous. Especially during adolescence, the fear of being rejected by the peer group is so strong that perceived expectations are not tested. "I wouldn't dare wear my hair that way; others wouldn't like it," "I couldn't possibly go with that person; what would others say?" "I can't carry this book around," and so forth. In this way, adolescents conform to perceptions of fictitious norms. Conditions of pluralistic ignorance can be diminished through explicit sharing, using group discussion.

Open sharing of norms allows each student to become more realistic about his or her peers' reactions to various behaviors. Sharedness requires that three conditions be present in the classroom group: (1) Students recognize what others expect them to perceive, cognize, feel, or do; (2) students accept others' expectations for themselves, abide by them, and in some instances exert pressures upon violators; and (3) students recognize that other students share in their acceptance of the expectations.

Usually, students perceive a more restricted range of legitimate behavior than most teachers will accommodate. Open sharing allows for a widening of the range of alternatives for perceptions, cognitions, feelings, and behaviors. Also, public sharing of norms produces greater social support for the agreement eventually decided upon. Changes in methods of working in the group are brought about most effectively when students are involved in planning the changes. Imposed alterations often bring about resistance and the development of counternorms that impede the class's group processes. Interpersonal support for a new norm is usually increased when group members are actively involved. Open sharing and discussion about classroom norms also can increase feelings of group solidarity. Students are more attracted to classes in which they can voice their perceptions and share in influencing the group's direction. Also, when students have trust in their classmates, they tend to apply group norms more to themselves. Sharing of those norms that are real and desirable contributes to higher involvement in the classroom group and often to more satisfaction with school.

Individual Reactions to Group Norms

Relationships between group norms and individual attitudes involve two-way influence and cannot be understood without considering both. Group norms have strongest influence over individuals' attitudes when the individuals willfully accept the norms, but some individuals are so constituted that they are influenced very little by interpersonal pressures, regardless of the strengths of group norms. Let us consider, first, reasons why group norms affect individuals in general.

Groups define social reality for their members. Many of the individual differences that occur in society can be accounted for by the different group memberships of individuals. For instance, a militant teachers' union defines issues and develops solutions that are quite different from those of an association of school administrators. There are considerable variations between the two groups in the information discussed, the attitudes expressed, and the actions considered. Social reality takes on different priorities and meanings in each group. Likewise, different student peer groups communicate various meanings and priorities to their members. Within any classroom group there are subgroups and cliques of students that define reality in somewhat different ways.

Individuals rely on group norms to guide them, especially when they are unsure about social reality. Uncertainty leads to a search for the social world as others see it. During the search, individuals notice that their social surroundings are commonly shared with the members of their group, and they expect the others to be experiencing the same reality. For students especially there is a pull toward the peer group to make the complex world of the school more understandable. For example, students perceive the teacher or a textbook and at the same time realize that their peers' perceptions are also converging on the teacher or text. It is reasonable, then, for the students to expect peers to be helpful in clearing up ambiguous events.

Students feel insecure when their personal response is in opposition to a group norm. Hoffman (1957) experimented with the relationship between anxiety and disagreements with group norms. He had students state opinions about a series of social attitudes, and then six weeks later each student was asked again for his or her attitude on the same items— this time after hearing the experimenter present false group norms. Hoffman measured anxiety, using galvanic skin responses. He found that subjects' anxiety was lowest when their opinions were in agreement with the norms both times. As the subjects changed their opinions from the first to the second time toward the bogus norms, there was a moderate degree of skin response; but for those subjects whose opinions both times were quite different from the group norms, there was the highest amount of galvanic skin response.

Many students fear being rejected by their peers and tend to go along with peers' perceptions of group norms in order not to be rejected. Students make the norms of the peer group their own attitudes as they become more and more involved in and rewarded by the group. High influence students in the peer group usually exhibit most allegiance to group norms and have attitudes very similar to the norms. Peer groups also have goals toward which they are moving, and highly involved students become committed to these. Students who are actively working toward peer group goals may willfully allow themselves to be infringed upon personally and even put themselves out in order to help the group.

Group norms also can influence individuals' attitudes through interpersonal pressures exerted over members to conform. An experiment by Schachter (1951) shows how group pressures can be brought to bear in ways that make it difficult to resist. Schachter asked groups to make a judgment on what to do about a juvenile delinquent named Johnny Rocco, who was awaiting a sentence for a minor crime. Group members each were asked to take a position on an attitude scale ranging from love and kindness at one end, to extreme and harsh discipline at the other. Three prompted subjects were involved in each group: the stooge playing the *modal role* took the typical position of the group; the stooge called a *slider* took the extreme punishment position, but eventually moved toward the softer, majority position; and the stooge playing the *deviate* differed most from the group, maintaining throughout that there should be extreme discipline for Johnny Rocco.

Schachter's results indicated that the *deviate* was rejected in groups with a high degree of cohesiveness and interest in the activity. The *sliders* received the most communication during the discussions, especially during the time that they were moving from the deviate to the modal position. The person playing the *modal* role did not receive special attention by group members. The strongest interpersonal pressures and most hostile criticisms were leveled at the *deviates*. Students who dare to adopt different attitudes from the predominant norms of the group may risk similar kinds of rejection in schools.

Group pressures need not always restrict individuals however. Groups can support and liberate their members so that each one can react as he or she personally feels. Milgram (1965) experimented with the freeing effects of a group when he had the group support a person's resolution of a value conflict in favor of the person's own values. He studied the effects of group support and pressure in a sequence of three experimental conditions. In all of them, the subjects were asked to teach a confederate of the experimenter a list of paired associates, by administering electric shock whenever the learner made a mistake. The subject was also told to increase the voltage intensity of the shock after each error. The subject was in front of a pseudo voltmeter which described the degrees of shock as slight, moderate, strong, very strong, intense, extremely intense, and dangerous-severe shock. Actually, the learner did not receive any shock at all. Clearly, the experimental situation sets up a conflict for the subject between the experimenter's demands to increase the shock and the pseudo cries, discomforts, and vehement protests of the learner.

In the first experimental situations, the subjects were with only the experimenter and the experimenter's confederate, the learner. Of the forty subjects, only fourteen withdrew before the completion of dangerous shocks. The majority of subjects continued to administer shocks at the highest voltage points. In the other two experiments, two additional confederates joined the subject. One read the list of words, the second informed the learner if he were correct, and the subject administered the shock. In the second experiment, even though the experimenter pleaded, prodded, and cajoled, the two confederates refused to continue after "very strong" shock was reached. Ninety percent of the subjects also defied the experimenter by refusing to continue. Just the opposite condition was set up in the third experiment. The confederates continued to obey up to the maximum shock and only 27.5 percent of the subjects refused to continue compared with about 35 percent refusers in the first experiment. Other data indicated that subjects outside the interpersonal pressure of the experimenter would not continue to shock to maximum levels. Thus, group support strongly influenced whether or not a person actually continued to shock the learner. This experiment indicated how group pressure can help or hinder an individual from resolving his or her own value conflicts.

It is interesting to note that these experiments on obedience and interpersonal pressures demonstrate the strength of normative phenomena in two other ways. First, the content of the experiments themselves indicate how powerful the norms of our society are for acting in the name of science. The experimenter in each of these studies dresses in a white coat and acts very objectively and distantly as he firmly directs the subject to administer shock. Indeed, Milgram's studies can be interpreted as demonstrations of the degree to which people have come to trust the scientist; the white coat and scientific demeanor have become very important legitimating symbols.

Second, these experiments also have pointed out that the evaluative norms in relation to science gradually are changing, at least in the psychological profession. During the last five years, as experimental psychology has rapidly increased in prominence, concern has also rapidly increased about the ethics involved in carrying out research. The particular techniques used by Milgram and his associates to study obedience have been criticized as examples of scientific procedures that may, in fact, have harmful or disturbing consequences on the subjects.

Other research has shown that group norms are influential when (a) the group is a highly cohesive unit, (b) when the norm is highly relevant or intense, (c) when the group is crystallized so that individuals know where the group is going and share its opinions, (d) when the group is a source of gratification for the individual, and (e) when the situation facing the group is ambiguous to the members. At the same time, the personality attributes that a person brings to a group situation also determine how much he or she will conform. Crutchfield (1955) in a study of the personality characteristics of conformists, found them to be less able to make decisions, more anxious, and less spontaneous compared with persons he called independents. Further he found that the conformists had pronounced feelings of inadequacy, low self-confidence, and unrealistic pictures of themselves; while the independents had high ego-strength, positive self-esteem, and realistic images of themselves. Conformists were more conventional and moralistic; independents showed greater tolerance for differences and ambiguities in their worldviews. Conformists also tended to be more dependent and passive in their human relations compared with the independents.

Jackson's Model for Norms

Jackson (1960) has developed a systematic framework for analyzing norms which can be useful for teachers. Jackson's model describes a norm as specifying the amount of particular behaviors that are expected of a person by using two dimensions, behavioral and evaluative. His behavioral category includes perceptual, cognitive, and behavioral norms as we have described them. The model specifies that for any behavior in a group, the amount of approval or disapproval felt by the group's members may fall anywhere along the evaluative dimension from highly positive, through neutral, to very negative. Figure 6.2 depicts a norm for verbal participation where low amounts of participation (three or fewer) are disapproved and where high amounts (eight or more) are also disapproved. For this group, emotional support is given for moderate participation. The curve in Figure 6.2 describes the behaviors that have "oughtness" attributed to them. It shows the amount of positive or negative *return* which members will *potentially* receive if their participation during a discussion is at different rates.

Jackson's Model serves only as a guide for plotting out classroom norms. There are many things that have to become known before the model can actually be used to understand classroom norms. Some of them are as follows:

INTENSITY OF A NORM. Some questions the teacher might ask about normative intensity are: What behaviors really make a difference to how class members feel? What behaviors really get a class turned on, positively or negatively? With students in nursery school and kindergarten behaviors concerned with sharing toys could constitute an intense norm. During the upper elementary years, norms about how students work together in class could be intense. During high school, strong norms tend to govern dress, dating, and classroom behavior.

RANGE OF TOLERABLE BEHAVIOR. The range of tolerable behavior, shown in Figure 6.2, depicts those rates of participation that are ap-

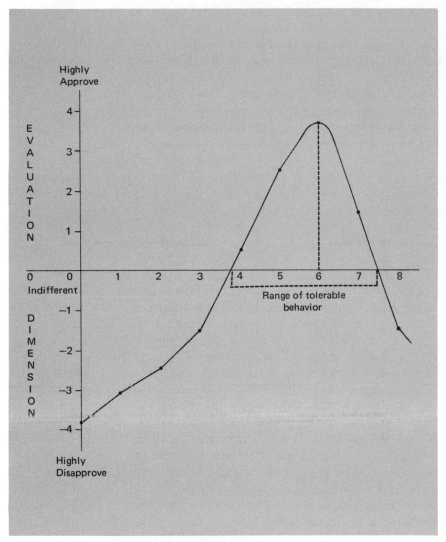

Adapted from J. Jackson, "Structural Characteristics of Norms." In *The Dynamics of Instructional Groups*. Chicago: National Society for the Study of Education, 59th Yearbook, Part 2, 1960.

FIGURE 6.2 / *Behavioral Dimension of Times Participating.*

proved by the group. Relevant questions about group tolerance are: Is the range narrow or broad? Is it low or high on the behavioral dimension? Classroom life could be threatening and insecure if only very narrow ranges were allowed for many behaviors. Moreover, if the narrow

ranges are close to the negative end of the behavior dimensions, re-
strictions are placed on individual students to withhold many behaviors.
For example, the likelihood would be quite great of breaking a norm
that specified that no class member may speak out without the teacher's
permission, for such a norm would constitute a restricted, unrelaxed
learning environment. The focus of attention would be on the teacher,
students would not be free to help one another, the peer group would
have little opportunity to become cohesive, and a great deal of the
teacher's time would be spent in enforcing rules.

CRYSTALLIZATION OF A NORM. Jackson uses crystallization to refer to
the degree of agreement among group members about what is approved
or disapproved behavior. The curve in Figure 6.2 was plotted by taking
the average curves for all members of a classroom group wherein there
was high agreement among the members and, consequently, high crystallization. In other classes or with other norms, subgroups of students
may differ widely in their approval or disapproval. Such low sharing in
the total group represents the condition of low crystallization of the
norm. High crystallization among the members of a group about the
appropriateness of important behaviors is a basic ingredient for an effective group and should be worked on through group discussions.

AMBIGUITY OF A NORM. Jackson uses ambiguity to refer to a special
case of low crystallization where there is high agreement within two
or more subgroups of the total group, but where these subgroups are
in disagreement, one from another. Classroom groups often exhibit ambiguity either in the beginning of the school year or when high conflicts occur within the class between two highly influential members.
Sometimes normative ambiguity occurs between two subgroups—one
of which is composed entirely of male students, the other of female students—each subgroup expecting the teacher to behave differently. In
some high schools, normative ambiguity for the entire school occurs between subgroups of students in different curricula. College-bound students often hold a norm for high involvement in the school programs
(curriculum, student council, and football). General or business students, on the other hand, sometimes are apathetic about the school's
educational goals and possess norms that are opposed to active school
participation. Such normative differences are maintained easily because
the two subgroups seldom communicate with each other. The ambiguity
of a norm is the presence of two opposing norms which are intense and
highly crystallized in themselves.

INTEGRATION OF NORMS. Integration of norms deals with how the
entire cluster of norms in a group relate to one another. Inconsistency
among them leads to confusion and frustration, e.g., a classroom in which

a norm for independent study exists, but in which the students also expect the teacher to monitor their behavior from moment to moment.

CORRESPONDENCE OF NORMS. Correspondence refers to the degree of depth to which a student personally holds an attitude which corresponds to the norm of the group.

CONGRUENCE OF NORMS. Normative congruence refers to agreements of norms across several groups to which one student belongs. Students have to deal with incongruent norms when expectations differ from one classroom to another. One norm that frequently differs from class to class is how much students should actively participate in classroom discussions. An example of norm incongruence in one school is depicted schematically in Figure 6.3.

Notice that a high amount of congruence does exist between classrooms A and B, but in classroom C, the norms do not support high student participation. Students moving from classroom A or B to classroom C will likely experience some confusion and will have to change their frames of reference, at least temporarily. Incongruences across classes are the bases of some interpersonal tensions in high schools.

To make use of Jackson's Model and some of these ideas about norms, the teacher should follow these steps: (a) Choose one behavioral dimension of high interest to the class, one that has a definite evaluative aspect, e.g., students following directions, student levels of participation, independence of students, behavioral manifestations of interest in the class or student productivity. (b) Plot a curve to show feelings of approval or disapproval of class members (an average) as you see it! Ask the students to draw a curve to make a composite of their reactions and yours; with regard to student productivity, for example, where do students "draw the line" for "how little" or "how much" work should be produced? (c) Check the range of tolerable behavior to see how broad or narrow it is. (d) If the curve turns out to be flat, check to see if it means that the norm has low intensity (is unimportant), or that there is low crystallization, or that there is normative ambiguity with two or more subgroups holding quite different norms. (e) Share the findings with the class to see if this is the sort of norm that the students wish to have; the teacher also should tell the students how he or she feels about the norm.

Peer Group Norms and Academic Performance

The peer group constitutes perhaps the most important normative force on students' school performance.

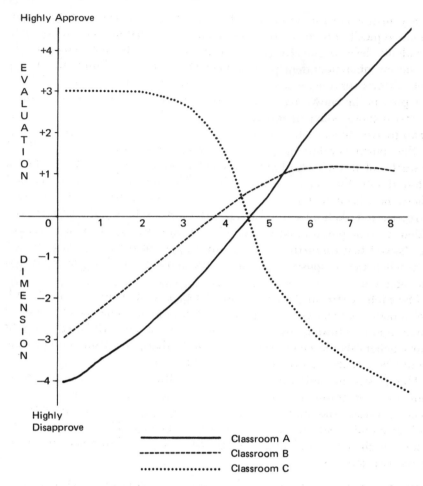

Adapted from J. Jackson, "Structural Characteristics of Norms." In *The Dynamics of Instructional Groups*. Chicago: National Society for the Study of Education, 59th Yearbook, Part 2, 1960.

FIGURE 6.3 / *Norm Incongruence.*

One particularly dramatic illustration of the power of the norms of the peer group in relation to school achievement was presented by David Hargreaves in his study of streaming in an English secondary school for boys (1967). Hargreaves studied the psychological impacts of the norms of several different types of peer group cultures. Although the extreme differences that he found among the several peer group clusters were obviously heightened by the traditional British custom of streaming students according to their scores on examinations, nevertheless his research is very instructive for Americans. Even though it is true that American schools typically do not make quite such blatant distinctions based upon a students' level of achievement, Hargreaves's results show how deeply the norms of a peer group can effect the behavior of individual students. Moreover, the norms of the British peer groups obviously are also present in many American schools and have, we believe, similar effects to those noted by Hargreaves.

Hargreaves focused his analysis of social relations in the peer group on the fourth (or last) year boys because they represented the "final products" of the schooling process and had spent the longest time being initiated into the values of the school. The fourth year class, like all others, had been divided into five streams upon entry into the school; Hargreaves studied only four of those streams, excluding the fifth stream which was composed mostly of retarded or minimally educable students. He showed that each stream had its unique set of norms which persisted even when the composition of the streams changed as boys were shifted among them.

The highest stream, labeled A, held norms that were consonant with the school's formal goals; boys valued academic achievement, looked down upon "mucking around" in class, discouraged fighting, thought that teachers should be obeyed, and thought that plagiarism and cheating should be strictly against the student code.

The B stream had quite a different culture; there was less correspondence of norms, i.e., less agreement among the boys on their personal attitudes and group norms. There were also norms incongruent with academic goals and procedures of the faculty. The following quote from a high status student within B illustrates the differences of norms in the two streams.

We don't like boys who don't mess about. We don't like boys who answer a lot of questions. If you answer all the questions, the lesson goes all the quicker, doesn't it. I mean, say you have two periods and you start having all these questions, right then it would take a period to do, and then you have another period and then you'd have to do some new work. If they start asking questions and we don't answer them they have to start explaining it all to us and it takes two periods. So we don't have to use the pen. (p. 27)

Stream C was composed actually of three subgroups. It was similar to B in that most of the members strongly devalued academic work, but, whereas in B, fun was valued more than work and "messing around" was encouraged for its own sake, the high status clique members of C apparently were primarily interested in behaving contrary to school values and defying the school administration. In other words, the C group was negatively oriented toward the establishment of the school, while the B group was more fun-loving. One subgroup in C, however, continued to hold norms very different from the rest of the C group. For example, this deviant C subgroup valued work, obeyed teacher demands, dressed well and attended school regularly.

The D stream had an even more diffuse leadership and norms in opposition to the school; in fact one criteria for status seemed to be doing poor academic work. Truancy was encouraged, physical violence was used against the low status boys who went along with the teachers, and delinquent acts of all sorts were frequent and valued by the high status clique.

Members of the four streams entered into very little interaction with one another except when students were switched from one stream to another and when there was some mixing while participating on the school's rugby team. Most participants in the school—both students and staff—held stereotypic conceptions of members in the different group. For example, the A's were viewed as snobby while the D's were seen as delinquent. Hargreaves also showed that the students' identifications with their own group were very strong. For example, at times the boys in the lower streams behaviorally showed the importance of the norms by decreasing their performance on tests purposefully so that they would not be moved up to a higher stream.

Hargreaves concluded:

> . . . that the streams exert a powerful influence on the extent and form of interaction between age-mates in the same neighborhood school. Boys tend to interact with and choose friends from boys in the same stream and only rarely from streams more than one removed from their own. As the predominate norms of each form become differentiated and the various barriers to communication between streams are erected, negative stereotypes develop. These serve to reinforce the normative differentiation and inhibit further cross-stream interaction, and thus the incentive value of the "promotion" system is undermined for the low stream boys. (p. 82)

Norms and the Evaluation of Performance

Evaluation of performance is an integral aspect of both formal and informal classroom life. Academic evaluation is typically represented by a formal static norm—teacher and students share the expectation that evaluation will often occur and that it will be issued by adult professionals and received by students in the form of a grade, a star, a missed recess, a pat on the back, or making a team. We believe that the evaluation of academic performance should take the form of a somewhat dynamic classroom norm—students and teacher questioning the processes of evaluation as a normal part of their daily interaction.

We suggest that evaluation should be organized so that it would occur equally across hierarchical levels in the classroom; for example, students would be involved in evaluating both their own performance and the instructional performance of their teacher. This radical departure from tradition would put teacher and students into a normative relationship of mutual accountability. Furthermore, we believe that evaluation should be used not only to assess individual performance within the classroom, but also to enable students and teacher to determine where they are as a group, and to formulate improved group processes collaboratively.

Summative and Formative Evaluation

Two ways of approaching performance evaluation have become prominent and are worth considering when thinking about modifying classroom norms. They are referred to as summative and formative evaluation (Bloom et al. 1971). Summative evaluation is the typical formal static norm; it is the assessment of what has finally been accomplished. For instance, a grade ostensibly reflects the level of mastery a student has reached in a particular subject. Summative evaluations are helpful primarily to policy makers and decision makers, e.g., should the student be encouraged to move on to a more advanced level? They are helpful to people such as teachers and parents who typically are in decision-making roles in relation to students.

Formative evaluation, on the other hand, helps to give information about the next steps that should be taken for movement closer to a stated goal. The astute teacher continuously sizes up the social situation to ascertain the next move. Informally, most teachers do use formative data as they are performing their daily functions; the teacher develops a sense of whether students are involved, bored, or excited about a particular assignment. A formal example of formative evaluation is a diagnostic performance test used with young students in particular skill areas such as reading. Test results give the teacher information about how to proceed in developing reading skills; its purpose is not to evaluate summatively (such as in giving a grade) but to pinpoint the skills the youngster lacks and to indicate the appropriate kind of instruction. Formative evaluation provides objective information to identify problems and to suggest alternative paths of action to solve the problems.

Multiple Accountability in the Classroom

Classrooms with norms in support of students evaluating students and of students and teacher evaluating one another can make use of both summative and formative evaluations in new, more equalitarian ways.

As such these traditionally elitist procedures of evaluation can become more constructive aids to the improvement of everyone's performance.

For students, evaluations by peers can be much more powerful than evaluations from the teacher. We already know this to be true, having watched the power of informal peer relationships. Why not use the power of the peer group constructively? Students can help one another in ways that teachers cannot help them. For example, a student can often hold the attention of a friendly peer for much longer periods of time than can the teacher. A student can also paraphrase concepts to another student successfully when a teacher's logic does not seem to register. A student can often recognize the difficulty another student is having because he or she experienced the same difficulty just a short time before. Our experiences in working with peer tutoring and in researching cross-age tutoring have proven to us that the tutors themselves often learn just as much as, if not more than their tutees.

Student evaluations of teachers, when expressed, also represent a very powerful tool for improving teacher performance. In fact, our experiences have indicated that student feedback can be more influential on teachers than feedback from the principal or from parents. In a careful field study, Tuckman and Oliver (1968) found that the instructional behaviors of teachers in the classroom were changed more often as a result of student appraisals than by the appraisals of colleagues or supervisors. A similar phenomenon was documented by Margaret Nelson (1972) in a study of change among substitute teachers. She simply supplied the substitutes with systematic feedback from students about their classroom behavior, and the experimental group showed major behavioral changes in a very short time.

In conclusion, norms are very powerful guides to classroom behavior. Most important are the norms that govern academic performances and the use of evaluation in relation to performance. When members of a classroom are guided by the value-position that each person—teacher as well as students—should be developing better ways of learning and developing as individuals and as a group, they will work collaboratively on generating formal procedures to evaluate one another.

Implications for Teachers

The following summary statements capture the most salient implications of this chapter for teachers.

—Norms are *shared expectations* of how the participants of a classroom should think, feel, and behave.

—Norms influence the perceptions, cognitions, evaluations, and behaviors of the individual class members.

—Classroom norms can be identified and measured.

—Student peer group norms frequently will be in opposition to the goals of the professionals of the school. Such opposition can be counter-productive to individual student growth and development.

—Classroom norms can be changed through the concerted, collaborative efforts of teacher and students. Learning groups can gain control over their own culture through group discussion methods.

Action Ideas for Change

Following are descriptions of classroom practices that were employed by teachers to develop more supportive norms for learning in their classrooms.

Clarification of Classroom Norms

The main goal of the activity that follows was to help the class discuss openly norms that were operating in the group. The teacher wanted the students to regulate their own behavior, and this was a first step toward encouraging them to take more responsibility for making up the rules of the class. The teacher presented the idea of a norm to the class by stating that it was a shared feeling in the group about the ways one ought to behave or the things one ought to do as a class member. She explained further that norms can be formal or informal. She then asked each student to write examples of formal and informal norms on a piece of paper. The students were given about ten minutes to write down their individual ideas. Then the students were asked to share their responses in small groups of five and to make up a group chart which represented the consensus items for that group. The various items of the five-person groups were recorded on a large sheet of paper for the entire class. As a continuing activity, the teacher and the students looked at the chart each week, made additions and deletions, and had discussions to make plans for changing some of the less helpful norms.

Planning a Time Sequence for Academic Work

A high school English teacher became concerned over the large number of incompleted assignments in one class and felt that his students' quality of work was very poor. He brought the matter up with them and discovered that papers and homework assignments in other subjects were falling due at about the same times. The students were unable to cope with these time pressures, so the class, with the help of the teacher, decided to plan jointly at the beginning of each unit to space the assignments in a convenient manner for everyone.

At the outset of each new study unit, the teacher held a planning session with the students. The scope of work was discussed, and dates were established for papers and exams. The students became actively involved in the decision-making for curriculum sequencing and also decided on the preparation of the final examination on the basis of student questions. The class was divided into three groups, each being responsible for one section (grammar, literature, or vocabulary). The test turned out to be difficult and long but was an excellent learning experience. These planning sessions helped the class to establish a norm of high productivity and of high participation in English.

Forming a Classroom Student Council

The teacher of an elementary group felt that her students lacked a sense of deep involvement in classroom affairs. She wanted the students to think that their contributions were worthwhile, and that they themselves would ultimately be responsible for the effective functioning of the classroom. She decided to establish a rotating student council that would concern itself primarily with the establishment and enforcement of classroom rules. The council, comprised of six students, made recommendations to the class, and each class member as well as the teacher had a single vote. Punishment for infractions of the rules were also recommended by the council and voted on by the class. In the beginning stages, the rules were very strict, and the punishments were harsh. The teacher voiced her concern about the narrow range of tolerable behavior but did not interfere with the harsh decisions of the group. Even though at times it appeared as though a kangaroo court might be forming, rotations of the council members helped the students to become more realistic and tolerant in their rule enforcement. The teacher was most pleased to see the students begin to internalize many of the rules and to feel more responsibility for the establishment of positive group processes.

Developing Norms of Interest and Relevance

A high school social studies teacher wanted to encourage his students to use community resources in their studies of social problems. He hoped to establish expectations that such an activity would be interesting and relevant. The class as a whole was doing a unit on careers and decided to find out what career choices were available in the community. They planned the general sequence of the study as a total class but broke up into small groups to tackle specific aspects, such as questionnaires, interviewing, compilation of data, writing up the study, and discussing ways of using the information to make choices. The experience provided opportunity for the taking of both initiative and responsibility in planning a research design. The students were highly motivated and involved at every step, and developed shared expectations that to participate actively in this class was a valuable thing to do.

References

Angell, R. C. *Free Society and Moral Crisis.* Ann Arbor: University of Michigan Press, 1958.

Asch, S. E. *Social Psychology.* Englewood Cliffs, N. J.: Prentice-Hall, Inc., 1952.

Bloom, B.; Hastings, T. J.; and Madaus, G. F. *Handbook on Formative and Summative Evaluation of Student Learning.* New York: McGraw-Hill Book Co., 1971.

Cohen, A. K. *Delinquent Boys.* New York: Free Press, 1955.

Crutchfield, R. S. "Conformity and Character." *American Psychologist* 10 (1955):191-98.

Hargreaves, D. H. *Social Relations in a Secondary School.* New York: Humanities Press, Inc., 1967.

Hoffman, M. L. "Conformity as a Defense Mechanism and a Form of Resistance to Genuine Group Influence." *Journal of Personality* 25 (1957):412-424.

Jackson, J. M. "Structural Characteristics of Norms." In *The Dynamics of Instructional Groups.* 59th Yearbook, part 2, edited by N. Henry. Chicago: National Society for the Study of Education, 1960.

Lynd, R. S., and Lynd, H. M. *Middletown in Transition.* New York: Harcourt, Brace & Co., 1937.

Milgram, S. "Liberating Effects of Group Pressure." *Journal of Personality and Social Psychology* 1, no. 2 (1965):127-34.

Nelson, Margaret. "Attitudes of Intermediate School Children Toward Substitute Teachers Who Receive Feedback on Pupil-Desired Behavior." Ph.D. dissertation, University of Oregon, 1972.

Schachter, S. "Deviation, Rejection, and Communication." *Journal of Abnormal and Social Psychology* 46 (1951):190-207.

Sherif, M. "A Study of Some Social Factors in Perception." *Archives of Psychology,* no. 187 (1935).

Sumner, W. *Folkways.* New York: Dover Publications, Inc., 1906.

Tuckman, B., and Oliver, W. "Effectiveness of Feedback to Teachers as a Function of Source." *Journal of Educational Psychology* 59, (1968):297-301.

Warner, W., and Lunt, P. S. *The Social Life of a Modern Community.* New Haven, Conn.: Yale University Press, 1941.

Wax, R. *Doing Fieldwork: Warning and Advice.* Chicago: University of Chicago Press, 1971.

Whyte, W. F. *Street Corner Society.* Chicago: University of Chicago Press, 1943.

CHAPTER 7

Communication

Communication is uniquely human; it is dialogue between persons. Through communication, persons both participate in groups and develop as individuals. It is primarily through communication with parents, siblings, teachers, and peers that youngsters come to know themselves as people.

Communication as Symbolic Interaction

Although animals emit sounds and make gestures, such as a hen's clucking to her chicks or a wolf's cuddling her cubs, they do not communicate or interact symbolically. Humans share in attitudes and feelings of others by giving and receiving symbolic messages. An outstanding difference between animal noises and human communication is the ability of the human to take the role of another person. It is distinctively human to read psychological states of others through the messages they communicate, whether they are verbal or nonverbal. For a teacher to look into a student's eyes, to know that there is hurt inside, and to respond with an affectionate hug can communicate nonverbally a strong message of concern, compassion, and caring. To say, "I feel bad" or "I care about you," so that the student knows how the teacher feels can be a tender moment of human empathy and compassion.

An infant's gurgling and cooing contain sounds of all languages. By hearing specific sound patterns repeatedly, he or she eventually expresses some of the potential sounds and forgets others. Preschoolers incorporate some sounds, begin to understand that certain sounds have referents, and develop understandings about themselves and others by imitating others' verbal exchanges or by rehearsing conversations within their thoughts. Beginning at about the age of three their discussions with peers become exchanges, play and language become interactional, and they respond to one another realistically rather than autistically. Both as a preschooler and as a student within the classroom, youngsters' sharing of feelings with others and the development of their self-concept occur simultaneously and interdependently.

Members of classroom groups can understand one another, even though all the individuals are different, by communicating verbally. Language, the primary medium for exchanging messages, is made up of symbols associated with referents, e.g., the sound "chair" calls up an image of something to sit on with a back, seat, and legs. Of course, there are varieties of "chairness" from an artistic creation to a hewn log, and additional words must be used to communicate the differences. However, most persons will know what another is talking about when the word *chair* is used.

Symbols involve more than shared meanings with specifiable referents, however. They also take on special connotative meanings that are not necessarily widely shared. Roger Brown (1965) told of a sophisticated British physiologist who identified a student to an American colleague by saying, "He is the nigger in your class." The American professor was shocked. To him, the word had highly repugnant connotations; to the Briton, however, the word "nigger" was neutral, having only the referent of a black person. Larger blocks of words also have meanings that will be taken differently, especially in the classroom where students are just beginning to learn the connotations of words.

Often differences in understanding occur in classrooms because of changes in inflection, mannerisms, or intonations. The teacher who says to a student, "Well, you certainly did a good job on that," could either be intending sarcasm or making a favorable evaluation. The student who says, "I'm up-tight with arithmetic," could mean either anxiety about arithmetic, or high interest and involvement in it, depending upon the cultural contexts and the manner of speech.

Communication as a Reciprocal Process

Verbal and nonverbal messages constitute core ingredients of communication. Although words are the principal means of communicating, the meaning of a verbal message is not based on words alone. It depends upon how the receiver interprets the words as they are augmented by such nonverbal cues as bodily gestures, intonations, situational factors and previous relationships with the communicator.

Some youngsters, as an example, often are exposed to contradictory verbal and nonverbal messages. Their mother says, "I love you," but gives off bodily messages of hostility and anger toward the youngster. If the child responds to the message of hostility, the response may be, "Why do you do that to someone who cares so much for you?" On the other hand, if the child responds to the verbal message of love, the response may be, "Don't hang on to me so much." The child's interpersonal interactions with the mother are continuously confused and confusing, and soon he or she is unable to respond appropriately to others' communications. The child's self-concept becomes as confused as the interpersonal environments, and the child begins to send unclear, confusing messages to others.

Messages with multiple meanings are frequently communicated. In fact, received messages are discrepant from the intentions of the sender in many settings, especially those involving children. This is often observable in a family with a new baby. An older sibling, learning the appropriate behavior toward a new infant, might say, "You're a nice baby," and then match the loving remarks with a hug resembling the hold of a Suma wrestler. The baby may get hurt physically, while being loved with words. Similar confusions occur daily in classrooms. The teacher gives an assignment and smiles. Some students read the message as pleasant and supportive, while others see it as a show of power and authority. Only continuous checking with students on what messages they actually receive will keep communication channels open and clear in the classroom.

Communication emanates from individuals' needs, motives, and desires; it involves the sending of messages about personal intentions, whether they are desires for control, information, love or anger. Effective communication exists between two persons when the receiver interprets the sender's message in the way the sender intended it. The bridging of gaps between separate individuals involves congruence among intentions, behaviors, and interpretations. This reciprocal communicative process is depicted graphically in Figure 7.1. In effective communication, the messages of the sender (person A) directly reflect the person's intentions and the interpretations by the receiver (person B) match the intentions of the sender.

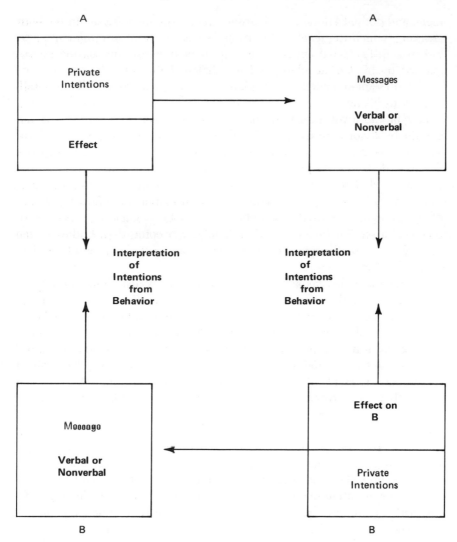

FIGURE 7.1 / *Reciprocal Communication Process.*

Miscommunication

Gaps between the message that is intended and the message that is received are miscommunications. They occur frequently because messages sent do not accurately reflect intentions. For example, Bill, a student, is embarrassed, guilty, and inferior when he is called upon to recite and doesn't know what to answer. He responds with defensive wise-cracking, which the teacher interprets as defiance and low subject-matter interest. Bill's actual feelings, which involve intentions to please, are masked by his verbal joking and nonchalant behavior. The teacher mis-reads Bill's inner state, becomes angry, and scolds him. Bill dejectedly returns to his seat, feeling rejected.

Part of the answer to why messages do not reflect intentions is that certain behaviors are more difficult than others for persons to perform; some words, phrases, or mannerisms are not even incorporated into some people's behavioral repertoires. In the previous example, the student lacked the skill required for transforming the feelings of embarrassment, guilt, and inferiority into appropriate verbal responses. Another instance of a discrepancy between intentions and actions occurs as people try to reveal affection for one another. Tongues become tied, bodies frozen, and eyes no longer make contact when some people attempt to show liking for another.

Discrepancies between intentions and messages also occur because of some confusion that lies between expressing oneself directly and trying to impress others so that they notice attractive attributes of the self. To *express* is to allow oneself to be known to others with authenticity; it is making the self transparent. To *impress* is to put on a face and to per-form in ways that hopefully will be attractive to others. Much classroom interaction arises from desires to impress. In class, students may present selves that are curious and interested in the curriculum, primarily to impress the teacher. The teacher may attempt to present an impression of omniscience or of distant control. In either case, real selves are being concealed in order to maintain a stable and predictable social scene. It is as though all parties are taking part in a play, with the classroom as the stage and class members as the actors. When class members, inten-tionally or unintentionally, attempt to impress, they set the stage for distrustful communication. Each becomes aware that others are playing the same game, but no one is able to change his or her own act because each is a crucial player in the drama.

To impress is not unnatural or always "phony"; it is a human phe-nomenon that allows persons to cope more easily with a number of superficial social events. Unfortunately, superficiality and the conceal-ment of self in teaching are detrimental to the development of auton-omous students and effective classroom communication. Teachers who continuously attempt to create impressions are inevitably discovered, thereby losing their students' trust. The "omniscient" teacher will at some time make a mistake that some students will notice. The teacher may attempt to hide the error by defending, justifying, or even falsifying the point, just to maintain the impression of omniscience. But students will perceive the behaviors as being defensive and soon will begin criticizing the teacher outside of the classroom. Eventually, they will challenge what the teacher is doing either covertly by not following directions or overtly by acting out in class.

Effective communication occurs in classrooms where trust and empathy reside. Teachers who communicate their own complex humanity directly by discussing their feelings and who listen to descriptions of students' feelings have a good chance of engaging students in effective dialogue. On the other hand, teachers who fashion false impressions encourage their students to play a game of impression-forming also, and increase the probability that the curriculum will be meaningless ritual. The teachers' warmth, concern, and acceptance help to facilitate interpersonal trust as long as these are communicated in a genuine sense. To behave as consistently accepting, when the teacher truly feels annoyed or angry, presents a phony facade which, over a period of time, will lead to less trust between students and teacher. Students, in our experience, tend to recognize as trustworthy those teachers who are open and honest about their thoughts and feelings. Authenticity on the part of teachers is more important than a rigid consistency of warmth and acceptance which has the ring of dishonesty.

Levels of Communication

Communication is an intricate bevy of spoken and unspoken behaviors occurring at several levels. Some parts of communicative acts are obvious and easily understood; other parts are covert and ambiguous. Using the analogy of a complex novel can be helpful for understanding communication as a multileveled process. Hemingway's novels, for instance, can be read simply as great stories with exciting details and action; the characters are real, facing authentic issues, and their lives are easy to grasp. Hemingway as the great storyteller and entertainer is communicating overtly, concretely, and descriptively. But those who read Hemingway's novels only at this level of communication miss a good measure of his complexity. The stories portray depth, compassion, understanding, and sometimes include allegory in the human existences portrayed. Basic psychological themes underlie the concrete events and lives of the characters, making up a covert, emotional level of communication.

Classroom communication can be just as complex as Hemingway's novels. Different levels of feelings, motives, thoughts, and intentions exist simultaneously. Some comments and behaviors are easy to understand, but others represent underlying messages in the lives of the teacher and students. Teachers are aware often that events must be occurring at home that are affecting the student's behaviors in school. Or perhaps a student, while talking to a teacher, is hopeful that some of his or her peers will overhear what has been said. Teachers may say something to the entire class, intending that only a few students will listen to it.

Increased awareness of these different levels by teachers should assist them in relating more effectively with the class. The teachers' talking about something that heretofore has been an unspoken subject or even a subject about which the students have not been conscious increases the likelihood of clarifying communication. Classroom groups have feelings, expectations, and thoughts that remain below the surface unless they are raised for discussion. When these hidden interpersonal processes are brought into the open for discussion, they can be worked on through group problem-solving actions. A classroom group that delves into these subsurface levels increases its freedom and ability to improve itself.

Four levels of classroom communication seem relevant:

SPOKEN-UNSPOKEN MESSAGES.   For communication to be clear in the classroom, the spoken and unspoken messages should be consonant. If they are in conflict, students will be confused and often will continue to communicate unclear messages in a circular fashion.

SURFACE-HIDDEN INTENTIONS.   Classrooms are constituted of a variety of personal goals, some of which are in conflict. In competitive classes, for instance, a surface intention of performing well may be accompanied by a hidden intention to do better than others. Both intentions will be communicated, but in much different ways; a preference for high performance may be communicated directly, while a wish to be better than others could be revealed in offhand negative remarks about them.

WORK-EMOTIONAL ACTIVITIES.   Messages communicated in the classroom about the curriculum typically have emotional meanings. Feelings about classroom work influence ways in which the work is accomplished. Long periods of inaction in improving feelings about work can lead to apathy and resistance toward learning.

TASK-MAINTENANCE FUNCTIONS.   Chapter 4 included a discussion of how communication can be directed toward moving the class along on its assignments (task), or toward keeping members of the class working together smoothly (maintenance).

Communication Patterns

Communicative acts in the classroom develop into routine and regular patterns, which are self-perpetuating. The teacher who dominates discussions develops students who don't initiate. The student who is ignored in discussions for a week stops speaking the next week, and may be ignored for much of the remainder of the year. Teachers and students can become victims of their own self-perpetuating routines unless they are able to raise subjects into awareness for more open discussion. Public recognition of communication patterns is the first step toward making constructive changes. Patternings of a classroom communication can be analyzed in several ways:

Verbal Communication

As many as twenty-six different instruments provide analyses of classroom verbal communication, capturing both affective and cognitive aspects (Simon and Boyer 1967). The affective systems measure classroom emotional qualities by coding the teacher's reactions to feelings of students. Cognitive systems deal with different types of information giving, questioning, and offering. They emphasize how the formal classroom curriculum gets communicated.

One system for analyzing classroom verbal communication warrants special consideration. It is the Verbal Interaction Category System (VICS), developed by Amidon and Hunter (1966), and based on Flanders' system of Interaction Analysis (1960, and 1970). VICS systematizes classroom verbal exchanges within an objective category system in order to describe verbal messages sent by teachers and students. By using the VICS, teachers can discover whether or not their verbal communications are consonant with their intentions. The VICS is a valuable tool for checking on what teachers actually are communicating, rather than on what they think or want to be communicating.

Its categories are:

Teacher-Initiated Talk:
1) gives information or opinions
2) gives directions
3) asks narrow questions
4) asks broad questions
Teacher Response:
5) accepts (a) ideas (b) behaviors (c) feelings
6) rejects (a) ideas (b) behaviors (c) feelings

Student Response:
7) responds to teacher (a) predictably (b) unpredictably
8) responds to another
Student-Initiated Talk:
9) initiates talk to teacher
10) initiates talk to another student
Other:
11) silence
12) confusion

After observations are collected, the data are compiled into a scoring matrix. Each square represents one characteristic; for example, teacher rejection of student responses, or extended student-initiated talk to the teacher or other students. By glancing at the matrix, the teacher can readily see what patterns of communication exist in his or her classroom. Teachers should read Amidon and Hunter (1966) for an array of details, situations, and skills on improving verbal communication in the classroom and Simon and Boyer (1967) for a variety of analyses of communication networks.

Research using the VICS or similar verbal communication systems has shown that verbal interaction occupies a great deal of class time, and that the preponderance of interaction is teachers "talking to students." One-way communication from teacher to students is not usually the most effective means for student learning. Many teachers wish to reduce the amount of talking they do by eliciting comments from students, but they are stymied as to how to do it. One way of increasing student talk is to change classroom norms so that the students expect one another to participate more. The following group activity sometimes serves as a springboard for arriving at classroom norms that support more two-way communication (Tesch, Lansky, and Lundgren 1972).

The class is divided into groups of about eight. One member of each group is chosen as coordinator, and another is asked to be a communication sender. The remaining six members are receivers. The coordinator signals when to begin, keeps track of the amount of time spent during each phase of the activity, and makes observations of the receivers' nonverbal reactions. To commence the activity, the coordinator gives two geometric patterns of rectangles to the sender without showing them to the receivers. The two patterns of rectangles, shown in Figure 7.2, are equal in complexity. One pattern is presented to the receivers in a one-way fashion; the other is given by two-way interaction. During both communications, the sender sits with his or her back to the receivers so that facial cues and hand movements do not influence the process. The receivers are asked to draw the patterns as accurately as possible. During one-way communication, they may ask no questions and must remain silent. In two-way communication, receivers are encouraged to break in at any time to raise questions and to interact verbally with the sender.

After the two communication episodes are completed, the coordinator assists the receivers in determining the number of correct placements in their drawings. A correct rectangle touches one or two other rectangles at the matching location on the sides of the other rectangles. It also should be oriented vertically, horizontally, or diagonally as on the sender's page. Scores in this exercise can range from 0 to 6 for each communication episode.

After each receiver scores his or her own drawings, the receivers and the sender might be asked to answer these questions: With which communication were you most satisfied? With which communication were you more frustrated or tense? Which type would you prefer to use as a sender? Which type would you prefer to receive? For each question, three alternative answers are possible, one-way, two-way, or no difference. The ensuing discussion is guided by the coordinator who uses the following questions as guides: When is one-way communication efficient in our class, and how might we improve it? When is two-way communication necessary in our class, and what can we do to improve our two-way communication? What are other implications of this activity for our class, and what keeps us from using two-way communication more often?

To complete this activity, each small group coordinator reports to the entire class on the primary outcomes of his or her group. All class members then discuss what they learned from the activity, and recommendations are made for improving communication. Perhaps a small committee of students could be constituted for continued work on improving clarity of communication in the classroom.

One-way and two-way communication are both useful vehicles for teaching and learning, provided they are employed appropriately. Although one-way communication places a student in a passive role, there is evidence that lectures are valuable for students who are highly motivated and who are eager to learn specific information. Students are ready to hear one-way communication when they are listening to answers to questions they have already raised for themselves. Two-way communication promotes more active inquiry and listening. It is especially valuable when the learning requires behavioral changes. For example, two-way communication is more valuable than one-way communication when students are asked to show insight into the real psychological problems of children, or to manifest the ability to act appropriately with disturbed youngsters. Two-way communication consumes more time than one-way communication does in getting work done, but generally, the work is of higher quality and is accomplished with less confusion and negative feeling.

Nonverbal Messages

Nonverbal messages usually involve expressing feelings by bodily changes, gestures, or various shades of facial coloring. A remarkable thing about classroom participants is that, while feelings are perhaps the greatest determinants of their actions, these feelings are the least communicated in words. In expressing emotions, too often language is used as a way of disguising real feelings rather than as a way of getting directly to them. Classroom communication would be enhanced more if a teacher caught in making mistakes would say, "I am embarrassed," or "I feel uncomfortable because of what I just did," rather than attempt to justify the error by covering up nonverbally.

Nonverbal messages are inevitably ambiguous, therefore the recipient is unclear as to what the sender is feeling. Expressions of feelings can

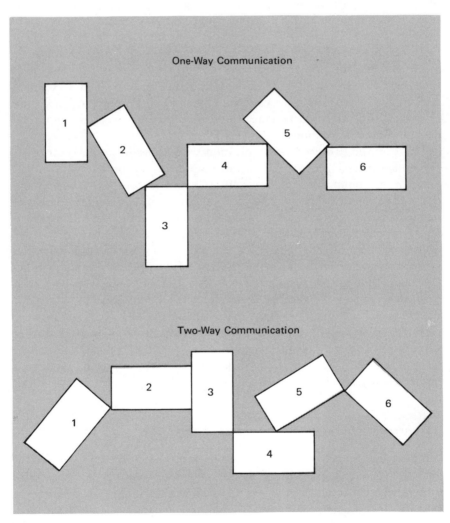

FIGURE 7.2 / *Geometric Patterns Used in One-Way, Two-Way Communication Activity.*

take the form of many bodily changes. Thus, a specific feeling, such as anger, can be expressed by great bodily motion or by a frozen stillness. Any single nonverbal expression also may arise from a variety of feelings, for example, a blush may indicate embarrassment, pleasure, or even hostility. Nor is a specific feeling always expressed in the same nonverbal way. A student's liking for a teacher may lead to a blush when standing near the teacher or watching from a distance—to bringing presents, or even doing work well. In perceiving nonverbal messages, the receiver must interpret the sender's actions. As these actions increase in ambiguity the chance for misinterpretation increases. The receiver's own emotional state is also very important in interpreting the sender's action. And so, for example, if the receiver feels guilty about previous actions, nonverbal messages of confusion might be received from the sender as accusations of negative judgments.

Nonverbal messages are continuously expressed among peers in the classroom. Nonverbal peer group communication gets triggered off especially when highly influential students are spoken to by the teacher. The response of a highly influential peer to a teacher's disciplinary action calls out a similar response in other observing students. If the disciplined student reacts with defiant gestures, quite often other students will follow suit; if the student submits to teacher influence by remaining silent, others will remain silent, also. Highly influential students may also induce others to do as they do, even when it is not their intention to influence others directly. Peers watch the nonverbal gestures of their highly influential peers to receive cues to guide their own classroom behaviors.

Seating Arrangements

Ecology deals with the physical arrangements of the classroom environment. Classroom communication flows through space and is influenced by physical phenomena, especially seating arrangements.

Some research sheds light on the effects of seating arrangements on classroom communication. Leavitt (1951) experimented with the effects of four physical structures on communication within five-person teams. The four structures placed different limitations on the teams. One pattern was formed as a *circle*. Each subject could communicate to persons on either side but to no one else. This structure was equalitarian; each subject could communicate with only two others, and no single subject was in a position to dominate. A second structure was in the form of a *line*. This was similar to the circle except that the subjects on the ends could only communicate to one other person. The two other patterns were more centrally structured in that they possessed focal points through which communication was to pass. One was shaped like a square with four subjects at each corner and the fifth subject in the center. This pattern was most central with most communication passing through the center person. The last was shaped like a Y with two subjects at the upper points, one at the juncture and two below the subject in a line. The four communication structures of Leavitt are depicted in Figure 7.3.

All four groups were given problems to solve calling for information exchange. The results showed diverse effects of the physical structures. Groups 3 and 4 were more efficient than the other two groups, but the errors they did make persisted longer, and their feelings of dissatisfaction with the exercise were much higher. The circle pattern, Group 1, was inefficient in terms of time, although few errors were made, and the subjects felt most comfortable compared with all other groups. The line pattern, Group 2, was also inefficient, but it did offer more satisfaction than Groups 3 and 4 reported.

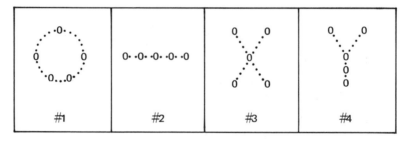

FIGURE 7.3 / *Leavitt's Four Communication Structures by Groups.*

Leavitt's research has implications for the classroom. Certain communication patterns give rise to feelings of being peripheral or not important. This would be clearest in classes where communication is centered on an elite peer group, or where it emanates primarily from the teacher in the manner of one-way communication. Feelings of being peripheral to the group leads to a reduction of communication with others, possibly resulting in the start of a negative circular process. It is clear that when the class is organized so that the possibility exists for communication to flow equally—as in the circle—everyone participates, more or less, during an hour's time. In the circular structure, communication remains open and is dependent on participation of most members. In classrooms where issues are discussed by almost everyone and where different people become central to the discussion at different times, greater feelings of involvement, satisfaction, and a steadier flow of communication will occur.

Sommer (1967) adapted Leavitt's ideas to carry out research directly on classrooms by studying the relationships between seating arrangements and classroom participation. The primary seating arrangements were *seminar style* (the students and instructor sat around in an approximate circle), and *lecture style* (the instructor faced the students, who sat in rows). In the seminar-style arrangement, Sommer found that students directly facing the instructor participated more than students off to the sides. In classrooms with straight rows, students in front participated more than students in the rear, and students in the center of each row participated more than the students at the sides. Sommer argued that direct visual contact between persons increases communication between them. It is important to note that there is no one best seating arrangement, since different goals may lead to different arrangements. For individual study, for example, eye contact should be minimized, while in small group discussion, maximum eye contact would be best.

Communication Skills

The skills described below were developed by John Wallen (1969) to facilitate more effective communication. The skills may appear simple, but they are difficult to execute well on a continuing basis. We have found that teachers think they are communicating effectively with students at times when they actually are not. The following skills should be employed to improve communication dialogue in the classroom.

PARAPHRASING. Paraphrasing involves restating what another person has said, using one's own words. It is a communication skill that implies a caring for what the other person has said, and a desire to respond with an accurate mirroring of that person's thoughts. Useful lead-ins to paraphrasing are, "I understand you to say that . . ." or "Did I read you to say . . .?" The function of paraphrasing in the classroom is twofold: checking to see that the student understood the communication; and communicating to the student that he has been understood.

BEHAVIOR DESCRIPTION. The skill of behavior description involves noting overt actions of another person, but without impugning motives, and without trying to place psychological meaning on the actions or making generalizations about the actions. Looking beyond behavior for psychological interpretations is a common cause of miscommunication and interpersonal friction. Some differences between behavior description and impugning motives are expressed in the following examples. "Jim and Sarah have talked the most during this discussion," and "That is the third time you interrupted," are behavior descriptions. "Jim and

Sarah are the only ones who are following the discussion," or "Why won't you listen to what I'm saying?" are not behavior descriptions and most likely will create defensiveness.

DESCRIPTIONS OF ONE'S OWN FEELINGS. The direct communication of one's own feelings is probably the least used communication skill. Unfortunately, its virtual disuse has the greatest potential for misunderstanding in the classroom. To express feelings directly places one in a vulnerable position with others, especially if there is little trust present. Because trust is often an unknown quantity in many classrooms, feelings tend to be expressed in indirect ways. Due to this indirect expression, therefore, these feelings are often misunderstood. The following examples illustrate differences between direct and indirect expressions of feelings.

Direct statement of feeling	*Indirect expression of feeling*
"I feel embarrassed."	
"I feel pleased."	Blushing-saying nothing.
"I feel annoyed."	
"I feel angry."	Withdrawing-saying nothing.
"I feel annoyed."	or
"I feel hurt."	"Why do you do such bad things?"
"I enjoy her sense of humor."	
"I like her ability."	"She's a wonderful person."
"I am impressed with her facility with language."	

IMPRESSION CHECKING. Checking of impressions involves the description in tentative fashion of what one perceives as the other's psychological state. It is similar to paraphrasing except that it involves interpreting the feelings and internal processes rather than the words and overt behaviors of the other. Impression checking is tentative; it attempts to free other people so that they want to describe their own feelings directly. When impression checking, the teacher should avoid implying disapproval until some dialogue has occurred and the feelings of the student are described directly. Some positive examples of impression checking are: "I get the impression that you are angry with me. Are you?" and "You appear disinterested in your work today. Is that right?" Some ineffective impression checks are: "Why are you angry at me?" or "Why aren't you doing what you're supposed to be doing?"

FEEDBACK. Feedback involves the giving or receiving of information concerning the effect that several persons have on one another. It may involve any of the four previous communication skills, such as *para-*

phrasing. What is your understanding of what I just said?"; *behavior description,* "This is the fourth time you've asked that. Can you say more about your question?; *describing own feelings,* "I felt antagonistic toward your behavior"; or *impression checking,* "You seem to feel very strongly about the point you were making." Feedback is one's own reactions; the person who is receiving it should be free to use it or not. Feedback does not oblige the recipient to change behavior. In the classroom, feedback should be given only after a careful assessment has been made of the needs of the student receiving it. For feedback to communicate and to engage the student in dialogue, it should arise out of empathy for the student, not out of a teacher's need for catharsis. Feedback tends to be helpful when it is specific and concrete rather than general; when it is solicited rather than thrust upon a student; and when it is checked to see if it was received accurately.

Closing the Communication Gap

Teachers are being spared from the necessity of employing one-way communication. Teaching machines, movies, audiotapes, television, and other technological developments have been created as effective ways of passing on information to students. Even though technological advances have opened the way for more possibilities of two-way classroom communication, impersonality and lack of dialogue still characterize many classes. Instead of using the advances for more humanized classroom relationships, teachers too often have generalized the "machine orientation" into their interpersonal relationships with students. The mechanical orientation is perhaps safer and more comfortable; teachers can remain aloof and uninvolved, thereby keeping themselves from being hurt by negative feedback from students.

True dialogue is not safe; it is unpredictable, and makes the teacher vulnerable to negative criticism. Yet its absence creates communication gaps between teachers and students. A communication gap occurs when there is an absence of consonance between the behavioral actions of the teacher and the interpretations of those same actions by students. Communication gaps are pervasive in modern society; they are basic to generation gaps, racial gaps, and international gaps. They occur when language is used to conceal and veil, rather than to reveal and openly express. The phoniness of a teacher's concealment leads students to be alienated from school and to feel cynical about the shallow adult world.

Implications for Teachers

The following summary statements characterize the key implications of this chapter for teachers.

—Communication involves the human capability to hear and to understand one another's inner thoughts and feelings. The core psychological process inherent in human communication is *empathy*.

—Communicative acts are reciprocal. Like the Circular Interpersonal Process, they involve the intentions and message of the sender and the interpretations of the message made by the receiver.

—Communication is both verbal (relying on language) and nonverbal (represented by bodily cues and voice sounds). As such, communicative acts exist on several levels at the same time and usually carry multiple meanings.

—Regular and stable communicative patterns develop between people, within groups, and within organizations over time. Along with group norms, we can speak of such regularized communication as culture.

—Environmental considerations, such as seating arrangements or physical positioning and proximity to the teacher, affect the patterns of communication.

—Miscommunications are the results of discrepancies between the meanings the sender intends and the meanings the receiver receives. Effective communication involves the receiver correctly interpreting what the sender intends to communicate.

—Communication can be made more effective by using the communication skills of paraphrasing, behavior description, description of own feelings, impression checking, and feedback. Teachers should incorporate these skills into their instructional behavior and deliberately teach them to their students.

Action Ideas for Change

The three classroom practices described here were created by teachers in order to reduce communication gaps in their classrooms.

Developing Communication Skills as Part of the Curriculum

The teacher spent a few weeks early in the year introducing paraphrasing, behavior description, description of own feelings, and impression checking. He then told the students that several times each week he wanted to check to see if the skills actually were being used. He introduced a plan of having three students fill out observation sheets and give feedback to the class about their observations. Before any observations took place, every member of the class was handed an observation sheet, shown in Figure 7.4, and the categories were discussed in a total class meeting. The observations took place during small group or total class discussions. After each discussion, the observers were asked

Evidence of Listening:

    a. Paraphrase   _____

    b. Relevant point
        to the discussion   _____

Contributions:

    a. Direct expressions
        of feeling   _____

    b. Describing other's
        behaviors   _____

    c. Contributing an
        idea or suggestion   _____

Perception Check:

    a. Checking feelings
        of others   _____

    b. Paraphrase to
        understand   _____

Feedback:

    a. Telling how others
        affected you   _____

FIGURE 7.4 / *Observation Sheet for Communication Skills.*

to give feedback on what they saw. The teacher then selected a few incidents for further discussion, and class members were at times asked to practice some of the communication skills over again.

Matching Behaviors to Intentions

The major goal of this practice was to increase students' awareness of the fact that any behavior may be expressive of several different intentions. The teachers who used this practice asked their students to enact, in the form of role playing, short vignettes as take-off points for discussion. At the elementary level, the teachers used the following situations: (a) you want the teacher to help you with your math; (b) you have finished your assignment before anyone else in the class is finished; (c) a classmate grabs from you a paper on which you have been working; and (d) you wish to welcome a new student to the class. In the secondary classes, the teachers used these situations: (a) you want to introduce one of your friends to your teacher; (b) you borrowed a pen from a classmate and accidently broke it; (c) you want to get to know another student in one of your classes; (d) someone asks you to go to a movie, which you cannot do, though you wish to go very much; and (e) you come to class late but it is not your fault.

Several students were asked to enact what might be their behaviors under each of these circumstances. After several enactments for one situation, the teacher raised some of these questions for discussion: (a) What do you think were the intentions of each of the role players? (b) What were the actions of that person which gave you that idea about his (or her) intentions? and (c) What other actions might have been taken to communicate those same intentions and to communicate why that person behaved the way he or she did; and how else might the person's intentions have been expressed? In some instances, other students were asked to enact how they would try to put their intentions into action. The exercise works best when the class is comfortable with role playing.

Closing the Communication Gap

A teacher wanted to set time aside each week for open communication about her class's group processes. Clearing the air was not always possible in the midst of daily activities, and so she sought special time, with no limitations or boundaries as to the content for discussion. One hour per week for "gap closing" was planned. The agenda was prescribed as follows: (a) identify individual and group concerns, likes and dislikes (try to use behavior descriptions and descriptions of own feelings); (b) class chooses one or two of the concerns for concentrated work;

(c) class divides into smaller groups to work on concerns; (d) plans for solving concerns made by each group; (e) small groups report back to total class; and (f) class evaluates the solutions and comes up with actions to be taken.

Initially, the students did not know what concerns were appropriate to discuss, and so the teacher made suggestions, for example, "Sometimes it's difficult to concentrate when the teacher is presenting a topic"; or, "I'm not very much interested in the way we are studying social problems." The students tried to test the teacher's limits by suggesting concerns such as doing away with grades, doing away with homework, and closing school early. The teacher had to be patient and persistent in her desires to find legitimate concerns for discussion. At first, even the most outrageous demands were explored as possible classroom concerns; but as the students developed trust in the teacher, they began to discuss critical areas that had possibilities for improvement. Before long, "gap closing" discussions were held each day for short periods soon after the problems occurred. Although problems in communication arose throughout the school year, few of them lasted very long.

References

Amidon, E., and Hunter, E. *Improving Teaching.* New York: Holt, Rinehart & Winston, Inc., 1966.

Brown, R. *Social Psychology.* New York: Free Press, 1965.

Flanders, N. A. *Teacher Influence, Pupil Attitudes, and Achievement.* U.S. Office of Education Cooperative Research Project no. 397. Minneapolis: University of Minnesota Press, 1960.

———. *Analyzing Teaching Behavior.* Reading, Mass.: Addison-Wesley Publishing Co., Inc., 1970.

Leavitt, H. J. "Some Effects of Certain Communication Patterns on Group Performance." *Journal of Abnormal and Social Psychology* 46 (1951):38-50.

Northwest Regional Educational Laboratory, *Interpersonal Communications.* Tuxedo, N. Y.: Xicom, 1969.

Simon, A., and Boyer, E., eds., *Mirrors for Behavior.* Title IV, ESEA of 1965 in cooperation with U.S. Office of Education, Research Contract #OEC, 1-7-062867-3053. A Regional Education Laboratory. Philadelphia: Research for Better Schools, 1967.

Sommer, R. "Classroom Ecology." *Journal of Applied Behavioral Science* 3 (1967):489-503.

Tesch, F.; Lansky, L.; Lundgren, D. "The One-Way/Two-Way Communication Exercise: Some Ghosts Laid to Rest." *Journal of Applied Behavioral Science* 8, no. 6 (1972):664-73.

Wallen, J. (See Northwest Regional Educational Laboratory, 1969.)

CHAPTER 8

Cohesiveness

Cohesiveness results from the many situational and psychological forces acting on students and teacher to make them feel that they are a part of the classroom group. Some situational forces that enhance cohesiveness are dispersed influence and attraction, as well as norms that support individual differences. Among the psychological forces are favorable attitudes toward others and high self-esteem. Cohesiveness refers to the sum of inclusion feelings held by every member in relation to the rest of the group.

We already have drawn a basic distinction between norms and attitudes; norms are a group-level variable, while attitudes pertain to individuals. Similarly, cohesiveness is characteristic of a group, and is to be contrasted with feelings of inclusion or involvement at the psychological level. A cohesive classroom group is made up of students who are actively involved with one another, who care about one another, and who help one another. Some typical psychological responses of students in a cohesive classroom are "I really feel good when I am in that class," "I am involved and a part of the action," and "I know that I can contribute in this group." When responses like these can be summed up as coming from many students, the class is highly cohesive.

Students who feel involved in their class are more likely to communicate often with others, to be more open in expressing their own feelings, and to attempt influence more often. One reason students may feel that they are not part of the classroom group is their belief that others do not hold them in high esteem or see them as contributing much that is of value. Successful efforts to raise the esteem levels of students represents one strategy for increasing class cohesiveness and also one that might have the beneficial effect of increasing the dispersion of influence, the presence of supportive norms, and communication clarity.

Indications of classroom cohesiveness are at times quite obvious and easy to observe; at other times—confusing and misleading; at still other times they are very subtle and difficult to measure. Obvious indicators of cohesiveness are class members hanging around together outside of class, a high proportion of the students saying "we," in contrast to "I" or "me" during class discussions, and active involvement among students during small group interaction. Misleading indicators are such phenomena as low rates of tardiness, absenteeism, or classroom vandalism since these depend for their meaning upon the norms of the group or norms outside the group. If students share negative feelings toward school, they may reveal their cohesiveness in high rates of tardiness, absenteeism, and vandalism. In other words, cohesiveness is related not only to student behaviors that are positively valued by adults; it may support concerted and spirited antiadult behavior, as in delinquent gangs or defiant classroom subgroups. Subtle indicators of low cohesiveness might be a great deal of daydreaming in the classroom, fragmented subgroups that cannot wait to leave the class to interact, and low amounts of clear communication among students.

Cohesion and Other Group Processes

Cohesiveness refers to all group processes that converge to influence students' feelings of inclusion and involvement. It helps in summarizing much of what has already been written in this book. Group processes concerning expectations, leadership, attraction, norms, and communication can all play a part in relation to cohesiveness. For example, interpersonal expectations that people will try new behaviors and develop new ways of interacting can encourage a variety of ways of relating among class members. Vicious negative interpersonal cycles can be broken when members openly discuss their expectations for others.

A teacher's leadership behaviors that encourage active participation and joint planning with students can lead to high feelings of involvement in the class. Students with interpersonal influence begin to say "we" instead of "I," while carrying out classroom activities. Democratic leadership stimulates interaction among students, which in turn leads to more dispersion of power in the peer group. As power is diffused, students' resources are used more easily by the group. The making use of students' resources by the group supports high involvement and increases feelings of personal contribution. In cohesive classes, students feel influential, contributions are considered relevant and worthwhile, and appropriate influence methods are agreed upon by teacher and students.

Attraction processes also relate to cohesiveness, but with more complexity than a mere summing of interpersonal liking in the class. Just as classroom cohesiveness is related to dispersed influence, so also is it related to dispersed friendship patterns. We found that classrooms with diffusely structured friendship patterns, those in which most students had at least one or two close friends, were more cohesive than classes in which the friendship structures were centrally organized, with only a few students highly liked, and few others strongly rejected, and most not chosen at all (R. Schmuck 1966). Cohesion is also based on several aspects of attraction working simultaneously for students, such as feelings of membership, identification with other group members, and good feelings about participation. Cohesive classrooms tolerate flare-ups and heated arguments, but are *not* characterized by sustained friction and hostility among members. The deep investment and involvement of students in the group support rapid solutions to interpersonal problems by means of joint collaboration to reduce tensions.

Generally, cohesive classes exert high interpersonal pressure on students to conform to the expectations of members. Members of cohesive groups invest energy in their interpersonal relationships, tune in to the expectations of others, and gradually make others' expectations their own. In this way group norms become strong and members feel pressure to conform. Such pressures need not lead to those dehumanizing pressures toward conformity which reduce the individual's autonomy and creativity. If the norms support individual differences and autonomy, then group pressures to abide by them will free students to seek ways to gratify themselves. One way of describing the relationship between cohesiveness and norms has been delineated by Seashore (1954) and generally replicated by Stodgill (1972) and is illustrated in Figure 8.1.

Seashore found that the performance of highly cohesive industrial work groups was either very low or very high. He argued that the U-shaped curve shown in Figure 8.1 was indicative of the role played by norms in relation to cohesiveness. Work groups whose norms opposed high output performed poorly, especially when the groups were cohesive. In such groups, cohesiveness actually diminished the productivity. Similarly, Stodgill showed that industrial groups had highest productivity when they were cohesive *and* when members possessed "high drive"—

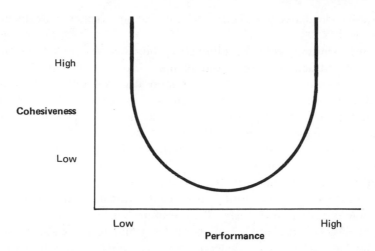

FIGURE 8.1 / *Relationship Between Cohesiveness and Performance.*

were motivated and enthusiastic about the group and its intended purposes or products.

Naturally, similar group processes could prevail in classrooms. Students who share negative attitudes about academic learning and who make up a cohesive class probably would achieve at low levels. Conversely, student groups with positive norms for learning would, especially as they increased in cohesiveness, attain high achievement. High cohesion means simply that students are more susceptible to interpersonal influence than usual; the *direction* of influence depends on the group's norms.

Classroom communication also relates to cohesiveness. Frequent interactions among students allow for possibilities of more cohesiveness to emerge; infrequent interaction generally keeps students from getting highly involved with one another. Bovard (1956) described the effects of different interaction patterns on two classroom groups. One class was characterized by "group-centered" discussions with students sitting in a circle, and the teacher participating as a member of the discussion group. In a contrasting classroom, "leader-centered" discussions were held, with the teacher at the front of the room as the focus for discussion, and most interaction involving the teacher talking to one student at a time. In the group-centered discussions, students made contributions that were more open and spontaneous; they were more active; and they became more cohesive. By contrast, all communications in the leader-centered group were channeled through the teacher; the students seldom talked to one another; they were more formal and less free to express feelings directly. The leader-centered class did not become as cohesive as the group-centered class.

Bovard's study presented a glimpse at the ways in which expectations, leadership, attraction, norms, and communication interrelated in a cohesive classroom. The relaxed and collaborative style of leadership employed by the teacher in the group-centered discussion encouraged more communication between students. The students gradually developed expectations that the teacher would support peers talking with peers. As peer group communications became more open, additional opportunities arose for the formation of friendships and for the occurrence of more mutual influence on the formation of norms. Changes in friendships and norms, in turn, encouraged more dispersed influence and increased two-way communication in the class. Furthermore, we believe that as involvement in the class increased, feelings of trust and security also increased, and that these latter feelings encouraged a reaching out to others to make additional interpersonal contact. Through these deeper contacts, personal experiences can be shared, feelings can be communicated, and involvement can be increased even more. In this manner, clear expectations, dispersed influence and friendships, supportive norms, two-way communication, and cohesiveness are part of the same enhancing group process.

Luft's Model of Interpersonal Behavior

Luft (1969) has described interpersonal relationships in a way that can be helpful for understanding some of the psychodynamics of cohesiveness. The four quadrants presented in Figure 8.2 are the basic ingredients of his graphic model. The Johari Awareness Model, named by combining the first names of its authors, can also be used by the teacher as an instructional device for helping the class to look at itself as a group. The basis for division into quadrants is the awareness of behavior, feelings, and motivation. An act is assigned, based on "who" knows about it, to one of four quadrants. Quadrant 1 refers to behavior, feelings, and motivation known both to self and to others; acts in Quadrant 2 are known to others, but not to self; those in Quadrant 3 are known to self, but not to others; and acts in Quadrant 4 are known neither to self nor to others.

Luft believes that productive working relationships with others can be facilitated by increasing the area of Quadrant 1 in relation to the other quadrants. This means that group members should interact openly in order to reduce blind spots and to reveal hidden areas of concern. We believe that as communication increases among students, more openness and spontaneity will arise among them. They will reveal more of

	Known to Self	Not Known to Self
Known to Others	**1. Open** Area of sharing and openness	**2. Blind** Area of blindness
Not Known to Others	**3. Hidden** Area of avoided information	**4. Unknown** Area of unconscious activity

Reproduced by permission of J. Luft, *Of Human Interaction.* Palo Alto, Calif.: National Press Books, 1969.

FIGURE 8.2 / *Johari Model of Awareness in Interpersonal Relations.*

what is on their minds, and will be less afraid of giving feedback to one another. Increasing the area of Quadrant 1 is one way of describing what occurs psychologically as a classroom group becomes more cohesive. Classes become more cohesive, and stronger as groups, when the students share more of what so often is hidden from public discussion.

Types of Classroom Cohesiveness

Students are attracted to classrooms for a variety of reasons. Some like the challenge of school work; some like to be rewarded for effort; some like to be near other students; others feel some prestige in the peer group as being part of a particular class. Just as one's classes are regarded differently by each student, so also can classroom groups be described as being cohesive for different reasons. Back (1951) carried out an experiment in which he investigated various "pulls" that groups have for individuals. In his research, the subjects worked in pairs cooperatively on a task. The pairs were formed to be either cohesive or noncohesive, and the cohesive pairs were arranged in one of three ways: (1) attraction to the group because of a liking for the other member; (2) attraction to the group because of high interest, mutually held, in the task; and (3) attraction to the group because of its prestige for the members. Even though the three types of cohesiveness were different, the groups that were cohesive in one way or another worked more effectively than the noncohesive groups.

These three sources of cohesiveness are visible in school settings. Liking for other students often is the primary source of cohesiveness for extracurricular clubs, for informal gatherings at lunch, and for parties. Common interest in an activity or task sometimes is the basis for cohesiveness in the school's theatre group or the basketball team. Prestige is often a powerful source of cohesiveness for the football team, the cheerleader's rally squad, and certain advanced classes. Indeed, any group in the school can possess one or more of these bases of cohesiveness, and each gains strength as it incorporates one or more of them. For instance, the student council will probably work in a concerted fashion if it performs activities which the members enjoy, or if it has some prestige in the school culture, or if the members like one another. Groups which have fewer bases of cohesiveness will work less coherently. Classroom groups often lack cohesiveness, especially when compared to other student groups, because friendship, prestige, and common interest in the tasks are missing.

The sources of attraction in any one group may also differ for the individual students. For example, an interview with a group of junior high students who were very enthusiastic about their class in local government produced a variety of answers to the question, "What do you like most about this government class?" Among these answers were: "I get to study with my two best friends," "It's interesting to find out how this town operates," "I'm going to have a chance to be a mayor for the day," "I'm getting a chance to know more people in the class," "I'm thinking about politics for a career," and "The work is fun to do." While each of these answers revealed a different individual interest and several different sources of cohesiveness, together they added up to a highly cohesive class.

Classroom groups increase in cohesiveness as students feel they are satisfying their interests, values, and needs. Such satisfactions, according to Back and to our observations of students, center in the activities, prestige, and friendships that a class affords its members. Students' feelings about themselves as students become increasingly or decreasingly favorable, depending upon how much their achievement, power, and affiliation needs are satisfied. Thus, carrying out a task productively can reward students' achievement strivings, being part of a group which others respect can reward power needs, and associating closely with friends can satisfy the motive for affiliation. If students continually fail at learning tasks, see the class as having low status in the larger student culture, and experience unpleasant interpersonal relations, their feelings about the class will be negative and their involvement will be low.

The teacher's classroom influence extends only to making it possible for achievement, power, and affiliation satisfactions to occur; it can not assure such satisfactions will be met. Students will attempt to satisfy their personal interests if they view themselves as valuable and contributing members of the group. The teacher can facilitate the emergence of such feelings by being clear about learning goals and by helping students to choose ways of arriving at the goals. It is in increasing the flexibility of arriving at learning goals, however, that open two-way communication is so important in the classroom. If channels of communication are closed, and feelings or concerns are hidden, little chance of establishing a variety of avenues for satisfying individual interests is possible. When many people participate actively and openly so that the air can be cleared and group process problems can be discussed, more opportunities arise for the students to find ways of satisfying their own interests.

For some individual students, however, cohesiveness can have negative consequences. Students who are attracted to the class and wish to belong, and who, at the same time, view themselves as being rejected by some of their fellow students, will experience negative feelings about themselves and their school work. Such negative outcomes often arise when a student's initial attraction and involvement are based on interest in the task or the prestige of the group. Subsequent interpersonal rejection, after becoming involved, can be psychologically painful. Empirical relationships linking sociometric status, self-esteem, and academic achievement are especially strong in highly cohesive classroom groups. Students who are accepted members of cohesive classrooms with a dispersed friendship structure have the best chances for achieving high self-esteem and for working up to their intellectual potential.

Diagnosing Classroom Cohesiveness

Perceptive teachers can easily make note of classroom behaviors that indicate how cohesive the class is. They can count the number of times plural pronouns in contrast to singular pronouns are used. Classroom groups in which "we" and "us" are heard are usually more cohesive than ones in which "I" and "me" are more often expressed. Members of cohesive groups see themselves not so much as individuals set apart from the other students, but rather as part of the class. Teachers might also watch for students to offer and accept help from one another. Generally, cohesive groups have the greater percentage of their cooperative relations internally and of their competitive relations externally.

Another indication of a class's cohesiveness is its internal flexibility. Students in a cohesive class take pride in the group, even in the physical appearance of the room, and can work easily with a variety of other students. Work groups can be changed easily; members take one another's place when a substitute is needed, and students want to fill in where they can be helpful. Another indication occurs when students participate with other class members in out-of-classroom activities, as when they play together at recess, have lunch together, walk home together, study together. Helpful, friendly, cooperative relationships with classmates both inside and outside the classroom are indications of cohesiveness. By the same token, competitive situations outside the classroom will find members of the cohesive group upholding and supporting one another.

The absence of these indicators of a cohesive class is no cause for alarm. In many respects, they are overly-ideal group processes, both for learning and personal development. Even so, the achievement of cohesiveness is worth the building of new and better teaching strategies.

Implications for Teachers

The following summary statements capture the key implications of the contents of this chapter for teachers.
- —Cohesiveness is an attribute of a group, not of individuals. A classroom group is cohesive when most of its members, including the teacher, are highly attracted to the group as such.
- —Attraction to a classroom group occurs for individuals when their desires for achievement, power, and affiliation are satisfied by acquisition of membership in the group.
- —In highly cohesive classrooms, students' involvement in learning may be high or low depending on the norms of the group. Productivity in learning will be high in classes where there is high cohesiveness *and* where the norms support academic involvement.
- —A summation of the dynamics of interpersonal expectations, leadership style, attraction patterns, and the flow of communication are the ingredients that go into a cohesive class. Cohesive classes can be created by open discussions of expectations, by dispersion of leadership, by developing several friendship clusters, and by the frequent use of two-way communication. The effects of building cohesiveness can, in turn, be made favorable for individual growth and learning by the holding of open discussions and problem-solving sessions in relation to the group's norms.

Action Ideas for Change

The practices described here have been employed successfully by at least one teacher to increase classroom cohesiveness.

Public Discussion of Cohesiveness

A junior high teacher wanted his students to discuss their feelings of involvement or alienation from the class. He structured the first discussion around the Johari Awareness Model by taking a few minutes to present the four quadrants and then asking each student to think about the question: "How do I feel about this class?" As an example, he began filling out a blank Johari model (described in Fig. 8.2) on the blackboard. The teacher next asked each student to fill out Quadrants 1 and 3 by themselves. After giving students about five minutes to work on each quadrant, he organized them into groups of four. All students in any small group filled out Quadrant 2 for all other students in their same group. Quadrant 4 was skipped altogether (see Fig. 8.3).

1	2
I don't like to read out loud. I like to have class discussions. I think this class is "cool."	You act mean when you get a score. You say "ah" a lot when you talk out loud in class.
3	4
I am afraid of making mistakes. I like to work with Joe.	

FIGURE 8.3 / *How I Feel About This Class.*

The purpose of the exercise was to get many feelings that might have been hidden, out into the open for discussion. Since a cohesive group is achieved by building trust and openness, it was important for this kind of sharing to occur. The exercise worked well, and it served to launch the class on fruitful weekly discussions about the group. It should be borne in mind, however, that some prior cohesion and attraction must exist in the group before public sharing will be carried out in a forthright fashion. The following activity can be helpful in producing a beginning level of cohesion.

Strength Exercise

An elementary teacher assumed that raising the self-esteem levels of students would increase group cohesiveness. The activity chosen to raise the students' esteem was a strength-building exercise, sometimes referred to as an "up with people" activity. The students divided into small groups of four or five. Each small group member spent time thinking alone about his or her own strengths as a student as well as the strengths he or she viewed in the other students of his or her small group. No admissions or observations of weaknesses were allowed. Time spent alone was followed by a general sharing of perceptions of strengths. It is important to emphasize strengths viewed in one's self, as well as in others; and it is important for the group to move to every student in its discussion so that strengths are identified for everyone.

Involving Students in Evaluating Classroom Activities

A secondary English teacher thought that her students felt close to one another but that their involvement did not extend to learning English. She thought that they were poorly motivated for academic work, even though they were already fairly cohesive, so she sought to modify norms in the expectation that the group would band together around the study of English. She hoped to involve them in curriculum building more than she had in the past, as a way of changing group norms.

She decided to begin by asking the students to report their feelings about class work that had already been accomplished. After developing a format for student evaluation of past classroom activities, she followed these steps: (1) discussed the reasons that evaluation of past events was important for building a more interesting English course; (2) presented an evaluation sheet for the past week's studies; (3) had the students fill out the sheets, and prepared a summary of the data for a discussion the next day; (4) made revisions in the curriculum based on these evaluations; (5) saw to having an evaluation sheet filled out every week; (6) received feedback that was given, together with revisions in the curriculum.

After carrying out several months of evaluations and incorporating them into weekly lesson plans, the teacher was convinced that students' ideas were useful and sensible. The students liked the procedure and, most importantly, from the teacher's point of view, the close relationships that existed in the peer group were put to work to learn English. Although this activity added more work for the teacher, the increased motivation and learning of the students reduced her frustrations and worries.

Discussing Commonality of Problems

A fourth grade teacher wanted to demonstrate that students often share similar interpersonal and emotional concerns. He wanted his classroom to be a place where students would feel free to discuss problems, and perhaps to receive help from other students. He also hoped to increase feelings of interpersonal support and closeness in the group. He began by using an "unfinished story" about a boy who wanted to learn to speak French but who didn't want to admit it to his friends. He had his students present some possible endings to the story. Later, he asked them to present real or fictitious problem situations to the class. Discussions were held by the whole class or by various subgroups. The teacher noted a definite increase in sharing and communicating among the students, a development which had an especially supportive effect on the increased involvement of the least active students.

References

Back, K. "Influence Through Social Communication." *Journal of Abnormal and Social Psychology* 46 (1951):9-23.

Bovard, E. "Interaction and Attraction to the Group." *Human Relations* 9 (1956):314-20.

Luft, J. *Of Human Interaction.* Palo Alto, Calif.: National Press Books, 1969.

Schmuck, R. A. "Some Relationships of Peer Liking Patterns in the Classroom to Pupil Attitudes and Achievement." *School Review* 71 (1963):337-59.

———. "Some Aspects of Classroom Social Climate." *Psychology in the Schools,* 3, no. 1 (1966):59-65.

Seashore, S. *Group Cohesiveness in the Industrial Work Group.* Ann Arbor, Mich.: Institute for Social Research, 1054.

Stodgill, R. "Group Productivity, Drive, and Cohesiveness." *Organizational Behavior and Human Performance* 8, no. 1 (1972):26-43.

CHAPTER 9

Sequential Stages of Development

Groups, like individuals, pass through discernible stages of development as they mature. Erikson's theory (1950) of an individual's psychological development presents some helpful hints for understanding the growth of classroom groups. He wrote that an individual faces a sequence of problems during his lifetime—problems that must be resolved before he can achieve maturity. As Erikson views it, psychological development is sequential and successive; each stage follows another in time, and solutions to problems at any later stage are dependent on the resolutions that were made during prior stages.

Classroom groups also pass through sequential and successive stages in developing their formal and informal social patterns; the resolutions to current interpersonal problems are dependent on the solutions to prior problems. As with the individual, classroom growth also can be arrested at a particular stage of development. For example, a classroom group would have difficulty carrying out an activity requiring group cooperation and interpersonal flexibility (in the form of a division of labor) if it had not previously developed trust between the members and established open lines of communication. Indeed, if the members of a class never develop a foundation of basic interpersonal trust and closeness, they will have a hard time proceeding to more advanced stages of group interdependence.

While both individual and group development are sequential and successive, they also are cyclical with very similar developmental issues coming up again and again in new social situations. In other words, even though certain psychological problems and group process issues seem to accrue more to specificity of times than others, individuals and groups continually face many of the same problems. For example, Erikson pointed out that the development of trust is the first significant problem faced by the infant. However, the psychodynamics of trust are confronted again when the child begins to have friends, again when adolescent dating occurs, and again when the marriage vows are made. Yet, to some degree, the interpersonal trust learned during infancy remains always with the individual as he enters new relationships. Analogously, group development is cyclical; issues of trust and accurate communication continually arise as the group copes with the dynamics of leadership, attraction, and norms. At the same time, a large reservoir of trust established early in the group's developmental history will reap subsequent benefits as the group is confronted with new challenges.

Of all class members, the teacher's influence on the group's developing climate is most critical. Teachers deliberately or unwittingly guide and direct the development of group processes in the classroom. In classes where most of the talk and all of the information comes from the teacher, and in which students infrequently hear one anothers' ideas, student members will not have the opportunity to develop interpersonal trust or to engage effectively in decisions about classroom activities. Such a "collection of students" will not be able to carry out learning tasks that require student planning, cooperation, and an interdependent division of labor.

At the same time, the teacher's power can be reduced significantly if the group's developmental history is at odds with the teacher's style. Ron Lippitt was fond of telling a story about his own experiences as a teacher-trainer that bears on the complex interplay between the power of the teacher and the strength of the classroom group. Early in his college teaching career, Ron was in charge of preparing teachers for schools in rural Illinois. He quickly learned that his ideas about shared decision making and equality between teachers and students did not take hold once the neophyte teachers were in the field. Even though his trainees could behave democratically in classroom role-playing, they seemed unable to do so in actual classrooms. After all, these neophyte teachers were moving into classes in which levels of trust and openness were low—the students shared firm expectations that the teacher was the sole authority and organizer. Faced with schools of this kind, the new teachers soon reverted to traditional, authoritarian practices. Subsequently, Lippitt revised his training program to include practicing "how to be a humane authoritarian teacher" and "how to move from autocracy to democracy" so that the prospective teachers would be able to cope wisely and effectively with the classes they would face.

We often work with neophyte teachers who are "turned on" to the idea of democratic teaching or open classrooms or who wish to make frequent use of small group instruction. Frequently, such teachers will hand over the reins of leadership totally to students who themselves are unprepared and unskillful in assuming initiatory roles. When the class falls into disunity and disarray, the teacher pulls back the reins of control and explains, "I tried it and it didn't work." But, as all teachers come to see, students cannot change their expectations, behaviors, and skills simply by administrative fiat—behavioral changes in student groups require understanding, planning, and practice over a long period of time.

Teachers who understand the sequential nature of developing classroom groups can planfully influence growth in productive ways. On the other hand, teachers who do not take into account the need for gradual development of skills and behaviors in attaining effective group performance will have classes that are thwarted or stilted in their development and cannot be optimal environments for learning.

Theories of Group Development

As we have noted previously, learning groups have a hidden world of emotional life, and the task of academic learning to accomplish as well. Both of these social dynamics—the emotional and task aspects of group life—develop simultaneously. Among the several theories that have been delineated on group development, three appear to be especially useful to our purposes. We include a brief description of each of these theories, because each focuses on different aspects of group development and all three have contributed to our understanding of the developmental stages of learning groups.

Schutz (1958, 1966) developed a theory about the emotionality of group members which was based on the members' expressed and desired needs for *inclusion, control,* and *affection.* Schutz's theory emphasizes personality dynamics of individuals. Parsons and Bales (1955) proposed a theory of group development that emphasized the roles or functions that members must perform in problem-solving groups; their theory is closer to a social level of analysis than a psychological one. The Parsons and Bales theory is helpful for understanding the activities that members must perform in order for learning in a group to occur. Finally, Gibb's (1964) theory of individual and group development contained essential ingredients of both emotionality and problem solving and therefore has been most useful to our understanding of learning groups.

None of the three theories has been used directly in research on learning groups in schools. Schutz's research included teacher-student dyads and sensitivity groups with educators, but was not carried out in public schools. Parsons and Bales made use of simulated problem-solving groups and real families. Gibb conducted experimental and field studies in several industrial and organizational settings. Even though these three theories certainly have limitations for understanding the school learning group, we believe that each presents useful ideas concerning possible developmental stages.

Schutz's Theory

According to Schutz, individuals want and express the three interpersonal needs of inclusion, control, and affection to different degrees and as a natural course of events. His theory states that in the beginning of a group's development the most predominant domain of interpersonal interaction focuses upon inclusion; this is followed later by control, which in turn is followed by affection. This cycle may recur several times prior to the termination of a group's life. The final three stages of a group's history, according to the theory, occur in reversed order with affection preceding control and ending with inclusion. These stages of group development are viewed as sequential, but also they are seen as overlapping and as continually intertwining, not as mutually exclusive.

Issues of interpersonal inclusion characterize the beginning of a group's life. In the classroom, the students and teacher confront one another's presence and raise questions such as: How will I fit in here? Who will accept me? Who will reject me? What do I have to do to be accepted? Academic work cannot easily be accomplished until these questions of inclusion are answered satisfactorily. Each person—student or teacher—cautiously reveals aspects of himself while gathering information about others. Schutz called the content discussed during this period "goblet issues" because he figuratively visualized persons picking up their goblets and gazing through them to size up others without at the same time revealing themselves. Issues of becoming included in the peer group may revolve around having friends in common, where one lives, what one's hobbies are, or clues about whether one is pleasant and considerate. Students reveal themselves bit by bit and issue by issue until each one considers himself or herself part of the class. Unfortunately, some students never achieve a feeling of membership.

After inclusion in the group has been achieved by most of the members, Schutz views groups as moving on to struggles with influence, which involve the development of decision-making norms, and the sharing of responsibility. He calls this the stage of control. It appears inevitable that students will test their degree of influence with the teacher as well as with other students. This period of testing for control discussed extensively in Chapter 4 finds each person attempting to establish a confortable level of influence for himself within the group.

Next, group members begin to confront the emotional issues involving affection and closeness. Who will like me? and Who do I like? are characteristic questions of this third stage of development. During this period of group growth, discussed in Chapter 5, each person strives for the optimal degrees of intimacy with others to suit his personal needs.

Basic to Schutz's theory of group development is the variable of interpersonal compatibility, which was discussed in the previous chapter as cohesiveness. He defines compatibility as the amount of comfort that exists between two or more persons by virtue of their satisfying each others' expressed and wanted needs. Compatible groups have members who want inclusion, control and affection and other members who express these same interpersonal needs virtually to an equal degree. Incompatible groups do not have members who complement one another's needs. For Schutz, groups will develop optimally only when the members are psychologically compatible. Most educators already know, as the Hargreaves' study on streaming in the British schools showed (see Chap. 6), that simply grouping students according to similar ability or achievement levels does not lead necessarily to cohesive work groups. While it may be difficult for schools to put students together solely on the basis of psychological needs, on some occasions psychological compatibility may be the best criterion to use. Letting students organize their own ad hoc or task groups may be one way to organize around personality characteristics—students often are accurate judges of who they, themselves, can best work with.

Parsons and Bales' Theory

This theory specifies that group members must perform certain roles for the group to solve its problems and remain viable. The two major clusters of roles are designated as *task* and *maintenance* functions; if both functions are not performed, the group will not be effective. Any member can, potentially, perform task or maintenance functions, but in most groups certain individuals engage in specific behaviors to a greater degree than others, and usually interpersonal expectations get set about who should perform which roles. According to Parsons and Bales, in contrast to the thinking of Schutz, personality characteristics are important determinants of group life only insofar as they explain why particular persons might take particular roles. Their theory specifies that groups develop in a predictable fashion regardless of the personalities within them.

Research on the Parsons-Bales theory of group behavior has been carried out on four- to eight-person groups with specific problems to solve (Bales and Slater 1955). The research showed the development of a group over a series of meetings as well as its development during one period of time. Stages labeled *phase movements,* for example, have been shown to occur within a single meeting. Three phases have been noted. The first phase generally involves giving and receiving information. During this period of time, information about the problem, background information and possible solutions are presented. Usually, the solutions are tentative and not well developed. The next (or middle) phase is characterized by exchanging opinions and evaluations. Members test out ideas, criticize one another's ideas, and jointly develop new ones. Decision-making about what actions to take also occurs during this period. Finally during phase three there is an increase in pleasant feelings and a decrease of criticism. Joking, the release of some tension and jovial laughter are typical during this final phase; members attempt to increase their solidarity and to turn their attention to emotional support of one another.

Particular groups will go through different phases in one session and different stages over a longer period of time. A single meeting is in some ways, however, a microcosm of total group development. For learning groups to gain strength and momentum, they should be allowed and encouraged to move through all phases during a single meeting.

Lippitt (1940) showed an instance in which a group of youngsters failed to reach the final phase of group development but remained instead at the stage of argumentation. In Lippitt's example, the group of students was floundering without direction, decisions were hard to make in the face of interpersonal conflict, and the leader attempted to intervene with controlling and dominating behaviors. The group ended on a note of divisiveness and with a large number of negative interpersonal feelings. Similarly, we think high amounts of negativism occur in classrooms, especially when the teacher gives the group freedom to solve a problem, but then steps in to control and alter the group's decision making.

In most classrooms we have observed, the beginning stages are fraught with ambiguity and unclear directions on the part of the students. How the resulting frustrations and insecure feelings get resolved is critical for determining the extent of student involvement in the group. Teachers who do not let the students' resources and feelings emerge and who take over in an authoritarian fashion may retard the development of the group.

Systematic patterns of group development also have been shown to arise over the duration of a series of classroom sessions. In one careful study, Runkel et al. (1971) documented the key developmental stages of task activities in a college class. The primary requirement in this large undergraduate course in social psychology was for groups of students to complete an independent research project collaboratively. The developmental processes of these research groups were documented by student observers who were using Tuckman's model of group development (1965). The observers reliably measured four distinct phases: (1) time during which members defined the task and set limitations on it; (2) emotional responses to the task usually in the form of resistance to carrying out the task; (3) the open exchange of information, feelings, and opinions; and (4) the generation of solutions and plans for work.

Heinicke and Bales (1953) found that over a span of four meetings, members gradually spent less time doing work and more time carrying out social-emotional functions. Although the first meeting was mostly characterized by cautious and polite behaviors, a great deal of negativism arose during the second meeting. The researchers labeled the negativism that was observed, "status struggles," parallel to what Tuckman called "emotional resistance to the task" and what Schutz labeled as the control phase. Heinicke and Bales noted that interpersonal conflicts arose mostly when the group was faced with making decisions. The groups that were unable to resolve their status struggles did not move on to become effective in problem solving, nor were the members very happy with the group. Groups that did move successfully through this stage proceeded to make plans for action, developed favorable feelings, and supported one another strongly.

One of the most consistent results filtering through the research on group development is the tendency of groups to alternate in a cyclical fashion between emphases on task and social-emotional concerns. When groups of students are asked to work together on classroom projects, it is only realistic to expect that they will spend nearly half of the available time dealing with emotional aspects of their interpersonal relationships. All groups, including student and adult groups, spend a great deal of time giving emotional support to the members. Learning groups that do not solve their emotional hang-ups also will have difficulty in accomplishing academic learning tasks.

Gibb's Theory

Gibb's ideas (1964) are highly relevant to classroom group development because of the way in which he described personal and interpersonal growth as occurring interdependently. His major themes were that groups grow into maturity only after they develop interpersonal trust, and that groups in which trust is not established do not help individual members to develop self-esteem.

His theory proposed four basic concerns of members while their group is developing. The first concern involves interpersonal acceptance and the formation of trust and confidence in the self and in the group. On the personal side, one's feelings of adequacy and self-esteem are at stake. For the group, concerns of membership, and trust in others are most prominent.

The second concern involves what Gibb refers to as "data-flow." During this stage, individuals think less about themselves and more about the group. They become aware of the ways the group is functioning and begin to evaluate whether they like what the group is doing. Norms begin to take shape about how the group will make decisions. If some degree of acceptance and trust has *not* already been established, decision making will be hampered by closed and guarded communication, and decisions will get made without deep commitment on the part of the members.

The third stage involves the achievement of goals for the individuals and the group. Individuals want to achieve something that helps them feel successful and competent. They will become **independent** and autonomous provided earlier concerns have been successfully resolved. At the group level, norms will be established about goals and procedures; if there is open communication, goals can be determined to compliment the individuals and the group will develop a comfortable and flexible task structure.

The final concern presented by Gibb was described as the control stage. Individuals feel independent and autonomous provided earlier concerns have been resolved successfully. For the group, norms are formalized, interpersonal behaviors are agreed upon, and the group is able to change itself.

We believe that these four developmental concerns describe well what goes on in the interpersonal underworld of many classes. Students cannot directly express their own ideas and opinions until they have learned that their peers and the teacher will not reject them. Those students who do not feel accepted will tend to withhold their ideas from discussion. They will feel alienated from academic learning, be directionless and poorly motivated, suppress their feelings, and not abide by the academic norms of the school. Students who learn to trust their peers will become more involved in pursuing their own goals in the learning group, and abiding by learning group norms.

Classroom groups naturally differ in these regards. In one class, the stages of development may not get worked through and the interpersonal relationships may become formalized and distant. Students do not get acquainted with one another very well in such classes because they do not communicate openly and personally. Some of the students become afraid to express their ideas; discussions, when they do occur, are awkward and lack spontaneity. The learning goals are presented to the students by the teacher, rewards are extrinsic, and the direction of the group is determined by the evaluations of the teacher. Classroom organization becomes routinized, norms are characterized by a narrow range of tolerable behavior and the teacher enforces classroom rules. This picture, unfortunately, represents the majority of public school classrooms that we have observed.

In a contrasting class, the same developmental concerns are confronted; but, because of different ways of working with the issues, the group develops differently. As the students cautiously reveal parts of themselves, the teacher accepts a variety of student behaviors. The students learn that their peers also are afraid to reveal themselves but gradually imitate the teacher's behaviors of acceptance. The students begin to reward one another for the expression of ideas, information is freely exchanged, and joint decision making begins to occur. Later the students begin to direct themselves and to establish things they want the class to accomplish. Norms are discussed and changed by the teacher and students as they prove to be no longer helpful to what everyone wishes to accomplish.

These differences in the developmental processes of classroom groups are strongly influenced by the teacher. Gibb identified two clusters of leadership behaviors, which he labeled as persuasive and participative that could influence groups to cope with developmental issues in different ways.

Behaviors of the persuasive teacher would emanate from an orientation of distrust; such teachers would lack confidence in their students. Persuasive teachers consider students as not mature or wise enough to make decisions for themselves, hence believe that they must make decisions for them. Such teachers see their role as setting goals for learning, and pursuading students that these are worthy goals to pursue. Their authority is clear; academic learning is formal and routine; and they set the norms for appropriate classroom behavior and enforce them.

In contrast, participative leaders begin by trusting and accepting their students. They place themselves in an equalitarian position in relation to their students by often functioning as one of the class members. They expect to be listened to just as they expect to listen carefully to the students. They encourage students to make decisions for themselves, to express themselves, and to participate in the determination of policies and procedures for learning and behavior. Participative teachers typically encourage a classroom climate that is informal, relaxed, and supportive.

A Practical Guide to Group Development

The necessary ingredients for the development of a positive climate for learning involve the skills and abilities of members to resolve problems and concerns at different stages of development. We will describe briefly the four developmental stages that learning groups move through, and refer to exercises and procedures that can be used to highlight the issues of group development at each stage. Many of these activities already have been discussed in previous chapters; we suggest here some additional ones also.

An exercise (or simulation) is a structured game-like activity designed to produce group processes that participants can easily understand because they will have just been manifested in the participants' experiences through the game. Each exercise is designed to make salient a certain type of group process, thereby making certain lessons easily comprehensible. No exercise is intended to match the complexity of the group's full reality, but rather to enable members to learn the advantages or disadvantages of specific forms of group behavior. In brief, each exercise has a particular content and product.

A procedure, on the other hand, refers to a group activity that does not, in itself, entail learning a specific content, but rather enables a group to accomplish its work more effectively. A procedure can be used for a variety of tasks or purposes. For example, the use of a certain form of decision making such as majority vote, or the use of a problem-solving sequence are procedures. Whereas, exercises typically are carried out only once or twice by a learning group, procedures can and should be used regularly throughout the life of a learning group.

Although our ideas are presented in a sequential format, we wish to emphasize that group development is also cyclical. Thus exercises that are used at the beginning of a group's life to resolve membership issues, for instance, may be appropriate at a later time because questions about belonging can come up over and over again during the life of a group.

Our primary criteria for including the sample of activities that may be used are three: First, that the techniques primarily emphasized issues of ongoing group processes and development, in contrast to abstract or theoretical items about social behavior that are in established curricula; second, that the techniques may be used by anyone, administrator, teacher, or student with a small amount of previous experience in working with classroom groups, and a modicum of time and energy; and finally, that the techniques do not require special materials that cannot be found in most schools. All of our suggestions are also presented in a general way to that they can be altered and tailored to fit classes of all ages.

Stage I: Inclusion and Membership

During the early period of the life of a classroom group, students seek a secure notch within the peer group. Each student is reticent and to some extent fearful of presenting a weak image; each is anxious about being rejected. The first weeks of the class represent critical times for finding one's own place in relation to others. Students usually are on their best behavior presenting ideal images to one another. Academic work tends to be carried out carefully and smoothly.

During this first period of development, by virtue of the traditional position of authority, the teacher takes on extraordinary power in setting the tenor of the group's future. He conditions the group for formal, routine, impersonal relationships, or for exciting and stimulating relationships. Not until later in the group's development do the students have sufficient information to decide whether the teacher's behaviors are worth following, ignoring, or rejecting. What is crucial, then, is that the teacher takes the initiative to help the members of his learning group toward establishing feelings of inclusion and membership.

During this period, questions such as, will they accept me? Will they like me? Who are they? and Can I get close to them? are asked implicitly and preconsciously by all students. Many classrooms unfortunately never develop past this stage; questions such as these remain unanswered throughout the life of such groups. There are many classrooms in which students have spent a whole term working next to one another without learning the names of their compatriots.

We cannot be precise about the length of time it will take for classrooms of students to achieve feelings of inclusion and membership. The intensity of the striving for inclusion and its eventual resolution will depend on the amount of time the students spend together, the past familiarity of students, the ages of the students and their previous experience in working out some of the developmental issues in a group. However, we believe that every classroom group will have to resolve first the basic issues of belongingness and membership in some way, even though their resolutions will take on quite different forms and patterns.

The following suggestions provide what Schutz refers to as the "goblets" through which teacher and students size up one another and cautiously reveal parts of themselves. These exercises and procedures emphasize the kind of interaction between teacher and students and between students and students that we believe will help move a class to a later stage of development.

ACTION PLANS FOR STAGE I. The two activities described here can be tried during the first few weeks of class to facilitate more rapid inclusion, involvement, and rapport among the students.

1) *Who are they?* Students are asked to work randomly around the room. The teacher gives a series of directions at three-minute intervals as follows: "Greet others without words or gross physical gestures!" "Say a brief word of greeting to all the people you see!" "Find a fellow student with whom you believe you may have something in common; talk for a few minutes about what you might have in common!" "Find a person whom you don't know very well and find out a few things about that person!" "Find someone you think you may be uncomfortable with and talk about why!", and "Find someone with whom you'd like to work and talk about why!"

2) *Where do I belong?* Students stand up and mill around the center of the room. Without verbal communication among them, they are asked to divide up into groups of four people each. The rule of four to a group is very useful unless the number in the group does not allow for this kind of division. As a subgroup becomes too large, members are asked to leave it to form another one. The teacher should not talk or suggest where students should move; he should just remind them of the rule of four to a group. After the groups have been formed the students discuss how this entire process felt, how it felt to have to leave one group and join another, and in general their reactions to forming and reforming groups. The teacher might ask: Was it easier to move toward some groups and not others? Were there verbal or nonverbal messages of acceptance or rejection given? If so, what were they like?

After the subgroups have had a chance to discuss each individual's experience, the entire group then should discuss what the exercise means for the whole class insofar as the group will be working together for a long time. The students should be encouraged to construct a list of behaviors that communicate acceptance of others and those that communicate rejection. The group might also make a list of feelings that students have when they are not accepted or when they do not feel part of a learning group. Finally, the students can discuss things that they might be able to do to help new student members feel more at ease and to become a part of the classroom.

3) *Other Activities.* In addition to the above two exercises, the reader is referred back to particular exercises and procedures discussed in earlier chapters. Each of the following activities might be used to increase stu-

dents' feelings of inclusion and membership in the class: "Encouraging Acceptance of New Members," "Interviewing," and "Role-Playing," all from Chapter 5; "Learning How to Communicate," "Matching Behaviors to Intentions," and "Clearing the Air," all found in Chapter 7; and "Discussing the Commonality of Problems" in Chapter 8.

Stage II: Establishing Shared Influence and Collaborative Decision Making

After the students and teacher build some security and sense that they do belong together in one classroom, two sorts of "power-struggles" typically become prominent. One has to do with testing the limits of the power of the teacher and typically involves the psychodynamics of dependency and counter-dependency; the other concerns the pecking order of the student peer group and involves the psychodynamics of domination and autonomy.

Traditionally the pattern has been for the teacher to maintain all important power over the students and, consequently, most classroom groups remain at the unresolved stage of control and influence throughout most of the school year. Underneath the surface of a controlled classroom, interpersonal conflicts and tensions exist between the teacher and students, and also within the student peer group. Teachers have been warned, "Don't smile before Christmas." This means that if they can maintain their formal control of the students during the first four months of school, they have a good chance of not having to face many disruptions or attempts to gain control.

Those teachers who manage to "keep the lid on," not only waste a great deal of energy in policing students' interactions, but also tend to miss the excitement—as well as the pain—of getting genuinely close to their students. It is very natural that conflict will arise over how things will operate and who will make those decisions. After all, such conflicts arise in all of the human sectors of life; they occur between child and parent, between friends, between spouses as well as in churches, in communities and between nation-states.

Attempts to control can be seen clearly at certain stages of child development. There is the invincible and incorrigible two or three year old who struggles with his parents as he discovers ways to be autonomous and independent. "I do it myself" he says, as he persistently and incapably tries to button a shirt, or "you go away" as he touches a forbidden object. He hears the word *NO* over and over as he attempts to establish his independent position in the world. Of course, his attempts at autonomy and influence are mixed simultaneously with wishes for love, acceptance, and security. Part of the control issue for youngsters involves testing of the limits of love and acceptance.

Very similar developmental phenomena occur in classroom groups. Just as the young child learns about autonomy and power through the way parents handle the inevitable control issues, so will students in the classroom learn about influence relationships from the behavior of the teacher. How the leader's role in the group will be resolved depends in part on what happened to the classroom group during its first stage of development. The teacher who has successfully maintained all power by *not* smiling before Christmas most likely will produce a well ordered, formal (possibly even a pleasant) classroom where no student makes any obvious attempts to gain power. Such classrooms also tend to have students who are alienated from the school and do not consider themselves an integral part of classroom life; but there won't be many public influence struggles, save for a few isolated bursts of counter-dependency.

It is not intended here to imply that teachers who have encouraged closeness, belongingness, and shared leadership in the beginning stages of the learning group's life will have an easy time during this second stage. After all, since the norms built during the first stage supported public discussions of conflict and of "clearing the air," movement toward collaborative decision making and shared influence can also be assumed to carry a great deal of tension and stress. But, we do believe that teachers who are genuinely committed to creating a classroom group in which learning is viewed as part of the process of living, and not limited to reciting the multiplication tables by rote, will endure the stress and strain in exchange for the joy of educating. And we also believe that it gets easier and easier, although not less joyful, once the teacher has experienced several groups of students who have become a healthy and productive learning group.

ACTION PLANS FOR STAGE II. Classroom groups that have successfully achieved a sense of belonging for all members typically are active and rather noisy places. Most members feel comfortable and secure in giving their own points of view. Consequently, discussions often become disorderly when people are so intent on giving their own ideas that they forget to listen to others. For this reason, the five procedures chosen for Stage II emphasize the right to talk as well as the right to be heard.

1) *The Chance to Listen.* Although discussions in a class can allow everyone to have his say, often there is too little regard for whether what was said was understood or persuasive. One procedure that can facilitate clearer communication and more even participation among participants is that before a student speaks he paraphrases what the last stu-

dent said. The same rule should apply, of course, to the teacher. Before a proposal is decided upon, also, several students should paraphrase the terms of the proposal so that everyone is clear about what is being decided. The teacher or a student might be charged with insuring that each participant, along with his right to be heard, is granted the right to listen and to be clear about communications within the group. This procedure might be tried first as part of an exercise for practicing paraphrasing, later attempted as a procedure within the steering committee, and finally employed during discussions of the entire class.

2) *Tokens for Talking.* This procedure as well as the one that follows can be used to help all students to participate in discussions and decision-making. For instance, when only a few students talk during discussion it might be suggested that time tokens be used to ensure wider participation. Each student is allotted the same number of tokens. At the point of making a verbal contribution he must give up one of his tokens to a spot in the middle of the learning group. He can speak only as long as his tokens last.

3) *High-Talker Tap-Out.* Another method for preventing domination by only a few students is the "high-talker tap-out." A coordinator (either the teacher or a student) monitors the group to see if any participant seems to be dominating the interaction. If one or two are dominating, then the coordinator hands each instructions asking that they refrain from further commenting—though the instruction might permit comment on group process. In this way, the remainder of the participation can be balanced out more evenly.

4) *Buzz Groups.* Another procedure that can be used to spread participation in a large class is the buzz group. The class meeting is temporarily interrupted while subgroups of four to seven students form to discuss an issue for a short time. This can be done to best advantage when important decisions have to be made and some students hesitate to express their contrary views in front of the entire class. When feelings are difficult to bring out, the buzz groups might have reporters summarize the ideas and feelings of their group without indicating which students expressed them. Summaries also make it difficult for any one group of students to dominate the flow of interaction.

5) *Fishbowl.* Since the problems of participation in a large class are much more complex than those in a small one, time tokens and tap-outs might not be very useful and practical. One procedure that uses some of the advantages of the small-group discussion, within the setting of the large meeting, is the fishbowl or theater-in-the-round. In a fishbowl arrangement, a small group is formed within a circle made by the larger group. The small group (which could be the steering committee, for

instance) discusses whatever is on the agenda while the other students observe. Empty chairs can be provided in the fishbowl, so that any observing student can come in and join the discussion with the understanding that his seating will be temporary, thus assuring wider participation.

6) *Other Activities.* In addition to these procedures, the reader is referred back to exercises and procedures discussed in earlier chapters: "Encouraging Students with Interpersonal Influence to Pursue Constructive Goals" in Chapter 4; "Improving Acceptance of Rejected Pupils" in Chapter 5; "Clarification of Classroom Norms," "Building a Time Sequence for Academic Work," "Forming a Classroom Student Council," and "Developing Norms of Interest and Relevance" in Chapter 6.

Stage III: Pursuing Individual and Academic Goals

Classroom groups are not ready to work diligently and productively on academic and personal growth until they have settled the issues of group membership and interpersonal influence to some degree, at least. This does not mean that classes have merely to "sit and rap" for their first few months of existence. Some academic work, of course, does get done during the early stages of the group's development, but not to the high degree that it does during this third stage.

One third-grade teacher in the public schools put the case very neatly when she described her three-staged design for the year. The first stage generally lasted from the beginning of school until December. Students carried out the usual tasks of skill development and reading but her primary goals were helping the students to feel comfortable with one another, to work independently, to make collaborative decisions, and to learn how to be cooperative. She visualized January through May as the period of high academic productivity. During these months students set their own goals and developed many projects that emphasized various academic skills. More academic work was accomplished during this time period than at any other time during the school year, this teacher believed. May and June were primarily given over to evaluating the students' work, setting goals for the students' next year at school, and getting the students ready to work with their next teacher.

One frequent complaint heard from teachers is that they waste too much time policing interactions in the class. Such complaints of unruly and undisciplined students indicate to us that the first two stages of group development have not been resolved to a sufficient degree to allow academic work and personal growth to become predominant themes. In our experience, students who have achieved feelings of membership along with the skills of shared influence and collaborative decision making in the classes do not have the great number of discipline problems that plague traditional classroom groups.

The third stage of group development is a high production period; it is the time when the norms and procedures established during the first two stages come to fruition in the form of attainment of academic and personal goals. This stage is most clearly visible in a class coming together for a short period of time to fulfill a specific function, such as a project. By the third stage the students know each other well and have an understanding of one another's resources. They have settled some of the leadership questions and are ready to set clear goals, divide tasks, and set deadlines for completing the tasks.

During this stage the antagonistic pulls between the production goals of the group and the students' feelings will become obvious and persist as a problem off and on. As indicated earlier in this chapter, research by Bales and Parsons showed that groups tend to swing back and forth between a focus on the task and a focus on the social-emotional issues. Some meetings are almost totally given over to individuals' feelings while others are directed toward production.

We believe concerns about students' satisfactions and feelings should take a good deal of time in classes, and that the time taken is not wasted in terms of academic learning. It is imperative that maintenance issues are handled if classes are to work productively. Classes that ignore the basic pulls and tugs of members' goals in conflict with academic goals will not be successful in their production efforts and will be missing a significant part of their productivity—the personal growth aspect.

The third stage is by no means all "sweetness and light," with students diligently and efficiently working on their goals. Group development is cyclical, as well as successive. Predominant in this stage is a constant oscillation between fulfilling the task needs as defined by the school and the emotional needs of the students. Some hours or days, even at the height of productivity, will be filled with conflicts about someone not participating properly or doing his job completely. This will also be the time when the conflict between the individual student and the class as a whole can occur with intensity. A class may come to a collective decision but there will be a minority who do not agree with that decision, causing conflicts which should of course, be publicly dealt with—immediately. And, it should be borne in mind that short-term groups which are part of a larger body will themselves represent in microcosm the developmental sequence of the larger group.

For students who have developed some degrees of trust and skill in communication and group decision making, the key problems of the first two stages can be resolved quickly and easily. Unfortunately, the majority of public schools do not provide the opportunities for learning about group development, consequently teachers with a group-skill orientation often have to spend a great deal of time developing in students the skills and competencies that are necessary for reaching decisions.

The third stage of group development focuses upon the pursuit of academic goals as well as individual student growth—the two primary reasons for which students should go to school. The following procedure can be used by students and teacher to reach both personal and academic goals; it can be used in group setting or by an individual.

A Problem-Solving Procedure. A systematic problem-solving procedure can help individual students and classroom groups work out new avenues for reaching their academic and personal growth goals. In this procedure, a problem is defined as a discrepancy between a goal state and present reality; between what ought to be and what is. The procedure emphasizes making clear statements about goals, diagnosing the situation as it is now, and establishing plans and commitments for future action.

The formal sequence involves seven rather detailed steps: (1) identifying the problem, (2) analyzing the problem, (3) generating multiple solutions, (4) designing plans for action, (5) forecasting consequences of intended actions, (6) taking action, and (7) evaluating the actions.

Step 1. State where you are (the situation) and where you would like to be (the target) precisely and specifically. Discuss with others how they see the two positions. Check out understandings of others!

Step 2. Think of all the forces that are keeping the group from moving closer to its target, and think of all the forces that are helping the group to move toward its target. Ask all group members to think about helps and hindrances. List the forces in order of importance.

Step 3. Think of ways in which the forces holding the group from its target might be reduced. It is usually more efficient to reduce hindering forces than to intensify helping forces. This is one proper stage in problem solving in which to bring in an expert who knows a lot about the substance of the problem.

Step 4. Make a concrete and specific plan of action. Be sure to get the help of the people who will implement the plan.

Step 5. Anticipate the barriers to carrying out the plan effectively. Simulate part of the plan and get feedback from others. Revise the plan if necessary.

Step 6. Put the plan into action. Make the first move and alter the plan according to how it works; and

Step 7. Evaluate the effects of the group's work together in terms of both the problem-solving effort and its interpersonal processes. Assess the changes that have occurred in the problem. If necessary, return to Step 1 and start all over again.

Other Activities. In addition to this procedure, the reader is referred to some exercises and procedures discussed in earlier chapters: "Training Students in Goal-Directed Leadership," "Giving Students an Opportunity to Teach Their own Lesson Plans," and "Students Teaching Students" in Chapter 4; "Developing Norms of Evaluation" in Chapter 6; and "Evaluating Classroom Activities" in Chapter 8.

Stage IV: Self-Renewal: Adapting to Changes

Healthy classes, like healthy students, eventually reach a condition of adaptive maturity. For the healthy student, reaching maturity is not an end but rather a state of readiness for continuous growth and for the broadening of competencies, skills, and interest. Adaptive maturity involves confrontation with the options in one's life, the ability to respond with choices, and the courage to accept the consequences of one's decisions. John Gardner (1963) applied the term *self-renewal* to this kind of adaptive group. Self-renewing groups can continue to set up new purposes and procedures out of their own internal resources and wherewithal, and they have the competence to adopt new processes when the old ones are no longer functional. They are termed mature because the members accept the responsibility for their group-life and are continuously striving to improve it.

Although this description may sound appealing, self-renewing learning groups are not easy to live in. They contain a continuous array of human problems such as intermittent feelings of exclusion and alienation, power-struggles and resentments, and frustrated goals. While they afford much satisfaction and comfort to the members, they do not allow for complacency. While they support individual growth and insight, they also are confrontative and challenging. An adaptive class may be viewed as one which is continually stimulating to its members.

Most of the exercises and procedures presented earlier in this chapter and in preceding chapters can be used at this point, therefore we will not present new ones. Even activities used once at the beginning of the classes' life can bring forth new issues and concerns at a later time. One exercise, "Building Work Groups to Change Classroom Liking Patterns" described in Chapter 5, represents a genotypic action plan that might be used at any time to counter an unhealthy social situation. Two other exercises, "The Johari Window: A Public Discussion of Cohesiveness," and "A Strength Building Exercise," both described in Chapter 8, are ideal to use in the later life of a class. They require class members to trust in and have knowledge about one another, and they are designed to explore new depths and dimensions of interpersonal relationships. Through activities like these, the chance for the class to stay adaptive to changing pressures and demands is increased.

References

Bales, R., and Slater, P. "Role Differentiation in Small Decision-Making Groups." In *Family Socialization and Interaction Process,* edited by T. Parsons and R. Bales. New York: Free Press, 1955. Pp. 259-306.

Erikson, E. H. *Childhood and Society.* New York: W. W. Norton & Co., Inc., 1950.

Gardner, J. *Self-Renewal: The Individual and the Innovative Society.* New York: Harper & Row, Publishers, 1963.

Gibb, J. "Climate for Trust Formation." *In T-Group Theory and Laboratory Method,* edited by L. Bradford, J. Gibb, and K. Benne. New York: John Wiley & Sons, Inc., 1964. Pp. 279-309.

Heinicke, C., and Bales, R. "Developmental Trends in the Structure of Small Groups." *Sociometry* 16 (1953):7-38.

Lippitt, R. "An Experimental Study of the Effect of Democratic and Authoritarian Group Atmospheres." *University of Iowa Studies in Child Welfare* 16 (1940):43-195.

Parsons, T., and Bales R. *Family Socialization and Interaction Process.* New York: Free Press, 1955.

Runkel, P. J.; Lawrence, Marilyn; Oldfield, Shirley; Rider, Mimi; and Clark, Candee. "Stages of Group Development: An Empirical Test of Tuckman's Hypothesis." *Journal of Applied Behavioral Science* 7 no. 2 (1971):180-93.

Schutz, W. *FIRO: A Three Dimensional Theory of Interpersonal Behavior.* New York: Holt, Rinehart, and Winston, Inc., 1958.

———. *The Interpersonal Underworld.* Palo Alto, Calif.: Science and Behavior Books, 1966.

Tuckman, B. W. "Developmental Sequence in Small Groups." *Psychological Bulletin* 63 (1965):384-99.

CHAPTER 10

The School Organization

In a reciprocal fashion, the primary building block of a school is its classrooms and what transpires in any particular classroom is influenced by the culture of the larger school organization. Classes may be organized as the traditional self-contained rooms that are relatively autonomous from one another, or they may be organized as modern flexible and fluid groupings in which subgroups and individual memberships frequently change. In whatever ways the classrooms are organized, the culture of the school organization makes its mark on them.

The school organization is constituted of many parts. It is the arena in which the various professional subgroups of the faculty are called upon to work together. It is the stage on which various committees are formed and on which crucial decisions get made. The school organization is composed of the formal and informal relationships among the faculty and between faculty and students. It is made up of the community and other external forces, and it includes the curriculum and other academic resources. A school organization is a living complex social system; classrooms are the key subsystems of this larger system. As a system, a school continually adapts to changes from within—its teachers, committees, students, and classes—and it responds to forces from without—budgets, parents, and school boards.

Many features of the school have a direct and immediate bearing on what happens in its classrooms. There are the obvious environmental facts about the school such as where it is placed and the characteristics of the surrounding neighborhood. These outside social forces are "givens"; a school staff can do little to control them. It can, however, develop ways of coping with them creatively and effectively. There are also the ongoing dynamics of the organization itself; these involve the ways and means by which learning activities are carried out, and they can be altered by the staff's careful planning. It is these ongoing social processes of the school that are the primary foci of investigation and intervention in the consultative strategy called *Organization Development.*

In this chapter, we will explore in depth some external organizational characteristics that have a direct impact on classroom life. We will also analyze the features of the internal organizational processes of the school and show how they can directly influence what happens in the school's classrooms. Finally, we will explain the purposes and activities of Organization Development, a consultative method that has been used to humanize industrial and school organizations.

External Organizational Characteristics

The obvious sociological characteristics of the school organization—its size, socioeconomic character, and neighborhood culture—are forces outside of the school itself. Each of these characteristics bears directly on what transpires in the school's classrooms, yet school faculties often do not take steps to cope effectively with "givens" of these sorts. At the same time, staffs with vision and courage can alter the detrimental effects of these external characteristics; they can use them, in fact, to their educational advantage.

Size

The number of students and staff members within one school is a critical factor that influences many aspects of the school's organization. There are some obvious effects, such as the average student-teacher ratio or the number of classes available to the student body. There are also some less obvious effects, such as the ways in which interaction among teachers and students take place. Barker and Gump (1964) and Baird (1969) have presented impressive empirical evidence on the relationships between school size and student behavior.

In both studies, it was found that although small and large high schools had about the same number of "behavioral settings"—facilities and activities in which students participate—a greater proportion of students in small schools participated in the activities offered by the school than students in large schools. The average number of extracurricular activities and the variety of kinds of activities for students in small schools were twice as great as for those students in large schools. Furthermore, a greater proportion of small-school students held positions of importance and responsibility, whereas in the larger high schools, fewer students proportionately held such positions. Students of small schools reported more personal kinds of satisfactions, e.g., developing new competencies, being challenged, participating in activities they considered important, and becoming clear about their values. On the other hand, students from large schools reported more impersonal satisfactions that were less goal-directed: vicarious enjoyments, affiliation and identity with the large groups, learning about persons and affairs, and receiving external rewards such as points for participation.

Even though small-school students appear to be more involved in relationships with peers, there is a greater probability that large-school students' attitudes and values are even more strongly influenced by the peer group. It is likely that youngsters in large schools become just as intimate with some peers as their small-school counterparts, except that these friendships more often take place outside of the school. A student in a large school is faced with many alternatives in the kinds of persons he will choose for friends. Such alternatives are not present within the relatively homogeneous group of small-school students. The student in a large school may choose people quite different from himself, and the peer structure of small cliques and dating couples are important factors in the developing of his personality. As a student chooses friends outside of his classroom experiences, the importance of school-related activities decreases and the influence of out-of-school peer relationships increases.

In studies of college environments, Pace (1967) and Astin (1968) reported that size was negatively and strongly related to college students' perceptions of their campus's friendliness, cohesiveness, and supportiveness. In the larger colleges they found less concern for the individual student, lack of involvement in classes, little familiarity with the instructor, greater competitiveness, and lower cohesiveness. Exceptions were found, but generally smaller sized institutions were more supportive environments for effective group processes.

These studies run counter to the prevalent argument that large schools are better than small schools because they can concentrate resources, develop more impressive activities, and stimulate more learning. Theoretically, at least, large schools can engage in many different activities and provide a diversity of curricula and events, which would allow a heterogeneous student body to follow a course of study best suited for each individual student. Such diversity and potential for satisfy-ing the needs of individual students would seem to support the argu-ment for big schools. However, research on school size suggests that the quality of the use that is made of facilities is more important than their magnitude or impressiveness. Students in small schools seem to make better use of their facilities, at least in terms of individual and group participation in educationally valuable activities. The data on size give clear evidence that the necessary ingredients for learning—involvement and participation—are not encouraged by large and impersonal schools.

How Can Educators Cope with Size?

Some schools have been organized in such a way that students can benefit from the multiple resources of a large school while also experi-encing the advantages of participation in the small school setting. For example, many small rural districts have become consolidated to derive the benefits of bigness. In such cases, the single school district could not afford to offer and to maintain the services that could be made available in the consolidated district. As a case in point, several rural districts in the Southwest sought to reach and educate students who lived in inac-cessible areas. These districts combined their resources to put together expensive programs of educational television and telephone to get to these isolated youngsters. In such cases of consolidation, bigness is war-ranted because no single district could afford the high cost of imple-menting creative educational strategies.

Bringing large numbers of students together within large urban cen-ters presents quite a different problem. Here bigness typically is detri-mental. In most American cities, schools are huge sprawling physical plants, housing hundreds and often thousands of students. And, for some decades now, educators have become concerned about the inevitable alienation, loneliness, and depersonalization of students in large urban schools. Yet urban districts typically do not have the money needed to tear down their schools and start all over again with smaller units.

Some urban schools have, however, taken creative steps in adapting to the impersonality of bigness; while, at the same time, maintaining a core of diverse resources. Some urban schools have established "houses" within a building; each house being a mini-school in itself with its own faculty, student body, and administrative cabinet. Several houses together use such facilities of the larger institution as language laboratories, movie equipment, and athletic playing areas. While lectures can be given in large groups, seminars about the lectures can take place back in the intimate setting of the house. This "school within a school" design can be an effective way of having smallness within bigness.

Small clusters of teachers within a large building can also make a difference by combining their efforts. Some teachers have found, for example, that by combining teaching activities with several colleagues, they can cope with the limitations that would otherwise be imposed while attempting to teach all subjects to their students. The "unit" plan is one method to help solve the problems created by increasing numbers of students and by increasing amounts of knowledge in several disciplines. A unit typically is made up of a team of four or five teachers; some are experienced teachers while others are neophytes. One member might be a paraprofessional. Usually, the unit is made up of about 125 students with a chronological age-span of from two to three years. In some learning activities, such as social studies, the students are in small groups and might remain in these same groups for the whole year. In other activities, such as reading or math, the students might be grouped according to performance, with individuals moving from group to group as they progress. In still other learning activities, the entire unit might be brought together for a movie, play, concert, or science demonstration. Following the large session, small groups would form to discuss the event.

Socioeconomic Character

The socioeconomic environment of the school is an important external organizational characteristic. Sexton (1961) found that the money spent for schools in one large city school district, as well as the quality of education offered, varied in direct proportion to the income of families in the school's neighborhood. Sexton found inequities in: (1) quality and adequacy of school buildings and facilities, (2) school and class space accommodations (crowding), (3) quality of teaching staff, (4) methods of testing and estimating student performance, (5) methods of selecting and segregating students, (6) quality of the secondary curriculum, (7) vocational and educational counseling of students, (8) opportunities for completion of secondary school and admission to college, (9) use of school buildings by adults, (10) enrollment in pre-first-grade programs, (11) health, recreation, and food service facilities, and finally, (12) total costs of educating students. All of these were correlated with the poorer school performance of lower-income students. These findings also have implications for race relations. In another city, appropriations for school operating expenses were almost 25 percent greater per student in white than in black schools, teachers' salaries were 18 percent higher, and nonteaching operating expenses were 50 percent higher (1963 Handbook).

These differences of school organization set the stage for differences in the psychological components of the classrooms. Herriott and St. John (1966) showed that both teachers and principals in low socioeconomic status schools were less experienced and less satisfied in their jobs than in high status areas. The principals in the highest status areas were considerably more satisfied with their teachers. In the highest status areas, 17 percent of principals wanted more prestige, compared to 43 percent in the lowest. Forty-two percent of teachers in the lowest compared with 18 percent in the highest status schools wanted a transfer to a school in a better neighborhood. The teachers in the lowest status schools were, on the average, younger, less experienced, newer to the school, and getting less pay. Poor physical conditions, overcrowding, out-dated curriculum materials, and inexperienced or harsh, punitive teachers made up the reality of the school for the lower-class students. Most indices related to teaching performance and the quality of classroom group processes were found to be somewhat poorer in schools of lowest socioeconomic status.

Finn (1972) found that teachers in predominantly lower-class urban schools had lower expectations for student performance and paid more attention to I.Q. scores and achievement tests in evaluating student work than did teachers in middle-class suburban schools. He pointed to the socioeconomic character of the schools to account for his findings. The teachers in the suburban schools had better teaching conditions with lower-class loads, more teaching resources, and more support from psychologists, counselors, and curriculum personnel than did their urban counterparts. The teachers in the lower-class urban schools did not have the resources, nor did they have the time to make sophisticated diagnoses of student problems. As a consequence, out of utter frustration, the urban teachers used the most direct cues—mental test scores—to determine the worth of a student's school performance.

Most of the available research literature indicates that classroom conditions, teachers' expectations, and the circumstances of family and neighborhood combine to reduce the likelihood that lower-class students will do very well in school. Students from low socioeconomic backgrounds require different types of teaching and need to acquire many skills already obtained by their middle-class counterparts. It is unfortunately the case that the low socioeconomic student has the lesser of all that is offered by a total school district.

How Can Educators Cope with Socioeconomic Characteristics?

We believe that the individual teacher can do numerous things to overcome the detrimental effects of social class differences within the classroom. First, if a teacher accepts each student as a unique person—with idiosyncratic strengths and weaknesses—he has come a long way toward reducing obvious social class biases. Second, if a teacher sets up a pattern of support so that students can expend their strengths and overcome their shortcomings, then students can learn to respect themselves. If the teacher is supportive and caring then students will be likely to follow in that same pattern, and a healthy and favorable climate for learning can be developed. If teachers reject or disapprove of students with poor academic skills—and these are often the students from homes low in the socioeconomic scale—patterns of distrust, competitiveness, and hostility will set the tone for classroom life.

Aside from typical interactions in the classroom, there are many constructive steps that school faculties can take to use the surrounding community for educational purposes. In our recent book, *A Humanistic Psychology of Education: Making the School Everybody's House,* we have described several plans that educators can use to work together with community resources. Some of those suggestions included using parents for tutoring or clerical work, special classes taught by parents with particular skills, cross-age tutoring programs using older students from the local neighborhood, or parent advisory boards with actual power to affect decisions in the school.

In addition, there are many curriculum materials that are now available which focus on human relations and an understanding of how people cope with environmental pressures. Most of these instructional materials have a component of direct application rather than being focused only on cognitive and theoretical understanding. For example, *Social Science Laboratory Units* developed by Lippitt, Fox, and Schaible (1969) use the topics and methods of social psychology to study issues such as decision making, social power, and group and individual differences. *Man, a Course of Study* (1970) combines the disciplines of anthropology, sociology, and psychology to present a generic understanding of human behavior. Ojemann (1958) has created a curriculum focused on the causes and effects of individual behavior. DeCharms (1968) offers an instructional strategy to increase students' initiatory behaviors. And Alschuler's program for training in achievement striving (1970) can be applied to helping students develop increased control over their personal lives. Finally, Stanford (1971) has demonstrated how the use of popular books, movies, and magazines can be creatively incorporated into a standard English curriculum with special emphasis on human behavior.

Peer Group Norms

Peers demand conformity as the price for acceptance, especially during adolescence. From middle childhood through adolescence, as the youngster's dependence on the peer group increases, peers' power to exact conformity is concomitantly enhanced. Also, of course, the trend toward conformity is enhanced as a youngster internalizes the peer group's standards because of loyalty feelings and fears of rejection.

Wilson (1959) provided evidence showing how peer norms influence adolescent aspirations about higher education. He first identified student aspirations in schools with predominantly three types of populations: (A) upper-middle-class white collar, (B) lower-middle-class white collar, and (C) industrial working class. Wilson found that in school A, 80 percent wanted to go to college; in school B, 57 percent wanted to go; and in school C, 38 percent wanted to attend college. Wilson found that each of these schools embodied a different normative pattern regarding college attendance. His data indicated that 93 percent of sons of professionals in school A wanted to go to college, while only 64 percent of upper-middle-class boys in school B wanted to go to college. On the other hand, only 33 percent of sons of manual workers in school C wanted to go to college, while 59 percent of the working class boys in school A wanted a college education. The situational influences of peer norms altered aspirations about college.

Peer norms can have powerful influence on students of all social classes and personality styles. McDill et al. (1967) attempted to measure the relative effects of the socioeconomic context and norms of a school on the behavior of students. Their analysis revealed that the effect of the socioeconomic context of the school tended to disappear when some critical personality and ability variables were held constant. However, even when the school's socioeconomic context and the personal attributes were simultaneously held constant, the various normative dimensions that were studied still had significant effects on students' perfomances.

In another study of normative peer influences, Winter, Alpert, and Mc-Clelland (1963) assessed the changes in values of a group of bright boys, from rural schools, who were exposed to a very intensive summer educational experience at an elite private boys' boarding school in New England. The results indicated that the boys who attended changed their values toward what the authors called the classic personal style. They became more cynical and sophisticated, had more self-control over impulses, and were characterized by antihumanitarianism. This value system was not only promoted by peers at the school, but was apparently quite effective in influencing the thinking of boys who were exposed to it for only six weeks.

In many schools the faculty is continually involved in a battle with the student peer group, especially when the norms of the peer group are antagonistic to the achievement orientation of the professionals. Educators frequently find fault with parents, neighborhood subgroups, or even the larger community for socializing youngsters who have little conception of the "value of education." Recently, it has been commonstance to see policemen within the hallways of many schools to keep order. In some of these instances, such as the Hargreaves' study on streaming in the British schools pointed out, social relationships within the school itself perpetuates and accentuates the antischool norms of the student peer group.

How Can Educators Cope with Peer Group Norms?

We believe that for effective academic learning to occur the faculty and student body should not be at odds with each other. Educators need to take the initiative in developing plans and procedures to work collaboratively with the students. Initiatives for overcoming the generation gap should come from those in authority. Principals can usefully heed the advice and concern of students before making decisions. Teachers can use plans made by a student steering committee to guide the direction and activities of classroom learning. Other ideas for heeding the voice of students can be found in Wyant (1973) and elsewhere throughout this book.

Internal Organizational Processes

How the activities for implementing the school program are carried out is synonymous with the internal organizational processes of the school. Such activities involve how decisions are made about goals; how the curricula are determined and implemented; and how professionals, non-professionals, and students relate with one another. In this section we discuss five important internal organizational processes which we believe school faculties have the power to change.

TRUST AND OPENNESS. The interpersonal relationships among a faculty set the stage for the ways teachers behave in their classrooms. If teachers have feelings of comfort and rapport in relationships with colleagues, they are supported in their feelings of self-worth and are better able to relate positively to students. Feelings of hostility, competition or alienation lead to anxiety and low levels of tolerance with students. In contemporary jargon, if teachers are "up tight" with members of the faculty, they will tend to be "up tight" with students. One simple indicator of trust and openness among the staff is how often teachers ask one another to visit their classroom to make suggestions for improvement. If fear and anxiety pervade staff relationships, innovative and creative teaching will not be encouraged, and feedback will not be offered. Trust and openness are necessary for sharing of ideas and improving classroom group processes. In schools where teachers are in competition or alienated from one another, good ideas are the property of one teacher, either because no one else knows about them or because others are reticent to "steal" the ideas for their own use. The curriculum of a classroom will suffer if teachers cannot stimulate one another with new ideas and practices.

SKILLS OF COMMUNICATION AND CONSTRUCTIVE OPENNESS. Attitudes of trust and openness may encourage favorable interpersonal relations and creative teaching, but, in themselves, they do not guarantee that staff members will help one another become better teachers. Staff members need to be able to use the communication skills of describing behaviors without impugning motives, of being able to paraphrase what another person has said, of communicating their own feelings directly, and of impression-checking with another colleague to see what he is thinking and feeling. Teachers who are able to perform such communication skills in relation to one another can more easily do the same with their students. In one project dealing with the communication patterns of the faculty, for instance, Bigelow (1971) found that teachers used their communication skills—learned with fellow staff members—in their classrooms even though none of the faculty training in communication was directly geared toward instructional behavior. The teachers in the project found ways of collaborating and solving problems together which they, in turn, used in involving their students in the routines and procedures of the classroom.

In addition to communication skills, we should also place emphasis on constructive openness. Constructive openness is feedback that guides the recipient supportively toward new alternatives for his behavior; it does not threaten the recipient's self-concept or challenge his competence. Skill in being open constructively is a necessary part, we think, of the culture of a school. And we do not mean by constructive openness mere sympathy. On many faculties there is some member who has a sympathetic shoulder; sympathy may ease the burden but not necessarily solve the problem that the colleague is facing.

Faculties that use constructive openness with one another as well as with the students represent supportive climates for helping to solve frustrating problems. For example, in informal staff discussions, comments of colleagues about how they view the relationship between a teacher and a student may help the teacher to look at the student in a new way. In this manner, constructive openness widens the myopic view of the teacher involved. In some schools that we have observed or worked in, the use of constructive openness has become formalized. Teachers formally observe one another with the intent of giving feedback to improve instruction or they present problems at faculty meetings in order to use others' perceptions and suggestions. Critical evaluation that does not demean or chastise is one important avenue for encouraging improved group processes on the faculty or in the classroom.

INFLUENCE POSITIONS OF TEACHERS. Members of authoritarian organizations often feel passive and sometimes incompetent in relationship to the organization's leadership. Members who get involved in decision-making feel more powerful and are usually more willing to go along with organizational decisions. In most schools, the administration makes most organizational decisions; in some others, teachers participate actively in running the school. Research on schools indicates that the satisfaction of teachers is related to their perception of the extent to which they can influence certain aspects of the school's decision-making. Findings by Hornstein et al. (1968) showed that teachers report greatest satisfaction with their principal and the school district when they perceived that they and their principal were mutually influential, and especially when their principal's influence emanated from his expertise. As teachers feel more influential and view their principal as an expert, they feel better about the school, and indicate more support in their contacts with students. As teachers become more involved in school decision-making, they take greater initiative in designing new programs for the classroom and in getting feedback from other teachers before carrying their plan to the principal. In schools with more equalized power relationships between administrators and staff, the quality of teacher-student relationships in the classroom also improves.

LEADERSHIP ROLE OF THE PRINCIPAL. Just as influence attempts of teachers have strong effects on classroom group processes, the principal's behavior can affect group processes of the school staff. Gross and Herriott (1965) showed that principals' leadership behaviors influenced staff morale, innovativeness and professional performance—even student learning. They developed a concept to describe the principal's leadership called Executive Professional Leadership (EPL). A principal's EPL score was determined by how much teachers viewed him as being supportive, collaborative, and helpful to them. Principals with high EPL scores were characterized by some of the following: (1) had constructive suggestions to offer teachers in dealing with their major problems, (2) displayed strong interest in improving quality of educational programs, (3) gave teachers the feeling that they, the teachers, could make significant contributions to improving classroom performances of students, and (4) made teachers' meetings a valuable educational activity. Teachers who credited their principals with high EPL were comfortable in their school work and were stimulated and encouraged to improve by the principal. Teachers who felt supported and encouraged were not fearful of trying new educational procedures and therefore could provide a better academic learning environment for their students.

In another study, Chesler, Schmuck, and Lippitt (1963) found that a teacher's willingness to try new educational practices depended greatly on the principal's support of innovative projects. Teachers who saw their principals as supportive and eager for new practices most often tried new plans and practices. However, in schools in which the principal was seen as supportive of innovation but the teaching staff was *not* seen as supportive, the influence of the principal was undermined in getting teachers to try new plans. Thus, although the principal typically has significant influence on the climate of the school, the faculty can counteract that influence, especially in relation to discouraging innovative programs.

ASSUMPTIONS ABOUT HUMAN BEHAVIOR. The ways staff members think about human behavior can have an impact on classroom group processes. McGregor (1967) has distinguished between two conceptions of motivation labeled Theory X and Theory Y. In simple terms, Theory X stipulates that people are lazy and passive, and must be pushed and prodded to action. Theory Y argues that people are curious and active and should be allowed freedom to find ways of doing things. Staffs with Theory X orientations tend to employ traditional modes of leadership characterized by authoritarianism, one-way communication, and restrictive norms. Staffs with Theory Y orientations allow for more student freedom, are more collaborative, and employ more two-way communication. No matter how autonomous a classroom is, it is part of an organizational system and the teacher's classroom behavior will be influenced by the prevailing attitudes of the faculty, especially with regard to what makes people want to work and learn.

Appleberry and Hoy (1969) have used the concepts of "humanistic" and "custodial" to describe an educator's orientation to human behavior. A teacher who scores on the custodial side of the scale tends to think about students as being in need of control and training; students are viewed as lacking responsibility and self-discipline. From the custodial perspective, the school is viewed as being responsible for the students' behaviors and authority is viewed as being appropriately hierarchical with administrators and teachers at the top, giving students little opportunity to make their own decisions. In contrast, the teacher with a humanistic orientation views the school as a community of persons engaged in learning through their interactions with one another. He believes that power should be shared by all participants, including the students, and that discussions should be initiated for those who are affected by them whenever possible. In their research, Appleberry and Hoy found the faculties typically have a fairly high agreement about their assumptions for human behavior and that these assumptions become operative within the organization of the school. "Open" schools have a prevailing humanistic orientation, while "closed" schools are more custodial.

Consultation in Organization Development

Organization development is a consultative strategy designed for helping the members of a school organization to look at their internal organizational processes and by dint of planning to steer the course of how they will work together. It is a method for helping school people to take action to change their own organization. Schmuck and Miles (1971) have defined organization development (OD) technically as "a planned and sustained effort to apply behavioral science for system improvement, using reflexive, self-analytic methods."

From the point of view of OD, the school organization is an open social system, contained within the environment, but constantly influencing and being influenced by it. Even though the external environment has a decided effect on what happens within the school, we believe—as do other advocates of OD—that the educators themselves possess considerable leverage for improving their organizational climates.

The Efficient Use of School Resources

A school's efficiency can be defined in terms of how completely the school's resources are used in developing its products. In Chapter 2 we defined classroom climate as all group processes working together to create a supportive interpersonal environment. Analogously, organizational climate denotes the interpersonal and group processes that facilitate movement toward academic productivity and positive staff relations. A positive climate for the adult staff includes dispersed influence and friendship structures on the faculty, supportive norms, clear communication and workable goals. It is this quality of group processes mediating resources and products which determine the efficiency of a school.

Many educators have tried to explain the problems of public education by emphasizing the inferior nature of the school resources, while largely ignoring the mediating group dynamics and organizational climate.

For instance, academically ill-equipped youngsters from culturally disadvantaged environments are viewed as causing many of the major problems of urban schools. A large amount of grant and government monies are being spent to increase the school skills of the culturally deprived child. Poorly trained teachers have also been held responsible for the failure of schools. One argument is that school teaching attracts those less capable college students who received inferior educations from poorly prepared college instructors who know little about the realities of the classroom. We do not believe this to be the case. Today almost all school districts have preservice or in-service education encouraging and economically supporting continued academic growth on the part of the teachers. Other inferior resources focused on are inadequate curriculum materials, teaching aids or physical classroom conditions. All of these resources are important and it is encouraging that they are being improved. However, teachers cannot alone solve the problems of education today. It is the interaction of students, teachers, and curriculum materials in all their various interrelationships that determines the efficient use of the schools' resources.

The energies of school administrators are spent inappropriately if they are primarily used in improving the resources. Naturally, the administrator should attempt to select the most skillful teachers and highest quality curriculum materials for her school, but she should be more concerned with the interaction of these resources; and insofar as she is able to work efficiently in maximizing production from whatever resources she is given, the administrator would be defined as an effective leader. Two examples of inefficient use of a school's available resources come to mind. Schools often order many curriculum materials that are placed in a storeroom or a central office. Retrieval of these materials is a critical problem for teachers with lack of time to browse through the locked storerooms. Many large and expensive machines and good materials remain unused, an inefficient use of nonhuman resources. This condition can be altered by better timing and planning.

Another example of the inefficient use of school resources is highlighted by the nonsharing, acollaborative norms that are present in many school faculties. Teachers who are doing exciting and successful activities often are reluctant to tell their colleagues about their success; other teachers are reluctant to "steal" another's ideas; and still others are just too busy to share. In most schools, staff meetings typically do not provide formal time for teachers to discuss their instructional innovations with one another.

Often organizational decisions are made and work is done that do not optimize the school's resources. But this condition is not necessarily inevitable. School faculties can improve their organizational climate through consultation in OD—when the OD aims at creating norms and roles within the school that can help the staff to review itself continually, and to test out ways that make full use of human potentialities. A successful OD program does not involve a preconceived structure imposed upon the school by an outsider, but rather a process through which a school staff can improve itself.

The Strategy of Organization Development

Consultation in OD for schools aims at increasing the trust and openness among administrators, teachers, and students; it focuses upon improving their skills of communication in relation to one another, at making their respective resources more available, at making influence among them more equitable, and at increasing their effectiveness in collaboratively solving problems. It strives to help the members of a school staff develop the skills, norms, roles, procedures, and group structures that will enable them to change their modes of operating in order to cope effectively with changing environments. Specifically, the objectives of organization development training include: increasing understanding of how the different participants within the school affect one another; establishing clear ways of defining goals and of assessing goal achievement; disclosing organizational conflicts and confusions so that they can be dealt with constructively; improving the group procedures for effective problem-solving in small groups; and involving more participants at all levels in decision-making.

There are five central guiding principles involved in training for OD. First, the organization development consultation will be more effective if it is carried out with all the members of a working subsystem (an organizational family) rather than just with individuals who do not work together closely. It is assumed that since the role each person plays in the school is carried out in relation to others, changes in a school's procedures will be brought about as the consultation offers new ways for the role-takers to interact. By total staffs being involved together, individuals can see that their colleagues are accepting new patterns of behavior and are acting upon them

Second, OD should generate valid data for the members of the school about their collaborative functioning. The data should concern the staff's own internal organizational processes, thus offering the staff members a mirror from which to view themselves clearly as a functioning unit.

Third, discrepancies between current performance and the performance goals of a school are used as leverage points for change. The goals for a school, are, of course, set by the school members themselves; the OD specialists do not determine the school's goals. By checking goals against data on how things actually are in the school, dissonance is created which can motivate the participants to become more involved in changing their modes of operating.

Fourth, consultation in OD makes use of the available resources that already exist within a staff to solve problems and develop new plans. The OD specialists do not offer ready-made solutions, but rather present a procedure to help participants think of a number of alternatives for their operations for the present and the future, as well as to think of developing plans of action for implementing alternatives.

Fifth, it is important that the OD specialist who facilitates the consultation is not a member of the subsystem receiving the consultation. An outside person has a higher likelihood of being neutral and objective, while a subsystem participant already has been too involved in the ongoing dynamics to offer a dispassionate point of view. Also, it is preferable for the OD specialists to work as part of an intervention team rather than alone. An effective consulting team can be more accurate and creative in assessing problems and in helping participants develop alternative styles of operating than any single individual consultant can be.

The OD Specialist

OD specialists, those who implement consultation in organization development, are typically in industry, university settings, private consulting firms, and school districts. Counselors and school psychologists often are in key positions within school districts to act as OD specialists. Many counselors and psychologists already have developed the skills to facilitate groups and often they stay at a distance from the ongoing dynamics of the school organization. For these reasons, we will focus primarily on the counselor and the school psychologist as role-takers who can appropriately function as OD specialists with school districts. However, other sorts of role-takers such as administrators and teachers have also worked successfully as OD specialists. Indeed, clusters of various types of professional educators can constitute a very strong OD team (for more details, see R. Schmuck 1971).

OD Specialist as Internal Process Consultant

There are primarily three ways in which the counselor or psychologist of a particular school, performing as an OD specialist, can strengthen the organizational health of his own school. All three of these types of consultation share some of the benefits of acting as an external consultant because each involves serving as an objective third-party consultant.

CONSULTING WITH STAFF GROUPS. The psychologist-counselor can serve as a process consultant during faculty meetings—observing the group in action, giving it feedback on how it is functioning, helping the group to check out how the members feel, and leading the group in discussions about its norms and methods of operating. He encourages the airing of problems and conflicts that would probably remain hidden; he helps the group discuss its communication patterns, problem-solving competencies, and decision-making procedures. Most importantly, the process consultant teaches members to carry on their own diagnoses and to discuss their own processes of work even when he is not present.

In most schools, the principal serves as the convener of staff meetings. Although some principals can convene group discussions effectively, we have found that a large number of principals do not have effective leadership skills. Group meetings can sometimes be improved by assigning the role of convener to other staff members on a rotational basis. Also the group might ask for an OD specialist to serve as a process consultant to the group. The process consultant, in this case, would serve also as a coach to the new convener each week. Counselors and school psychologists can serve as effective process consultants so long as they can remain detached from the major content issues of the meeting. For elaboration on these points, see the sixth chapter of Schmuck, Runkel, Saturen, Martell, and Derr (1972).

CONSULTING WITH CLASSROOM GROUPS. Another way that the OD specialist can help to improve his school's interpersonal processes is to serve as a consultant to classroom groups. In this sort of consultation, the client is the entire learning group (not just the teacher) and the target is to improve the climate of the group. Although we have aimed this book primarily at the classroom teacher, the counselor or school psychologist could use its contents with teachers—in a workshop, for example—as an aid to improving their classroom group skills, or he could use the contents as a basis for consulting with classroom groups. By employing such consultative techniques as observation and feedback, communication skills, simulations and games, and innovative procedures, the consultant strives to help the class improve on such group issues as clarifying expectations, dispersing leadership, increasing attraction, establishing supportive norms, clarifying communications, and increasing cohesiveness.

CONSULTING WITH SCHOOL GROUPS. Most consultation to improve the system functioning of schools to date has been aimed at either the staff or classroom levels. There is now considerable interest in bringing students and teachers into more effective collaboration, especially concerning the development of educational alternatives and individualization of instruction.

Some staffs have tried to involve students in important decisions about how the school will operate, only to face frustration and disappointment with the low amount of interest and the low amount of skill displayed by students. This situation is not surprising; for students to become integrally involved in a school's decision-making processes it will take a considerable amount of planning, training, and relearning about the responsibility of a student in relation to faculty members. To change a traditionally organized student government, for example, from a rubber-stamp council dealing with inconsequential matters to a fully functioning, interdependent body in relation to the faculty will take considerable time and know-how. The OD specialist can serve as a consultant to a staff-student group—to improve its communication skills, to develop diagnostic competencies, and to develop norms of constructive openness. The OD specialist might also serve as a process consultant in meetings to which students, teachers, and administrators are brought to work on real issues and concerns.

Case Example of Counselor as Internal Process Consultant

The sixth-grade teachers in an elementary school referred a few of their students to the counselor because of some acts of vandalism in the school. Because of the amount of anger and irritation presented by the teachers over these acts and because of the counselor's suspicion that the problem resided deeper than a few random behaviors of vandalism, he decided the issue involved the sixth graders and their mode of operating as groups, rather than just a disciplinary issue concerning a handful of students.

In starting the consultation, the counselor interviewed the sixth-grade teachers, several students (some of those ostensibly involved in the vandalism), the principal, one cook, and the custodian to assess the nature and the magnitude of the problem. He organized a planning committee made up of some of the teachers, a few students, and the custodian (whom the counselor had recognized as being involved in the problem). This committee met three times in all. At the first meeting, they discussed the vandalism, deciding as they did so that they did not have sufficient information to suggest concrete actions. They wanted to have the teachers', students', and principal's views as to where the locus of responsibility was. After the counselor collected some data, a second meeting was held to review the data and to stake out action plans. The counselor discovered that almost everyone perceived the students as being responsible; at the same time he offered the students' view that they acted out of frustration and on impulse and that they felt the teachers and principal were not listening to their concerns. The committee decided to try a two-day conference for the sixth-grade classes to arrive at some solutions. The committee met with the sixth graders to outline their findings and their recommendations.

The two-day conference included the teachers, students, the custodian, and at times the principal. The counselor served as convener and trainer. The training involved communication skills, cooperation in groups, and group discussion skills. Next, the counselor fedback the data he had collected. The data were used on the last day of the conference as part of a problem-solving sequence. The problem-solving dealt specifically with the problem of vandalism. As a result, some minor punishment was suggested for the offenders, objectives and procedures were set up to prevent future problems involving vandalism, and several plans of action that involved communications among the principal, custodian, and students were decided upon.

The planning committee met one more time to design a half-day follow-up session to determine if the action plans were being executed and how they were working out. Before the half-day session, the committee members interviewed students, teachers, the principal and the custodian; the data that were collected were presented back to the entire body at the session. At the session, it was decided to institute a full time planning group which would meet once each month to determine whether other problems were arising and to develop ways of working on such problems before they became too difficult to manage.

OD Specialist as Member of an External Team

Another way in which a psychologist or counselor can perform as an OD specialist is as the member of a consulting team which intervenes in another school in the district or in a nearby district. Cadres of OD specialists can be constituted not only of school psychologists and counselors but also of teachers, principals, curriculum specialists, and assistant superintendents. Each cadre member receives training in such substantive topics as communication, effective meetings, conflict and interdependence, problem-solving, and decision making, as well as a supervised practicum and lengthy education in the theory and research on organizations. Counselors and psychologists are invaluable members of cadres, bringing their special knowledge and skills. Their knowledge of social psychology and group dynamics, previous roles as third party members between teachers and students, and skills in interpersonal communication and conflict contribute significantly to the resources of the cadres (for a detailed report on cadres of OD specialists, see Schmuck and Runkel 1971).

*Case Example of a School Psychologist as Member of
an External OD Team*

The coordinator of a cadre of OD specialists in a school district was asked by the principal and the cabinet of a junior high school to carry out an OD project with the entire faculty. The coordinator asked two teachers, a principal, and a school psychologist to constitute the external consultant team. The team designed and implemented three major training events as follows:

THE FIRST EVENT. Training began with a six-day laboratory late in August. Almost the entire building staff was present. The fifty-four trainees included all the administrators, all but two of the faculty, the head cook, head custodian, and head secretary. During the first two days, time was spent in group and intergroup exercises and communication skills designed to increase awareness of interpersonal and organizational processes; e.g., the NASA trip to the moon exercise, the five-square puzzle, planners and operators, and paraphrasing. Although these exercises were like games, they demonstrated the importance of effective communication for accomplishing a task collaboratively. After each exercise, the school psychologist and his consulting colleagues lead discussions in small groups of the faculty on ways in which the experience was similar or dissimilar to what usually happened in their relations with one another in the school. All staff members then pooled their experiences and analyzed their relationships as a faculty. The OD specialists supported openness in giving and receiving feedback about perceptions of real organizational processes in the school.

During the last four days of the six-day laboratory, the faculty went through a problem-solving sequence, working on real issues that were thwarting the school's organizational functioning. On the third day, after a morning of discussion and decisions which also served as a practice session in decision-making skills, three significant problems emerged. Each of three problems was assigned to one group who followed a five-step procedure: (1) identifying the problem through behavioral description, (2) further defining the problem by diagnostic force-field analysis, (3) brainstorming to find actions likely to reduce restraining forces, (4) designing a concrete plan of action, and (5) trying out the plan behaviorally through a simulation activity involving the entire staff. Each group worked mostly on its own; the OD specialists served as group facilitators, rarely providing substantive suggestions and never pressing for results.

This first training event culminated with a discussion to highlight the resources of the staff. Members described their own strengths and those of their colleagues. Finally, they discussed what their school could be like if all the faculty's strengths were used.

SECOND EVENT. Early in the fall, the school psychologist and his consultant-colleagues interviewed all faculty members and observed several committees and subject-area groups to determine what uses they were making of the initial training. The data indicated that problems which remained unresolved were closely related to misunderstandings in communication, the overload of duties in some jobs, and difficulties in work groups using the problem-solving procedures effectively.

During the second intervention—held for one-and-a-half days before Christmas vacation—the OD specialists focused on these three problems; they also explored additional ways for department heads to be communication links between teachers and administrators, to increase problem-solving skills of the departments, to help the faculty explore ways of reducing the burden of duties on some staff members, and to increase effective communication between services personnel and the rest of the staff.

THIRD EVENT. This training event also lasted one-and-a-half days and took place before Spring vacation. The main objective was to evaluate staff progress in solving the problems of resource utilization, role clarity, and staff participation. Another objective was to revivify any lagging skills. Faculty members tried to devise ways to halt the cases of backsliding by modifying the school's procedures. They continued with these activities in departmental groups during the remainder of the Spring without the OD specialists.

Major Stages of Organization Development

Organization development specialists typically proceed through three major stages during the consultation:

Improving communication skills through simulation. The specialists build increased openness and ease of interpersonal communication among the trainees by using simulations of typical school situations to train them in such communication skills as paraphrasing, describing behavior and their own feelings, taking a survey, and giving and receiving feedback.

Changing norms through problem-solving. After the specialists help the participants to identify their most vital organizational problems, they present a sequence of problem-solving. By using real school problems, they help the participants to proceed through the steps of problem-solving in an orderly fashion.

Structural changes through group agreements. The specialists help the participants to transform the results of their problem-solving into new functions, roles, and procedures. These new organizational patterns can be formally decided upon by the participants, and agreements can be made about the action steps for carrying them out. Some structural changes might include a faculty senate with well-defined decision-making powers, some procedures for teachers and students regularly giving feedback to one another about teaching, and some new teamwork procedures for helping students with special problems.

References

Alschuler, A. S.; Tabor, Diane; and McIntyre, J. *Teaching Achievement Motivation; Theory and Practice in Psychological Education.* Middletown, Conn.: Education Ventures, 1970.

Appleberry, J. B., and Hoy, W. K. "The Pupil Control Ideology of Professional Personnel in Open and Closed Elementary Schools." *Education Administration Quarterly* 3 (1969):74-85.

Astin, A. W. *The College Environment.* Washington, D. C.: American Council on Education, 1968.

Baird, L. L. "Big School, Small School: A Critical Examination of the Hypothesis." *Journal of Educational Psychology* 60 (1969):253-60.

Barker, R., and Gump, P. *Big School, Small School: High School Size and Student Behavior.* Stanford, Calif.: Stanford University Press, 1964.

Bigelow, R. C. "Changing Classroom Interaction Through Organization Development." In R. A. Schmuck, and M. Miles, ed. *Organization Development in Schools.* Palo Alto, Calif.; National Press Books, 1971.

Chesler, M.; Schmuck, R. A.; and Lippitt, R. "The Principal's Role in Facilitating Innovation." *Theory Into Practice* 2, no. 5 (1963):269-77.

DeCharms, R. *Personal Causation.* New York: Academic Press, 1968.

Finn, J. "Expectations and the Educational Environment." *Review of Educational Research* 42, no. 3 (1972):387-410.

Gross, N., and Herriott, R. *Staff Leadership in Public Schools.* New York: John Wiley & Sons, Inc., 1965.

Handbook of Chicago School Segregation. Compiled and edited by Education Committee Coordinating Council of Community Organization. Chicago: 1963.

Herriott, R., and St. John, N. *Social Class and the Urban School.* New York: John Wiley & Sons, Inc., 1966.

Hornstein, H.; Callahan, D.; Fisch, E.; and Benedict, B. "Influence and Satisfaction in Organizations: A Replication." *Sociology of Education* 41, no. 4 (1968):380-89.

Lippitt, R.; Fox, R.; and Schaible, L. *Social Science Laboratory Units.* Chicago: Science Research Associates, 1969.

Man, a Course of Study. Washington, D. C.: Curriculum Development Associates, 1970.

McGregor, D. *The Professional Manager.* New York: McGraw-Hill Book Co., 1967.

Ojemann, R. "Basic Approaches to Mental Health: The Human Relations Program at the State University of Iowa." *Personnel and Guidance Journal* 36 (1958):198-206.

Pace, C. R. *Analyses of a National Sample of College Environments.* Final Report, Cooperative Research Project No. 50764. Washington, D. C.: Office of Education, U.S. Department of Health, Education, and Welfare, 1967.

Schmuck, R. A. "Developing Teams of Organizational Specialists." In *Organization Development in Schools,* edited by R. A. Schmuck and M. Miles. Palo Alto, Calif.: National Press Books, 1971.

Schmuck, R. A., and Miles, M., eds. *Organization Development in Schools.* Palo Alto, Calif.: National Press Books, 1971.

Schmuck, R. A., and Runkel, P. "Integrating Organizational Specialists into School Districts." In *Current Technologies in Organization Development,* edited by W. Burke. Washington, D. C.: NTL Learning Resources Corp., 1972.

Schmuck, R. A.; Runkel, P.; Saturen, S.; Martell, R.; and Derr, C. B. *Handbook of Organization Development in Schools.* Palo Alto, Calif.: National Press Books, 1972.

Schmuck, R. A., and Schmuck, P. A. *A Humanistic Psychology of Education: Making the School Everybody's House.* Palo Alto, Calif.: National Press Books, 1974.

Sexton, P. C. *Education and Income, Inequaltiy of Opportunity in our Public Schools.* New York: Viking Press, Inc., 1961.

Stanford, B. "How Innovators Fail: Teaching Human Development." *Media and Methods,* October 1971, pp. 26-35.

Wilson, A. "Residential Segregation of Social Classes and Aspirations of High School Boys." *American Sociological Review* 14 (1959):836-45.

Winter, D.; Alpert, R.; and McClelland, D. "The Classic Personal Style." *Journal of Abnormal and Social Psychology* 67 (1963):254-65.

Wyant, S. "Power to the Pupil: An Annotated Bibliography of Student Involvement, Student Power, and Student Participation in Decision-Making in Public Secondary Schools." Eugene, Oregon: Center for Educational Policy and Management, 1973.

Index